Love Among the Archives

Love Among the Archives

Writing the Lives of Sir George Scharf, Victorian Bachelor

Helena Michie and Robyn Warhol

EDINBURGH
University Press

© Helena Michie and Robyn Warhol, 2015

Edinburgh University Press Ltd
The Tun - Holyrood Road
12(2f) Jackson's Entry
Edinburgh EH8 8PJ

www.euppublishing.com

Typeset in 11.25/13 New Baskerville by
Servis Filmsetting Ltd, Stockport, Cheshire,
and printed and bound in Great Britain by
CPI Group (UK) Ltd, Croydon CR0 4YY

A CIP record for this book is available from the British Library

ISBN 978 1 4744 0663 5 (hardback)
ISBN 978 1 4744 0665 9 (webready PDF)
ISBN 978 1 4744 0664 2(paperback)
ISBN 978 1 4744 0666 6 (epub)

The right of Helena Michie and Robyn Warhol to be identified as the authors of
this work has been asserted in accordance with the Copyright, Designs and Patents
Act 1988, and the Copyright and Related Rights Regulations 2003 (SI No. 2498).

Published with the support of the Edinburgh University Scholarly Publishing
Initiatives Fund.

Contents

List of illustrations

Preface

We are not afraid of telling over and over again how a man comes to fall in love with a woman and be wedded to her, or else be fatally parted from her. Is it due to excess of poetry or of stupidity that we are never weary of describing what King James called a woman's 'makdom and her fairnesse', never weary of listening to the twanging of the old Troubadour strings, and are comparatively uninterested in that other kind of 'makdom and fairnesse' which must be wooed with industrious thought and patient renunciation of small desires? In the story of this passion, too, the development varies: sometimes it is the glorious marriage, sometimes frustration and final parting. And not seldom the catastrophe is bound up with the other passion, sung by the Troubadours. For in the multitude of middle-aged men who go about their vocations in a daily course determined for them much in the same way as the tie of their cravats, there is always a good number who once meant to shape their own deeds and alter the world a little.

George Eliot, Middlemarch

This book is a love story – no matter how embarrassing these words are to write or, perhaps, to read. In the most obvious sense, the book is a story about Sir George Scharf – Victorian antiquarian, man-about-London and founding director of the National Portrait Gallery – and his loving relationships with male friends. It is also, however, about other kinds of loves – George Scharf's and our own. In *Middlemarch*, another (female) George reminds her readers of the existence of an alternative love plot, another beloved that must be 'wooed with industrious thought and patient renunciation of small desires'. This is, of course, the plot of work or vocation: we see signs of this love in the playful curlicues of George Scharf's drawings; in the time he spent each day sketching, reading, making notes and recording these activities in his diaries; in the attention he paid to the details of the portraits he examined, copied and arranged; and in the hard-won pocket money he expended travelling to great English country houses to catalogue their collections. The self-educated son of an immigrant artist, Scharf loved his work and the surprisingly elevated social life that grew up around it with titled friends and younger fellows.

The work or professional plot for George Scharf was, perhaps even more than for many other Victorians, entangled in familial structures of feeling. While love might not have been the only thing he felt for his father, the artist George Scharf Sr, the term is capacious enough, we feel, to include George Jr's quarrels with and attempts to separate himself from this man so similar to and so different from himself. By contrast, Scharf's relationships with his mother and his aunt seem simply a matter of unambivalent love, a feeling which he himself turns into narrative in his diaries through the recording of gifts and visits and the careful memorialising of their deaths in his annual entries. Traces of love for all three of his relatives show up in the most unexpected places, for example, in Scharf's meticulous (and tedious) bookkeeping, where the attentive reader can find among the neatly aligned figures notations for gifts of cream and wine for his mother or warm clothes for his father. We see traces of those gifts and that love in Scharf's often hasty letters home from the country houses and on the stationery of the rich, in which he refers mainly to money matters and to his increasing familiarity with his social betters. Announcing unapologetically one December that he will spend Christmas away from the family at a stately home, he encloses a drawing of his hostess's splendid Christmas tree for his German-born father, whose Teutonic love of the Christmas trees of his youth is part of the Scharf family lore.

George Scharf (Jr) also loved food. In many stories this would be a peripheral, if not slightly shameful, category of desire, but from our very first encounter with Scharf through his scrapbook of menus and invitations, we have been made aware of the importance of eating to Scharf's daily pleasures, his friendships and even his professional life. While food may not shape any of the plots to which we have had recourse in writing Scharf's life (in Chapter 2, the Marriage Plot; in Chapter 3, the Family Romance Plot; and in Chapter 4, the Sensation and Inheritance Plots), food is clearly part of his story – and of the story of our engagements with the archive of his life.

No one has ever written a biography of Sir George Scharf. Strictly speaking, this is still true, though Scharf's life – as glimpsed through his archival remains – is the subject of this book. From the beginning, this project has been as much about our love stories as about George Scharf's. If we became interested in him through our shared love of food (Scharf's, Robyn's and Helena's), our interest was sustained over fifteen years by what we call in the introduction to this book 'the romance of the archive' and in its title, 'love among the archives'. We fell in love with Scharf's ephemera, accidentally found in the British Library; we have loved our sojourns in the archival stacks at the National Portrait Gallery (and our tea breaks in their wonderful café); we loved our brisk walks through London from wherever we happened to be staying to the place where 'our' archive resides. We loved talking, talking, talking – with each other over those cups of tea and with colleagues at conferences where we presented pieces of this project – about 'George', and we loved writing about him together. Somewhere along the way we seem even to have fallen in love with George himself, despite his lack of glamour, good looks or lasting fame.

Even when we were most involved with the minutiae of Scharf's life, with his miniature diaries and his widely dispersed letters, we understood ourselves not merely to be talking about (although sometimes we found ourselves talking to) this one man. George Scharf is for us a way into and out of the larger stories that literary critics and historians tend to tell about Victorian life, especially those that have to do with sexuality, class and profession. Scharf's personal letters and diaries have allowed us to reconstruct – and sometimes to flesh out – a world of middle-class male households and to capture in part the elusive dailiness of masculine domesticity. His family papers and institutional records have produced for us a startling story of class ascendance and, at the same time, what might be a representative narrative of professionalisation in a moment when increasingly prestigious careers in the public sector were beginning to open up for non-university men. Scharf's life and the traces of it necessitate the creation of new identities and more nuanced narratives about what it meant for a mid-Victorian to be a bachelor, a professional, an artist, an expert, a host, a guest and a diner-out.

Scharf, as we meet him in these pages, is one among Eliot's 'multitude of middle-aged men', with or without cravats, who struggle to insert themselves into a meaningful story of personal and professional development. These stories are, as Eliot suggests, inextricably linked. The realist reader of Eliot's novels and Scharf's life can find new subjects for narrative and new names for objects and plots of love. *Middlemarch* is one of the few novels Scharf left any record of having read; as with virtually all aspects of his archive, his comments about the novel remain tantalisingly incomplete. He wrote from Brighton, where he was convalescing from scarlet fever (one of the many illnesses that marked a ten-year downturn in his health): 'Finished Middlemarch & was disappointed in the conclusion. Had seawater footbath for last time' (D 1 February 1876). Incorporated into the timeline of Scharf's life, George Eliot's novel disappoints at the moment when its plots come together. Our subject was, unaccountably, disappointed with the novel's closure, and we are, as usual, disappointed that we have no idea why. We like to think of Scharf's life and our account of it, however, as a long, productive and detailed description of middleness composed in the spirit of Eliot's great novel. Middle-aged, middle-brow and complexly middle-class, Scharf's life can be read not for its closure or the ends of his plots but for the possibilities that it offers those of us who linger with him.

Acknowledgements

A project so long in the making as *Love Among the Archives* risks taxing the patience of friends, colleagues and families. We are grateful to the many interlocutors with whom we have shared George Scharf's story and the story of our archival journey.

Given the longevity of the project and how many times we took George on the road, we cannot thank everyone who heard and responded to the project individually. We must mention two colleagues who have most profoundly shaped our work: Lara Kriegel, who inspired us to turn our initial discoveries into a book and who persuaded us we had a story worth telling; and Jules Law, our generous respondent at a Rice Feminist Research Group (FRG) seminar. Victoria Ford Smith and Lindsey Chappell were invaluable research assistants, and the inimitable Theresa Grasso Munisteri worked her characteristic magic on our manuscript.

Many groups have provided lively and helpful feedback, most notably at the Project Narrative Symposium on Queer and Feminist Narrative Theories, the Freiburg Institute for Advanced Study (FRIAS) and the FRG at Rice. Colleagues at the North American Victorian Studies Association (NAVSA), the Narrative Conference, MLA and the Dickens Project have had to endure many instalments of 'George': we thank them for their abiding interest, their questions and their suggestions. We are also grateful to the English Departments at Rice University and the Ohio State University, as well as to OSU's Dean of Arts and Humanities and FRIAS for generously funding our travel.

Though it might be going too far to call them fans of George

Scharf, several people have faithfully followed the many episodes of our story: Rosemary Hennessey, Susan Lurie, John Jordan, Jonathan Grossman, Rebecca Stern, Jay Clayton and Eileen Gilooly, in particular. Catherine Robson may get the prize for having heard the most versions of the project. Her fortitude is, we hope, rewarded by our finishing the book.

Our title reminds us of the labour and generosity of our many guides through the archives, including staff at the British Library, the British Museum, the Society of Antiquarians of London and the National Portrait Gallery, where Bryony Millan has played an especially important role. We thank the University of Edinburgh Library for giving us access to the Laing collection.

Our warmest gratitude goes to Robert Sackville and Bridget West for graciously inviting us to visit the private quarters at Knole.

We are fortunate that the publication timeline of this book has allowed us to thank those people who entered late in the process: our wise and witty copyeditor, Nicola Wood; our professional and supportive editor at EUP, Jackie Jones; and those staff members at the British Library, the British Museum and the National Portrait Gallery who supplied images and permissions for our illustrations. Since the majority of our images come from the NPG, and most had to be photographed especially for this project, we are particularly grateful to Emma Butterfield, who efficiently helped shape and streamline the permissions process in a way that would, we feel sure, have made the founding director proud.

Our families have lived more intimately with the exigencies of this project than anyone else. We are, as always, thankful for the forbearance of our sons, Ross Michie-Derrick, Seth Warhol-Streeter and Paul Michie-Derrick. It was a shock to realise that this project has almost spanned Paul's lifetime – and it has probably felt equally long to Ross and Seth, who can't remember a time when their mothers were not running off to London to 'work on George'. To them, to their fathers Scott Derrick and Tom Streeter, to our spouses (that same Scott Derrick and Peter Kriff) and to Robyn's stepson Max Kriff, we extend our most heartfelt thanks.

And finally we thank each other. For all these years we have collaborated (as Helena once wrote in inscribing a book to Robyn) '(almost) without sororophobia'. It has been a continual rediscovery of love among the archives.

A vita for Sir George Scharf (GS)

George Scharf in his youth

1816 George Johann Scharf arrives in London, sees people looking at white cakes in shop windows in Piccadilly.

1817 Two paintings by George Sr exhibited for the first time at
the Royal Academy.

1820 George Scharf Jr (GS) is born on 16 December to George
Scharf Sr and his wife, Elizabeth Hicks, co-owner with her
sister of a grocery shop in St Martin's Lane. They married
four months before GS's birth.

1830 GS attending University College School with his only
brother, Henry, two years younger. Scharf family living at
No. 14 Francis Street, near Victoria Station.

1836 Queen Victoria orders three copies of George Sr's drawing
of three giraffes displayed at the British Museum.

1839 GS, age nineteen, travels with Sir Charles Fellows to Turkey,
stopping on the way in Paris. Sketches Xanthus marbles in
situ.

George Scharf in his twenties

1843 GS goes again with Fellows to Turkey.

1845 GS, age twenty-five, begins his diaries, using a single-volume
format.
George Sr returns to Germany, spends two years there with

a sick brother. Makes the last three paintings he will show at Royal Academy.

1847 Macaulay's *Lays of Ancient Rome* published with illustrations by GS.

1848 GS with mother, aunt and father (back from Germany) moves to 1 Torrington Square in Bloomsbury, where rent is expensive.

GS gives lectures on art to young ladies at Queen's College, his father providing large-scale illustrations.

1849 GS travels to Rempstone, home of Lady Caroline Sitwell, probably his first visit to a great country house.

George Scharf in his thirties

1850 GS visits Embley, home of the Nightingales.

1851 GS begins travelling to cathedrals in southern England, making sketches for John Murray's guide.

1852 Election of GS to Society of Antiquaries. Lord Stanhope (then Viscount Mahon) supports his election.

First dinner-party table diagram in GS's diary. Father at head of table, 'I' at foot.

GS giving drawing lessons to ladies, including anatomy.

1853 GS's mother begins keeping a diary. For two years running, every day, she writes just 'bread, milk, ale'.

Brother Henry, an actor, has by now emigrated to the United States.

Scharf family falling behind in payments to tradesmen and shops.

1854 GS applies for position of secretary of the National Gallery, presents recommendations from twenty prominent academics, artists, noblemen, clerics and British Museum administrators; does not get the job.

GS visits Cambridge University, finds his British Museum connections are an advantage there.

Spends Christmas at Rempstone Hall. Promises to sketch tree for his father.

1855 Mother's diary notes once a month 'George had a smoking party'.

Scharf family having increasing difficulty paying their bills.

1856 GS, mother and aunt move to 1 Eastcott Place in Camden

Town; father moves to separate one-room lodging at 37 Preston Street nearby.

GS designs sets and costumes for Charles Kean's production of *The Winter's Tale*.

GS travelling with photographer to make images of cathedrals for *Murray's Guide*. Gives successful lectures in Oxford and Leeds.

GS appointed art secretary to the Manchester Art Treasures Exhibition; begins visiting great country houses to select paintings for exhibit.

1857　GS starts using 'Lett's Professional or Monthly Diary' format. Lord Stanhope appoints GS secretary of the new National Portrait Gallery (NPG) at 29 Great George Street, determines that salary should be liberal and secretary should live on the premises.

GS sketches Florence Nightingale at Embley.

Manchester Art Treasures Exhibition opens, with sixteen thousand works on display, many chosen by GS.

GS moves to apartment over NPG. Mother and aunt come for overnight visits from Camden Town.

1858　GS visits Chevening, Stanhope country estate at Sevenoaks in Kent, for first time.

GS makes first sketching excursion to Knole at Sevenoaks.

Lord Stanhope's professional communications with GS have been impatient and critical. After a trip he and GS make to Canterbury, he is more cordial.

GS retires from Queen's College, gives series of lectures in Birmingham.

1859　Mother's diary reports her servant, Ellen, had been embezzling funds intended for tradesmen. Ellen is dismissed and prosecuted for 'frauds'. Ellen had been with the family since Torrington Square.

George Sr, still living alone, applies to Artists' Amicable Fund for a sick allowance to be added to his pension.

GS frequently visits 'my good friend Miss Bayley' at Wimbledon.

GS produces catalogue of pictures at Blenheim Palace.

George Scharf in his forties

1860   Lord Stanhope gives permission for GS's mother and aunt to move into the third-floor space above his apartment at the NPG in Great George Street.

George Sr sells his large watercolours of the ruins of Parliament for only £2 10s.

Henry Scharf returns for a visit from America, where he has worked as an actor and a teacher of anatomical drawing.

GS regularly visiting Chevening and Blenheim.

George Sr in his final illness moves to Great George Street apartment, where he dies.

1861   Charles Dickens comes to NPG for a private viewing.

Prince Albert consults GS about portraits at Windsor Castle. GS, not treated as a guest, has to buy his own refreshment in Windsor that day. GS goes back to Windsor Castle twice that year.

Prince Albert suddenly sickens and dies. GS takes the loss very hard.

1862   First mentions of Jack Pattisson in GS's diary's year-end summary.

Sale of the late George Sr's drawings to British Museum brings in substantial revenue for GS's mother.

1863   GS's list of titled friends expands to include the Duke and Duchess of Marlborough, Lord Bristol, Lord and Lady Darnley and the Archbishop of Canterbury.

1864   Death of GS's Aunt Mary at Great George Street leaves only his mother in the upstairs rooms.

Staying at Chevening, GS receives from Lady Mary (Stanhope's daughter) a pair of slippers she made for him.

Jack Pattisson spends almost every evening with GS and his mother above NPG. GS's diary says this 'has done me a great deal of good & kept me very steadily at home'.

For the first time GS accepts an honorarium for cataloguing a private portrait collection, having asked Lord Stanhope's permission.

GS's mother and Jack's mother exchange visits.

GS's relations with the Stanhopes and Marlboroughs are increasingly friendly.

1865   GS's year-end summary says Jack Pattisson is 'like a brother'.

1866   Pattisson again cited as 'like a brother'.

1867   GS travels abroad, visiting Paris and making sketches at the Louvre and the World Exposition.

Pattisson's constant presence keeps GS home in the evenings and gives him an unprecedented 'pleasure in home'.

1868   Pattisson and GS often attend theatre and opera together, at GS's expense.

GS dismisses his maid, Anne, for having a man secretly in her bedroom.

GS's mother often ill but cheerful to the end, singing 'old songs' at home in the evenings.

GS's 'dear old friend' Miss Bayley dies at Wimbledon. Leaves GS a £500 legacy and a piano. GS gives Jack a £25 share.

1869   GS's mother dies. Pattisson and GS are the only two people at her funeral.

GS makes contact with brother, Henry, in America.

GS for the first time invests 'in the public funds', in the amount of £400.

Jack Pattisson, 'more brotherly than ever', takes a job in Ireland as secretary to Lord Dufferin.

NPG moves from Great George Street to South Kensington. GS takes lodgings at 8 Ashley Place.

GS sends his old piano to Pattisson in Ireland as a gift.

George Scharf in his fifties

1870   GS stays at Chevening, visits Knole as guest, stays at Blenheim Palace.

GS celebrates fiftieth birthday, thankful for how 'little bodily illness I have known & how few disappointments of any kind'.

GS's diary reports he has thought of writing to his brother in America, but does not have time.

1871   Pattisson spends much of his summer break at 8 Ashley Place with GS; they attend Freemasons' meetings, plays and operas together.

Scharf dreams of being beheaded, wakes upon remembering he ought to write to his brother Henry.

1872   Pattisson is often home from Ireland, staying with GS at 8 Ashley Place.

Pattisson leaves a message for GS saying he has become engaged.

Lord Dufferin, now governor of Canada, assigns Jack to a Canadian posting.

GS hosts bachelor party for Pattisson, pays for carriage with footman and postilions to carry Jack, Jack's brother and GS to the wedding.

Pattisson marries Ellen Miller in London, moves with her to Canada.

GS begins 'walking Masonically' in his room late at night to retaliate for loud piano playing downstairs.

1873   Piano Wars continue at Ashley Place.

Nellie Pattisson in Canada is presumed pregnant for nine months, and doctors are puzzled when she produces no baby.

Lady Stanhope dies. GS: 'Another link with my former belongings! Gone!'

1874   GS is initiated as a Freemason, becomes master of his Lodge.

Pattisson tries for a new job in London; Lord Dufferin reassigns him to Ireland four years before he is scheduled to leave Canada.

GS shaves for the last time, begins to grow his beard.

GS is ill from October through end of year. Permanent stiffness in left arm and hand are the aftermath.

1875   GS proposes extended visit to Knole, stays several weeks to sketch and arrange pictures.

GS is frequently at Chevening. Lord Stanhope is ill, dies in December. GS has scarlet fever, misses Lord Stanhope's funeral.

1876   GS recuperates at Brighton; he reads *Middlemarch* and is disappointed by the ending.

Mrs Lee, household servant to GS since 1868, leaves GS's service and 'is heartily tired of it'.

Piano Wars continue at Ashley Place.

GS hires Mr and Mrs Ball and rents modest 'villa' in Vauxhall for them to live in. Before they start work he makes complete inventory of his silver-plate flatware.

GS stays at Chevening, Knole, Blenheim and Bayham Abbey. When at home GS has many dinner guests.

Jack and Nellie Pattisson produce a daughter, Winnie.

GS in October and November makes unusual references to enjoying romps with children at country houses.

Two days before Christmas GS's scullery is swamped with

water that came in through the roof after a storm. GS: 'It was hard work for Mrs Ball.'

1877 GS begins practising piano at the villa in Vauxhall. The exercise helps with stiffness in his left hand. He also increases frequency of walks in London and is 'not increased in bulk'. GS spends most of the summer at Knole.
Application to NPG for pay raise by GS fails.
The night before an Ashley Place dinner party, GS has a nightmare of being beheaded.

1878 GS spends June at Knole. Goes back in October to find most of the servants have left over a dispute with Lord Sackville. GS advises under-butler to stay on.
GS spends Christmas at Knole.

1879 GS's New Year's entry says, 'My size of body is not less. But I take exercise & live regularly.'
GS visits Knole. Gives an 'extremely successful dinner' at Ashley Place serving gifts sent from Knole, including venison, chestnuts, gorgonzola and oranges.
GS writes letter to editor of *The Times* correcting identification of some portraits at the South Kensington NPG.
The Times runs an article on need for bigger space for NPG, praising GS's clever devices for co-ordinating the direction of light with the direction of light in the paintings.

George Scharf in his sixties

1880 Jack Pattisson becomes private secretary to William H. Smith, first lord of the Admiralty, in London. According to genealogical website he is lodging alone in the home of a telephone clerk.
Freeman 'Donny' O'Donoghue, age thirty-two, on staff at the British Museum, becomes a regular at GS's dinner parties and is often at Ashley Place in the evenings to work on GS's catalogue of brief descriptions of artists.
Piano Wars continue with downstairs neighbour. O'Donoghue falls asleep on the sofa one night despite the noise.
GS takes Donny on excursions to Windsor and Hampton Court.
Pattisson frequently dines 'with us', GS and Donny. Donny now sits at the foot of the table.

GS notes the death of George Eliot.

GS remonstrates with his servant Mr Ball for inebriety of Mrs Ball, the housekeeper.

1881 Donny constantly at Ashley Place in the evenings. Pattisson and other friends often there for dinner.

GS in pain from loss of teeth; gets fitted for false teeth. Rheumatism in the foot and knee also bother him.

1882 GS promoted from secretary to director of the NPG.

1883 GS dismisses Mr and Mrs Ball after overhearing her using foul language during an argument between them in the kitchen.

GS dreams again of being beheaded.

Times runs an article calling GS 'the most competent living authority on royal portraiture'.

1884 Donny makes a rude remark at dinner, which GS resents.

GS's diary declares Donny 'not a good manager or companion in a crowd'.

1885 GS awarded CB (Companion of the Order of Bath).

Spending Christmas at Chevening, GS becomes ill. His neck becomes stiff, requiring him to hold his head always bent down.

1886 Last card in GS's album collected this year.

GS very ill for over six months, suffering from inflamed gums and a dry cough. He is at first 'quite miserable and could eat nothing'.

GS finds the boardroom at the new NPG site too draughty to be healthy.

'Donny the faithful' still visiting almost every evening, per GS's diary. He is 'very nice & thoughtful'. Pattisson also visits several times a week during GS's long illness.

Servant Mr Carter disappears on a drinking binge for several days after GS gives him a guinea; GS does not dismiss him.

GS suffers deafness as a result of his long illness. His diary says he cannot hear conversation at table and is 'irritable and depressed'.

GS has more teeth removed and replaced with false ones. Frequently he has turpentine poultices applied, which leave painful rashes on his chest.

In July GS takes Donny on a holiday to Margate. They have a cabinet-card portrait taken together.

By year's end GS is feeling well and sleeps comfortably. The deafness has abated in the right ear. He is taking long walks in London.

1887 GS's diary says he has 'become fat and old'. Still deaf on the left side, he can hear on the right and can carry on one-on-one conversations. By December he believes he has fully recovered his hearing, but later developments prove otherwise.

At the National Gallery GS runs into the Crown Prince of Germany, who recognises him and reminds him he purchased a GS sketch of a Raphael painting.

GS consults Pattisson on changes to his will.

Donny still constantly there in the evenings.

GS's diary's year-end summary says he now 'enjoys a full sense of comfort, happiness, love of friends, & I hope also proper contentment'.

1888 Health much improved, GS appreciates continual presence of friends and notes 'Donny still closer'.

Servant Mrs Carter complains loudly of having to wait on Donny as well as GS, because she contracted only to work for 'one family'.

GS still visits Chevening and South Park but finds beds at South Park too soft and has to sleep on sofa in his room.

By year's end GS's 'powers of walking are very limited' and he stoops with 'head thrust forward'.

1889 Philanthropist William Henry Alexander donates the money and the government donates the land in St Martin's Place for the present NPG building, behind the National Gallery at Trafalgar Square.

GS's diary complains of weakness and lassitude but reports improved cheerfulness.

Donny still a constant companion in the evenings, beating GS at cribbage almost every night.

Going to visit Donny in his new lodgings at Clement's Inn, GS gets lost by mistakenly going to Clifford's Inn and has to walk several blocks to find the right place.

One night Mrs Carter serves up delicious strawberries and cream for dessert and, afterwards, anchovies on toast, 'too much both for Donny and me'.

At Chevening in September, GS enjoys sunlight in the garden and writes, 'I have rarely felt a sense of intense beauty & enjoyment of life as during that half hour.'

GS notes in year-end summary that he is in debt, but only for small amounts for clothing and piano repair.

George Scharf in his seventies

1890 GS now has great difficulty walking in London, due to 'very hard breathing'.

GS complains that at an Ashley Place dinner party his friends 'spoke inaudibly'. His deafness increases.

GS still has difficulty with breathing, painful gums and fatigue, but diary reports gratitude that he sleeps so well.

1891 Pattisson, now working at the Treasury and commuting by train from Eastbourne to London, assists GS in making further changes to his will, to the benefit of Donny and three other friends.

GS, now seventy-one and still in his NPG director position, receives from the Treasury a circular about compulsory resignation after age sixty-five. Writes to Lord Hardinge, chair of NPG Board, about it.

1894 GS's diary, now and in previous two years, dominated by daily inventory of physical symptoms and problems with elimination.

When going out, GS orders a carrying chair. Going up and down stairs he must be carried. Donny often assists.

On GS's birthday in December, seven old friends come to dinner. GS notes that Pattisson is abroad until January and cannot come.

For the first time, ladies come to Ashley Place to visit GS in his illness, including the younger Lady Stanhope.

1895 Now GS can only go to the office in a Bath chair and be carried upstairs. This keeps him often at home.

GS still enjoys rich meals at home.

GS is awarded KCB by Queen Victoria. He is now Sir George Scharf. Insignia and dispensation arrive at Ashley Place by mail.

In February Donny's sister dies, and in March his brother dies; Donny's mother has also been ill. GS's diary says Donny is 'terribly pulled down'.

GS can no longer tolerate much company besides his medical attendants, Donny and, occasionally, Pattisson. He is easily fatigued.

GS retires from directorship of NPG and is replaced by Lionel Cust. GS appointed as an NPG trustee.

Bedridden in great discomfort, GS dies 19 April. His last diary entry is dated 15 April.

1896   NPG moves to new building in St Martin's Square.

1

Introduction:
adventures in the archives

THE ALBUM IS HUGE.[1] *Depending on which librarian brings it to the circulation desk, you might be offered a cart to carry it to your seat in the British Library Reading Room or you might have to tote it yourself. Its vertical length is at least two feet; its width nearly as great. The covers are a dusty red-brown, faded and scratched, and the binding is broken so that the album must be tied with a flat cord to keep it from falling open when lifted. Inside, musty pages of heavy paper require you to stretch out your whole arm to turn them. Neatly affixed to the pages in rough chronological order are a variety of items in card stock: calling cards with the names of English dukes and duchesses in elaborate scripted fonts; handwritten menus for French meals served in grand country houses; seating charts for dinners large and small; printed bills of fare for restaurant banquets. The pages, despite their slight yellowing and a faint but perceptible yellowish smell, have an aura of faded opulence. Some of the menus are charmingly illustrated: in the four corners of one are the heads of three dogs and one fox, adorably drawn in the style of particularly cunning children's illustrations; another is bordered by gambolling cherubs eating, drinking from pitchers, ringing a dinner bell and having a smoke; many feature floral borders. Some, recurring every few pages, are three-dimensional. Flattened into crosses, if you fold them – as we did many times – they become tiny blue and white boxes with the name 'Knole' in gold letters on what becomes the top of the box. Fifteen years ago, the first time we saw the album, the cards and sheets of stationery were pristine, the pages of the album properly bound. Today many of the pages have come loose, and someone (surely not us?) appears to have turned them carelessly, so as to bend and crease some of the cards (Fig. 1.1).*

When we first ordered the album – having found an intriguing entry in

1

Fig. 1.1 Page from George Scharf's album of menus and invitations.
©The British Library Board, 1887.c.14.

the British Library's newly available online catalogue of Special Collections, 'A Collection of Invitation Cards, Menus, etc. from 1869 to 1876' – our interest was in Victorian food. As we turned the pages of the album, we became fascinated by the paper objects that recorded and memorialised the transitory act of eating. After a few days of browsing, our questions became biographical. We wanted to know the name of the man who had put the album together, a question we had elided in our initial eagerness to touch and to explore with our eyes the evidence of his dining. The man's name was Sir George Scharf. We had never heard of him, and neither had our Victorianist colleagues. While we might have come to our knowledge of him through footnotes in books about museum history, art history, Victorian archaeology and travel history, or even theatre history, as it happens we encountered him in an undigested archive for which we had neither context nor provenance. As a result, we thought of him for a very long time in terms of what he ate.

With the privilege of hindsight, we know George Scharf, the almost-famous subject of this book, to have been dying throughout 1895. He had suffered for over a year with a variety of debilitating symptoms, including swollen legs, a sore left foot that had to be continually 'pricked' and 'punctured', sudden urges to urinate and defecate, blood in his urine, diarrhoea and chills. There were, however, compensations big and small. On 12 February of that fateful year, he received, in acknowledgement of his distinguished record as the founding director of the National Portrait Gallery (NPG), royal orders making him Sir George Scharf. His diary, meticulously kept until the very end, notes: 'Royal Grant signed by the Queen for my KCB. [D]elivered Sunday afternoon 24th February, at lunch time' (D 24 February 1895). The temporal markers with which this announcement ends – the precise date and the salient time of day – suggest compensations of another sort: the satisfaction of his diary-writing itself, with its careful financial and professional accounting that chronicled a fifty-year upward journey through London society, and the pleasures of the dining-table recorded in those diaries and commemorated in the album.

Sir George Scharf – as we must call him after that crucial date in February of 1895 – ate his last fully recorded meal alone. Despite his considerable digestive troubles, the meal was a pleasure to him. On 19 February, after the announcement of his KCB, before the Queen's official signing of the grant and two months before his death, Scharf wrote in his diary: 'Excellent dinner alone in Library.

Gravy soup. Mutton cutlet. Ptarmigan [grouse]. Cold rhubarb tart. Cheese. Coffee. Claret (good).' We do not know if this assortment of rich foods aggravated his symptoms; if we take Scharf on his own terms, the gravy soup, the tart, and even the claret were simply part of an 'excellent dinner'. This is a case where our twenty-first-century sense of what is medically dangerous was approximated by the Victorians who attributed, as we know, all manner of diseases to rich diet (see Porter and Rousseau, Chap. 1); it is no anachronism to say that Scharf was risking his health for the pleasures of the (in this case solitary) table. This coming together of Scharf's pleasures, professional and gustatory, illustrates two aspects of his personality as we have come to understand it: the social climber and the diner.

We realise that terms like 'social climber' and 'diner' are not traditional answers to the question, 'Who was George Scharf?' a question made more urgent (at least for those who might consider reading this book) by his surprising obscurity in the nearly 130 years since his death. Sir George Scharf does have more conventional claims on the attention of Victorianists, art historians and the community of gallery and museum goers more generally. As the first director of the National Portrait Gallery, he presided over its development from a tiny collection located in a crowded and undistinguished London townhouse to the monumental tourist attraction in Trafalgar Square that it is today. He was responsible not only for the acquisition of thousands of portraits but for research on their provenance and authenticity. By the time of his death he was acknowledged as the nation's expert on British Royal portraiture, and his opinion was sought by both amateur and professional collectors when it came to authenticating (or exposing as fake) a particular portrait. Over his lifetime he illustrated dozens of books, among them Victorian editions of Keats's and Milton's poetry, an edition of Macaulay's *Lays of Ancient Rome*, a British edition of Horace's works, an English translation of Dante's *The Divine Comedy* and a translation from the German of Theodor Panofka's *Manners and Customs of the Greeks*. A theatre enthusiast, he produced a book of *Recollections of the Scenic Effects of the Covent Garden Theatre, 1838–39* and designed scenery and costumes for at least one production by Charles Kean. He was a drawing master for young ladies: his pupils included a granddaughter of Lord Byron.[2] He was the art secretary of the Manchester Art Treasures Exhibition of 1857. Although he had not been formally educated beyond grammar school, he lectured on ancient art to university audiences as well as to groups of professionals in London, Bath, Manchester and other cities. While he was still a teenager, he accompanied Sir Charles Fellows on the expedition to bring to London the Xanthus marbles, assigned to sketch the ruins as they lay before Fellows and his team of archaeologists/despoilers took them to exhibit in the British Museum, where some of them feature prominently today.

If these accomplishments make Scharf exceptional or singular, differentiating him, for example, from his father (the failed and bankrupt immigrant artist George Scharf Sr), George Scharf Jr was also in some ways a representative Victorian of a certain class and professional status. Tracing the trajectory from his father's gentle failure to his own robust social success, we can see that his ascent in the world required a lot of effort. Like many of the Victorians we love to hate for their boundless energy, he was a joiner: he was a member of the Royal Archaeological Society, both the Reform Club *and* the Conservative Club, the Institute of British Architects and the Worshipful Company of Brewers, to name just a few of his affiliations. His life brushed up against many of definitional Victorian institutions to the point where he might seem almost parodically familiar, even to those who have not heard of him. He was involved not just with the NPG and Covent Garden Theatre but also with the British Museum, the Manchester Art Treasures Exhibition and even the ubiquitous Crystal Palace, for which he authored and illustrated official guides to the Greek, Roman and Pompeian courts. He was connected to, but not entirely one with, the great and the titled, mostly the titled. For us, his status as a representative Victorian was made official when Scharf appeared in Dickens's correspondence as the recipient of a brief thank-you note (*Letters*, p. 695).

Over the years that we have been working on this project, we have struggled to name and to describe the man at its centre. When we speak to each other about our work together, we call him – and the entire project – 'George', coincidentally a name Helena's family has long used as a form of placeholder, a substitute for 'what's-his-name'. When we describe our project to others, we tend to use his most institutionally legible title and to call on his identity as the director of the National Portrait Gallery. The process of writing this book, however, has involved trying out, collecting and often discarding a series of identifiers for our subject: some traditional, some less so; some nouns, some adjectives; some satisfactory, most of them not. Although we will not discuss all of them here, we offer a grammatically and ontologically unparallel list of many of our operative terms: 'professional', 'bachelor', 'middle-class', 'queer', 'snob', 'diner', 'eater', 'artist', 'Sir George', 'George Junior', 'Scharf', 'diarist', 'guest', 'host', 'fat man', 'extra man', 'socialite', just plain 'George' – and on bad days in the archives, 'The Most Boring Man in the World'.

The impulse to name – and indeed to place – George Scharf is, of course, itself worth scrutinising. Our need to do so comes in part from the archival fantasies that we discuss at length later in this chapter. We were excited to have stumbled on this little-known Victorian, but if our project was to mean anything, to contribute to the sum of knowledge in this field or in that, Scharf himself would, we felt, have to be meaningful. How that meaning might be identified or communicated was, of course, a major issue: was this a recovery project that (re)inserted Scharf into his proper place in a canon of art history, museum history or Victorian studies? Was he worth the many years of research and writing that we had spent on him (already a revealing formulation) because he was singular or exceptional, or was it because he was representative of groups of other professionals, artists, bachelors or diners?[3]

Identifying George Scharf

One way of providing a sense of Scharf's identity and importance is to produce a list of his accomplishments, like the one above. 'Accomplishments' in this context are almost always professional; in current academic circles these would be the sort of thing one would put on a curriculum vitae (literally, 'current of life'), a genre we have come to think of as a kind of shorthand life-writing. While Scharf's professional and personal lives were, perhaps, even more than most people's, inextricably linked, we would like to lead with the professional context of which the c.v. or the vita is a reminder.

In some sense Scharf was an artist, but the term seems both too grand and too narrow to describe the many things he did with pencils and charcoal: while he was not a painter or a sculptor of what we would still call great art, while he was not a member of the Royal Academy, while he did not, after his youth, exhibit his work in galleries, he was, nonetheless, much in demand throughout his lifetime for the artistic skills which he put to such a variety of uses.[4] It is a pity that there is no English noun that comes directly out of the verb to 'draw', at least none that does not freeze George Scharf – singularly inappropriately for someone so mobile – into part of a piece of furniture. 'Draw-er' won't do, but 'draughtsman' seems too mechanical, though it is a word that aptly focuses on skill. 'Illustrator' captures something of his often secondary or derivative status, but it strikes us as too literal and confining. It also substitutes the end for the process in a way that elides what to us was most characteristic and compelling about his work. He was, for example, an illustrator of Fellows's successful *Introductory Remarks to Lycia, Caria, Lydia* (1847). His published drawings for the book included careful renditions of the horses, lions and human figures that appeared on the Lycean tombs so central to Fellows's archaeological project. The illustrations selected by Fellows are, in the main, fairly traditional architectural drawings, although there is something in the upward curl of the mouth on the lions of the Lion Tomb that suggests the energy and personality of the sketches that explode over the pages of Scharf's own notebooks recording the trip. In contrast to the official record, Scharf's personal pictorial journals from that expedition include everything from even more animated versions of the marbles, to page after page of Turkish turbans (he loved costumes), to vignettes of locals eating and drinking (we know he loved food). 'Illustrator' does not account for the energetic proliferation of images in those sketchbooks.

Perhaps, then, George Scharf was a 'sketcher'. This word, if it can be called a word at all, links him to his father. George Scharf Sr, too, was always sketching; it is to him that we owe a detailed and gorgeous visual record of the rebuilding of London during the Regency and, more generally, a lively visual lexicon of lower-class street life that predated the unillustrated articles by Henry Mayhew in the *Morning Chronicle* which were collected in 1851 as *London Labour and the London Poor*. 'Sketcher' suggests, at least to us, not only the compulsion to record the world around them, which father and son evidently shared, but (to borrow from the nineteenth-century literary genre of the 'sketch', as in Dickens's *Sketches by Boz*) also an attempt to capture that world through freezing a moment in time. 'Sketcher' shares with 'draw-er', however, the inadequacy of the suffix to turn all things and actions into the people that perform them; as of this writing 'sketchers', spelled a little differently, are a brand of athletic shoes.

Any identity constrained to Scharf's professional life narrowly construed is also not faithful to how we first came across him and, thus, to the archival process which is as much the subject of this book as is Scharf himself. As our epigraph recounts, our first encounter with the person whom we came to identify as George Scharf was through his album. The records of the private dinners, we came to realise, were traces of his work as a consultant on portrait collections, and the restaurant menus were souvenirs from dinners of the professional societies to which he belonged. Before we even thought to look at the name of the man who had produced this collection, we had – as we have said – unconsciously identified him in terms of the food he ate. He was, to us, an eater. Discovering his name and his professional profile laid down a parallel track of public accomplishment, but the detailed menus, of which we will speak much more later, were formative of our sense of 'George Scharf' and of the project that we hoped would embody him.

The term 'eater', however evocative, is not part of an identificatory canon any more than are 'sketch-er' and 'draw-er'; descriptive of neither a job nor a relationship, 'eater' seems at best insufficient, amateurish, even distasteful as a way of describing or summing up a life. And yet, far from being a hobby or pastime (or even a pathology), the consumption of meals – whether he was eating in or dining out – was for George Scharf an important part of his professional existence. The menus and place cards he kept and so carefully pasted into his album were individually and collectively signs of his professional, as well as his social, success. Scharf, then, could be said to be a professional diner whose rising reputation depended in part on a previous record of having been a dinner guest.

Although we want to keep all of the terms we explored in play, we were especially attracted to 'diner'. Despite the fact that this word, too, suffers from the reification problem, 'diner' is also a word used to describe people. People at restaurants (or even at diners) are 'diners'; they are, signally, 'dining out'. After some fifteen years spent with his papers, we have come also to see Scharf as a host whose (inevitably all male) dinner parties at home formed a crucial part of his emotional life; we will say more about this identity later. The album memorialises him primarily as a guest, a diner-out rather than a diner-in. The regular diner-out has a long tradition in Victorian and early twentieth-century literature; the man who always dines out is sometimes represented as a fraud or a parasite who is simply avoiding paying for his own food, like Mr Twemlow in Dickens's *Our Mutual Friend,* about whom we will have more to say as a literary instantiation of many of George Scharf's attributes. Scharf, as his meticulous financial accounts reveal, had persistent trouble making ends meet and was probably grateful to have good dinners frequently offered to him at no direct cost. For Scharf, however, there was no such thing as a free dinner; even his professional travel appears usually to have been out-of-pocket: his trips to aristocratic homes like Knole and Chevening in Kent always involved some financial outlay – cabs, trains, articles of formal clothing, tips to the servants. Of course, those trips might result in paid work or work that would raise his professional stature, so it is hard, even when you follow the beautifully precise and rounded figures of his daily accounting, to come up with a financial cost/benefit analysis of his dinners. Part of our project is to try to determine what he gained from these dinners in terms of class and reputation: the professional and snob value that could not be (directly) recorded in his bookkeeping.

All the dinner invitations we have seen are addressed to 'Mr George Scharf' alone. As there never was a 'Mrs Scharf' after his mother died, George conducted his social life as a bachelor, another of the identities with which we have experimented. To be sure, the term 'bachelor' was used more neutrally then than in the 1950s, where it began to signify a man who was highly but not monogamously (hetero)sexually active, or today when, to the extent that it is used at all, it gets paired with 'confirmed' to become a euphemism for 'gay'. Scharf's bachelorhood seems to have been a given; we have not read a single letter or diary entry in which he or anyone else suggests that Scharf should or could – or might want to – marry. Like many of the most powerful identifiers, 'bachelor' remains unspoken in Scharf's diaries and letters until, as we explain in Chapter 2, the unexpected marriage of the young man Scharf loved brings the word into play, attaching itself to Scharf by way of contrast and, we believe, of mourning. That first appearance of 'bachelor' on the record occurs in a note Scharf wrote, inviting male guests to dinner to celebrate the beloved young man's impending wedding (GS to W. F. Beauford, 20 September 1872; JP 72). While we explore in Chapter 2 the limits and possibilities of words like 'gay' and 'queer' both for Scharf and for the narratives he – and we – tell about his life, we deploy 'bachelor' as a way of thinking about Scharf's representativeness and of what his life might have to tell Victorianists about a world in which both marriage and sexuality appear to be absent. Neither the always-about-to-be married nor the sexy man about town, Scharf seems to have lived in a world without recourse to sex. In Chapter 2 we talk about the tension between

9

that surface world and the possibility that Scharf had one or more male lovers, but for now we want to linger on the possibility that sex was not central – discursively or otherwise – to Scharf's life and identity. This absence – and again we are, as it were, only trying it on – brings to the foreground other bodily experiences and expressions. Without sex we can focus on eating, drinking, walking, physical pain, reactions to heat and cold, sketching and the physicality of writing. Each one of these activities, of course, can be assumed to be a sublimation or a compensation for a missing sexual experience, but again, we want to take the experiences themselves seriously, to live with them and with Scharf until we understand more about their pleasures and their pains before reabsorbing them into a sexual narrative. The word 'bachelor', usually a sexual category, can, we feel, be used – at least temporarily – as a way out of the hegemony of the sexual.

During the time we have been working on the project, another dining-based identity has emerged in what we will call later in this chapter the 'institutional archive' of the National Portrait Gallery. The NPG website offers two virtual 'journeys' for website visitors interested in Scharf: 'Official Scharf', which includes 'Father of the Gallery' and 'Researcher', and 'Private Scharf', which includes 'Victorian Socialite' and 'Londoner', thus distinguishing his professional from his social identities. We were surprised during our own predictable rush to the *OED* that the term 'socialite' did not seem to be explicitly gendered. The first entry, from 1909, does not mark the sex of the 'ultra socialites' that 'were wont to gather at the bidding of the lovely daughter of the house', and examples from the last fifty years use the word to describe people of both genders. We felt, nonetheless, that 'socialite', for most people, is gendered female. While we liked the ambiguity of the term – the tension between its official relation to gender and its quotidian uses, as well as its slightly anachronistic feel – we felt that another term from twentieth-century dining culture had even more possibilities.

For George Scharf's social life, being a bachelor signified the ability to play 'the extra man'. As far as we can tell, 'extra man' is a locution of the mid-twentieth century, but we have taken it up for its special applicability to Scharf's social function. While Victorians seem to have been quite at ease with dinner parties at which there were more men than women, the opposite was clearly not the case.[5] Men could go down to dinner from the drawing-room unpaired, but an extra man was useful for walking unaccompanied women to the dining-room and sitting between them at table. 'Extra' here means single, available and serviceable. Scharf's 'extra-ness' – by no means to be confused with extraordinariness and often probably opposed to it – had everything to do with his singleness, which is not to say his singularity.

In thinking about what it might have meant to be an 'extra man', we had characteristic recourse to the literary example we have already briefly mentioned, *Our Mutual Friend*'s Mr Twemlow, the subject of one of Dickens's famously overextended metaphors – in this case a metaphor, among other things, for overextension itself:

> There was an innocent piece of dinner-furniture that went upon easy castors and was kept over a livery stable-yard in Duke Street, Saint James's, when not in use, to whom the Veneerings were a source of blind confusion. The name of this article was Twemlow. Being first cousin to Lord Snigsworth, he was in frequent requisition, and at many houses might be said to represent the dining-table in its normal state. Mr. and Mrs. Veneering, for example, arranging a dinner, habitually started with Twemlow, and then put leaves in him, or added guests to him. Sometimes, the table consisted of Twemlow and half-a-dozen leaves; sometimes, of Twemlow and a dozen leaves; sometimes, Twemlow was pulled out to his utmost extent of twenty leaves. Mr. and Mrs. Veneering on occasions of ceremony faced each other in the centre of the board, and thus the parallel still held; for it always happened that the more Twemlow was pulled out, the further he found himself from the centre, and the nearer to the sideboard at one end of the room, or the window-curtains at the other. (Dickens, *Our Mutual Friend*, p. 6)

Both ubiquitous and peripheral, Twemlow is part of the furniture of the social class to which he belongs. The grander the party, the less central he is, although he is always present and always accounted for. As 'an innocent piece of dinner-furniture' he straddles the divide between the human and the non-human, deadwood and the wooden 'leaves' of upper-class dining-tables. We do not know how Scharf's hosts constructed their guest lists, whether they started with Scharf, added him in at the end as a gendered make-weight or thought of him as central to an amusing evening. We do know that he was often present at great homes when other guests were not, straddling other lines between the professional and the social, as we explain in more detail in Chapter 4. We know from his diaries and correspondence that he valued after-dinner conversation with lords and ladies and, perhaps, especially with lords. Unlike Twemlow, of course, Scharf was not a poor relation of the aristocracy descending

the social scale; he was an ambitious professional man whose presence at dinner parties signalled a rise in status. Fancifully, perhaps,
we could think of Scharf and Twemlow passing each other on the
social scale, pausing as it were to dine – and to dine again.

And dine he did, ultimately qualifying Scharf for another of the
identities we have tried on, the 'fat man'.[6] Portraits, cabinet cards
and cartes-de-visite in the NPG collection show his increasingly
rounded girth, though the Santa Claus beard that made him look
in later life like an affable elf did not get started until 1874 when, at
age fifty-four, he 'ceased to shave' (D 11 October 1874), an event he
was to note on its anniversary for many years afterwards. Considering
what George Scharf ate every day, it's not surprising that he got fat.
'Very much butcher's meat' – as Lucy Snowe says of the ungainly
painted *Cleopatra* – 'to say nothing of breads, vegetables, and liq-
uids' went into constituting his 'affluence of flesh' (Brontë, *Villette,*
Chap. 19). We have found it difficult, from a twenty-first-century
viewpoint, to get a perspective on George Scharf's eating. As we will
explain in more detail below, his middle years were punctuated by
frequent banqueting on a scale almost unimaginable today. Even
after having recreated and consumed our version of a sumptuous
meal recorded in the menu Scharf saved from an ordinary evening
at Knole, we can't be certain whether any middle-aged Victorian
men actually ate all the dishes in all the courses of such dinners.[7]
There is nothing middling about the calorie content of such meals.
One dinner in 1868 was divided into two parts: the *premier service*
offered two soups (a consommé and a purée of peas), two fish (a
turbot gratin and a salmon with hollandaise *and* lobster sauces),
three entrées (slices of foie gras with truffles, chicken timbales and
calf's sweetbreads with asparagus formed into peas), two relevés
(braised fillet of beef with tomatoes and roast saddle of mutton with
salad and *ponche à la romaine*), followed by the *seconde service* of roasts
(duckling with watercress, small chickens with bread sauce and sole
in mayonnaise) and accompaniments (asparagus, petit pois, pine-
apple ice cream, strawberry Bavarian cream, apricot savarin) and
– finally – a savoury of pastries made with cheese.[8] Even if Scharf,
in the face of all this temptation, were to take a serving of only one
option in each of the courses, he would be consuming thousands
of calories in foods and sauces during a meal, not to mention the
wines that went with every course and – of course – with the gentlemen's cigars after dinner. When Scharf especially liked a dish at
one of these dinners, he would ask for the recipe, as he did once

at Chevening after tasting 'Imperial Sandwiches': 'Finely chopped Tongue between two slices of buttered toast and a layer of toasted cheese on the top. Served very hot. N. B. sometimes the yolk of an egg, boiled hard and mashed, may be used instead of the cheese' (D 6 August 1869). While that sounds to us like enough food – or at least enough calories – for an entire meal, Scharf enjoyed 'Imperial Sandwiches' after two complete services on the scale of the dinner we described above. His enthusiasm for the referents of those menus he so carefully preserved made him fat, but it must also have made him an especially welcome dinner guest.

Although the album, our first glimpse of Scharf, was overwhelmingly a record of his career as a guest, the diaries and letters we subsequently read invited us into a parallel reality in which he served as a host to a group of mostly younger men at his various lodgings in London. Scharf's depictions of his London life, and the intimate dinners he carefully arranged for friends, opened our eyes to his complex gender and sexual identifications. They also suggest links between his identities as a diner and a sketcher, since many diary entries about dinner parties future and past include seating charts, with the names of his friends radiating from a central rectangle representing the dining-table (Fig. 1.2). Hannah Arendt sees the (dining-)table as an object so powerfully implicated in the construction of the social self that it 'comes into visibility [. . .] only when [it] [. . .] fails in its function' (p. 56). Scharf brought the table into visibility and into his own visual idiom; although the pen-and-ink squares in his diary are by no means as elaborate as the menus or seating charts that signify his status as guest, his role as host is so crucial that it interrupts the textual format of his diary entries, foregrounding the names of his friends and the table that provides a structure and a context for their friendship.

A drawer, a sketcher, an eater, a diner, a bachelor, a socialite, an extra man, a fat man, a host: we have deliberately held these identity markers aloof from the received categories of race, class, gender, sexuality, age and nationality to learn what insights can come from working inductively, moving out from the evidentiary details of Scharf's life to the general terms that might taxonomise them, rather than beginning with familiar identity categories and seeking out the examples that fit from the diaries and letters. To make our project legible to ourselves as well as to our readers, though, we come back from these more fanciful designators to age, class, nationality and period with an eye to the differences we might

13

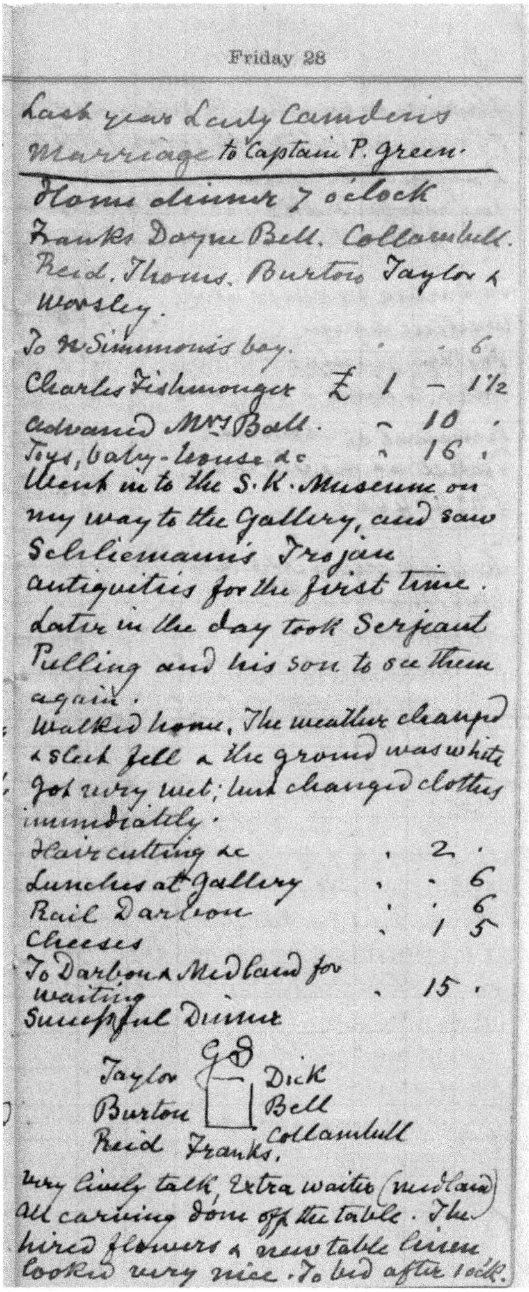
Friday 28

Last year Lady Camden's
Marriage to Captain P. Green.

Home dinner 7 o'clock
Franks Dayne Bell. Collambell.
Reid. Thoms. Burton Taylor &
Worsley.

To Mr Simmons's boy.	.	.	6
Charles Fishmonger	£ 1	–	1½
Advanced Mrs Ball.	–	10	.
Toys, baby-house &c	–	16	.

Went in to the S.K. Museum on
my way to the Gallery, and saw
Schliemann's Trojan
antiquities for the first time.
Later in the day took Serjeant
Pulling and his son to see them
again.
Walked home. The weather changed
& sleet fell & the ground was white
Got very wet; but changed clothes
immediately.

Hair cutting &c	.	2	.
Lunches at Gallery	.	.	6
Rail Darbon	.	.	6
Cheeses	.	1	5
To Darbon & Midland for waiting	.	15	.

Successful Dinner

GS
Taylor Dick
Burton Bell
Reid Franks, Collambell

very lively talk, Extra waiter (midland)
All carving done off the table. The
hired flowers & new table linen
looked very nice. To bed after 1 o'clk.

Fig. 1.2 Seating plan for a dinner hosted by GS in 1877.
©National Portrait Gallery, London.

perceive between preconceived ideas about the categories Scharf occupies and the specifics of his life experience. We find George stubbornly stuck in the middle of the more familiar identity categories he occupies: middle-aged, middle-class, middle-brow and mid-Victorian.

Expanding middles

Our adventures in the Scharf archives did not begin at the beginning of his life, and they took up a large chunk of our own middle years. We seemed always to find ourselves in the middle of writing, of gathering information and of the record of Scharf's life. Of the thousands of pages of diaries and letters we read, the vast majority were composed during Scharf's middle age, that segment of life when long repetition establishes the patterns by which one is likely to continue to live. A daily concern of middle age for everybody is, of course, the litany of physical complaints inevitably resulting from longevity, especially for those who love to indulge in food and drink. In middle age Scharf's body had become so inflexible he needed his housekeeper's husband to help him in and out of the bath. Until his advanced old age, when he had to order a Bath chair to go to the NPG offices, Scharf was far from sedentary; like the typical Londoner even today, in mid-life he walked everywhere, going out of his way to and from work many days to look at the progress on construction sites, to admire the urban parks and trees and simply to be out in the weather he so scrupulously observed and recorded. He sometimes fell down in the street, though, and once injured his hand in breaking the fall. Scharf, like many of his generation, drank plenty of alcohol every day, though there is no indication that his falling down was due to drunkenness or that he shared the addiction that seems to have bedevilled his brother, Henry. The financial notations in the diaries show that Scharf bought a lot of claret and port in this period, sometimes replenishing his stores more than twice a week. He also frequently sent his young friend and assistant, Jack Pattisson, out to buy cigars. The expense of his middle-aged habits always outstripped his income, which must have made his many invitations to dine out especially welcome. The earliest item in the scrapbook of his gustatory adventures among the wealthy dates from 1864, when Scharf was forty-four; his 'diner' identity overlaps with his middle years.

One of the persistent questions we asked ourselves – and which we got asked by other people as they heard segments of this project – was so simple it seemed naïve: What class was George Scharf? When we first turned over the pages of the album holding Scharf's ephemera, we saw not only menus but calling cards from such luminaries as the Duchess of Marlborough, the Duke of Devonshire and Lady Augusta Stanhope. This must, we thought at first, be the collection of a person who was part of that social echelon. He was, after all, Sir George Scharf. We vaguely pictured the carriage of some noble man or woman pulling up *chez* Scharf and leaving a card for Scharf's butler or footman to place on the silver tray in the front hall. Our next archival stop, reading the British Library's copy of a collection of recommendations from very prominent people for Scharf's application to become director of the National Gallery (a post, as we now know, he did not win), began to solidify our impression of his social prominence.

The more we thought about it, though, the less likely it seemed that a real aristocrat would fill a scrapbook with other noblemen's calling cards. Once we delved into the diaries, the picture of Scharf's acquisition of the dukes' and duchesses' cards got much blurrier and, then, suddenly clear. As we came to learn that Scharf shared a small flat with his mother and aunt, that he, sometimes impecunious, had to borrow money to pay his rent and that he was bourgeois enough to write down the cost of every pin he purchased, the illusion that Sir George Scharf was the social equal of the Duke of Devonshire or the Duchess of Norfolk quickly crumbled. The mystery came together when we found at the Portrait Gallery Scharf's directorial notebook entitled 'To call and see'. The many professional appointments with titled nobility and the explicit instructions to Scharf's assistants to admit any peer to the Portrait Gallery 'upon presentation of his card' cleared it up (AB 59/end of book). Those calling cards never came in at the front door of Scharf's home(s); they had been used as tickets of entry to the NPG, where the director had eagerly picked them up for his souvenir collection. Our vision of Scharf's social status came into focus: he was upwardly mobile, but never got high enough on the social scale not to be impressed with the grandeur of his circle of acquaintance. The 'Sir' that had initially suggested to us an inherited title turned out to be an honorary one; Scharf was no more an aristocrat than (Sir) Elton John. He belonged in some sense to that capacious and hard-to-define but, according to Eric Hobsbawm, surprisingly small group: the Victorian middle class.[9]

In Chapters 3 and 4 we look carefully at some of the many conflicting signs of Sir George Scharf's class status: his shopkeeper mother, his impoverished father, his constant petty debts and his lack of university education, on the one hand, and, on the other, his seeming intimacy with titled patrons and, more importantly, with their families. Of course, even in England, class designations contain the possibility of movement (up or down) and of narrative (euphoric and dysphoric). As R. H. Gretton notes, the term 'middle class' could be aspirational for some, for others, 'a confession of failure' (p. 1). Arguably, striving to get into or out of the middle class is itself a middle-class value. If so, Scharf's life embodied those values and in some sense the identity associated with them.

Scharf both does and does not fit into traditional narratives of Victorian class ascension. As we discuss in Chapters 3 and 4, Scharf's sense of class success depended in part on dividing his past from his present, his home from his work. But the division was not always neat and seemed to come along with an equally powerful impulse to bring family and work together – as did many working-class families – under one roof. Ironically, Scharf at least partly resolved these issues, it seems, by abandoning his ambitious artist father and by incorporating his ex-shopkeeper female relatives into his domestic arrangements.

It is tempting to talk about Scharf's class in terms of the simplistic arithmetic of averaging: his birth family, with its lack of servants and its itinerant domesticity, was artisan or upper working-class; the endpoint of his life had him associating with the rich and famous. If we split the difference, take a median or a mean, we get a term that we can use, however unhappily. We also think of Scharf's class more schematically and perhaps affectively: for us he could only be middle class by clinging, as it were, to its two opposite edges. With one foot in the world of his family as it scrabbled for respectability, and the other in the world and in the homes of titled friends with whom he routinely socialised, Scharf belonged to what we like to think of as 'an expanding middle'. And in some ways, by Scharf's middle-age, class categories were multiplying if not expanding. As we discuss in Chapter 4, Scharf was a (somewhat unusual) member of an emerging professional class, part of a growing civil sector. As with many of the categories we have tried on for Scharf, 'middle-class' works curiously in tandem with other identities.

Although not given to using the term 'middlebrow' in other contexts, we find this word helpful when thinking about Scharf's reputation, his degree of celebrity and, perhaps, even his intellect. 'Middlebrow' signals to us what one might now call Scharf's B-list celebrity. He lived on the fringes of greatness and sometimes in the houses of the great, but he was not 'of' them. Tied to the question of class, but by no means coterminous with it, is the issue of his fame. Although certainly not famous in our time, Scharf was well enough known during the second half of his life for him to be traceable in the public press. Starting in the 1850s his name began, for example, to appear in the advertising section of the London *Times*; as an illustrator, as a tutor and as a lecturer. In September of 1854, we see advertisements for Scharf as a drawing master who offers 'Figure drawing for Ladies' (25 September 1854). Surrounded by advertisements for shorthand classes, cures for stammering and courses on reading and elocution, this ad positions Scharf as one of an almost innumerable series of teachers trying to make a respectable living. He began to come out of the shadows in 1856 when his movements as art secretary to the Manchester Art Treasures Exhibition are reported in several short articles. One of them noted that 'Mr G. Scharf, jun., the art secretary, has recently returned from visits to Kimbolton Castle and Hagley-park [sic] the seats of the Duke of Manchester and Lord Lyttelton, Gladstone's brother-in-law' (29 December 1856). In the 1860s Scharf moved onto the social pages as one of the very last names listed at the queen's levees, among the handful of 'messieurs' following the titled and the clerical.[10] In the 1880s he was frequently cited as an expert on portraiture and in articles about the National Portrait Gallery. By the time he made it to Buckingham Palace, he truly had arrived on the B-list, or maybe even on the bottom of the A-.

In 1888 Scharf also appears in his own professional persona as the author of four long letters to *The Times* editor about portraits of Mary, Queen of Scots. His knighthood is, of course, the subject of a brief article, and his death the subject of quite an extensive obituary, in which he is described as having, among other 'gifts', 'an eye of remarkable accuracy [. . .] an extraordinary talent for testing likenesses, and [. . .] a still more extraordinary memory' (*The Times*, 20 April 1895).[11] Scharf's reputation continued after his death; he was quoted as an authority on portraiture until the mid-twentieth century. Scharf himself regularly registered his rise in status throughout his life; as we shall see in Chapter 4, his yearly diaries often end (or begin) with a summary of his accomplishments for the previous year; while the tone of these is sometimes difficult to read, one keynote is surprise at how far he has come, especially in terms of the social and professional connections he has made.

We found a beautiful visual illustration of George Scharf's B-list celebrity status among the exhibits at the National Portrait Gallery. One might expect that the gallery's founding father would merit a portrait among the luminaries of his time, and, indeed, the gallery's holdings include a splendid oil painting of Scharf by William Walter Ouless, which was commissioned in 1886 to hang in the boardroom at the NPG (Fig. 1.3). The painting shows Scharf holding a sketchbook in one hand and a pencil in the other, looking up at the portrait painter and sketching Ouless while he works. It is accessible now on the NPG website of portrait holdings, but it does not hang among the other eminent Victorians on the public gallery walls. What was on the walls when we went looking for Scharf for the first time, though, was an enormous painting of sixty-six elegantly dressed men and women gathered at what looks like an art opening, *Private View of the Old Masters Exhibition, Royal Academy, 1888* by Henry Jamyn Brooks. As the NPG website describes the group, it 'presents a varied portrait of the late Victorian Establishment, with prominent artists and critics alongside politicians and leading members of the aristocracy'.[12] If you stand in front of the picture with a key to the painting in your hand, you can see everybody who was anybody in London's art world – including Sir John Everett Millais, Sir Philip Burne-Jones, Lawrence Alma-Tadema, Sir Frederick Leighton, William Holman Hunt and the painter, Henry Jamyn Brooks himself – chatting with the likes of John Ruskin, William Gladstone and Mr Humphrey Ward (maybe the 'unidentified woman' standing next to him is his distinguished Mrs). In the farthest corner on the right side of the painting, you can just make out a bald head, a white beard, and – yes! – a sketchbook in the hand of George Scharf, turned away from the rest of the people in the room and copying one of the portraits on the wall, a posture he assumed thousands of times in public and private over the course of his career. To be sure, our middle-class, middle-brow hero is by no means in the middle of the crowd, but instead on the periphery where a person of middling importance ought to be. Scharf is just barely there. That he *is* there, much to our satisfaction, signifies his marginal but marked presence on the scene in a visual parallel to his appearance at the very end of the queen's levee lists.

No account of Scharf's middleness would be complete without some attention to the period in which it unfolded. A figure

Fig. 1.3 Portrait of GS by Walter William Ouless, 1865.
©National Portrait Gallery, London.

who lived – and whose middle expanded – in close step with his queen, Scharf was born at the beginning and died near the end of the Victorian period, rising to prominence in those heady mid-Victorian years from the 1850s through to the 1870s. The key transition in Scharf's life from journeyman to professional, about which we have quite a bit to say in Chapter 4, happened in the mid 1850s; that transition was made possible in part by a shift in cultural attitudes towards professionalism, one of whose instantiations was the consolidation of a professional class. While Scharf remains unusual in class terms – for example, as a director of a major gallery who did not attend Oxbridge or a public school – the existence of a professional class made his entry into public life possible and, indeed, made his accomplishments visible to the Board that hired and worked so intimately with him on his various projects for the improvement and expansion of the NPG. According to Andrea Geddes Poole, the National Portrait Gallery was unique among similar institutions in the extent of its reliance on professionals as well as aristocrats to staff its boards – in part because it required historical more than aesthetic expertise in the building of its collection. Scharf's transition to the directorship marked not only a move to a public and salaried position, but also a new and emerging form of institutional professionalism.[13]

If Scharf's relationship to professionalism was both slightly advanced for and in many ways characteristic of the mid-Victorian period, so, in a different way, was that of his boss and chairman of the NPG Board, Lord Philip Stanhope, 5th Earl of Stanhope. Although the Stanhopes had long been involved in more traditional ways in public service through their work in the two houses of Parliament, it was Philip, born in 1822, who redefined public service to include the leadership of numerous boards and associations, from the Society of Antiquarians, where he might first have met Scharf,[14] to the Historical Manuscript Commission, to the Royal Literary Fund and, of course, to the NPG. Stanhope was also a highly placed advocate for art, literature and intellectual culture more generally; he was active in the passage of the Literary Copyright Act of 1842 and was himself a published historian with numerous books to his credit. Stanhope's father, the 4th Earl, resisted his son's desire to take up a profession before entering Parliament; although he was by all accounts proud of his son's numerous public activities, the 4th Earl was obviously not entirely comfortable with these markers of a new generation of aristocrats (Newman, p. 251). It would be silly to think of the 5th Earl of Stanhope as belonging to a professional class, but one can think of him approaching and becoming involved in professional culture from above as Scharf approached it from below. The meeting of the two men in the middle was not always easy: as we discuss in Chapter 4, Stanhope sometimes had to make clear (not always patiently) the difference between aristocratic notions about business, art and punctuality and those of men who had to work for their living.

If George Scharf Jr, as distinct from his father, found a class niche where he could appropriately display and be rewarded for his talents, he also found ways of living in, and evidently taking for granted, an almost exclusively masculine world. Before the Oscar Wilde trials, which were to take place the year of Scharf's death, masculine worlds were not so quickly pathologised or found lacking. Scharf shared with many heroes and minor characters of mid-Victorian fiction a flexibility and, indeed, a creativity in his domestic arrangements. During his lifetime, he had five different addresses, all of them lodgings in London. He was able to produce – and to reproduce – a series of households, none of which were occupied by or defined in terms of a nuclear family. When Scharf was a boy, the household included his mother's sister as well as his parents and brother. For lower-middle-class Victorians this was not an unusual arrangement, but during George Scharf Jr's twenties his father was abruptly ejected from the family home, and his elderly aunt and mother came to live with Scharf Jr in the attic above his lodgings at the National Portrait Gallery. After the deaths of his mother and aunt, Scharf's flat became 'home' to at least one of his male friends.[15] While these latter arrangements would have been possible earlier and later, the key fact about them in the period in which George created them was that they were unremarkable or, at least, unremarked upon.

In arguing that Scharf was something called a mid-Victorian, we, of course, risk simplifying not only a very complex social history but also Scharf's uneven status as both representative and exceptional. We hope to keep both in play throughout this book. While we still believe that Scharf's primary emotional investments were in a group of younger male friends, there is no easy term for his sexual identity, no secret or not-so-secret solution to the 'problem' of his sexuality. As with his class, his sexuality challenges received categories of identity (his) and epistemology (ours). Like his profession, his sexuality leads us to think about and through certain terms that are not often central to biography or, for that matter, to a lexicon of identity. George was a single man, a middle-aged man, an extra man. He loved food. He loved his mother. He loved his friends.

So many archives

Scharf's equivocal class and status, his odd mixture of success and obscurity, make him an unusual biographical subject. Scharf is also somewhat at odds with another kind of biographical subject: the one whose 'life' is written (and rewritten) because of the inherent interest of story or character. Some people become the subject of life-writing because their life is full of incident. While we do not know everything that happened to Scharf, the things that we know are not dramatic in narrative or novelistic terms. As literary critics, we would have to say there was relatively little plot to his life and, to extend the idiom, not much character. This is not to say that George Scharf had no interior life, but if he had one that was complex or interesting, the ample record he left behind gives little access to it. The sketchiness of his story is inseparable from the nature of his archive: records of paintings purchased for the National Portrait Gallery; letters arranging visits to the NPG; that album of menus; some fifty portraits, a few of them drawn by himself; and notebooks containing hundreds of sketches. Even his 'diaries' are predominantly account books; looking for something like a life story, we were forced to trace his conflicts and appetites through his daily summary of expenses and income. And yet, as we discuss in Chapter 2, there are moments when something that we think of as a personality surfaces through the figures and the somewhat formulaic prose of the diaries: Scharf is devastated by the death of his mother, nervous about giving dinners, transfixed by a new telescope and by patterns of light, angry at a noisy neighbour, thrilled by increasingly intimate relationships with the titled, opinionated about portraits and affectionate to and about his young male friends.

This transient and equivocal payoff to years of research seems at odds with the fantasies of the archive we brought with us across the Atlantic: fantasies personal and professional, theoretical and practical, that we came to think well worth exploring on their own terms. The more we thought about what we were doing, the more we realised that while archives offer an opportunity for going abroad, they perform a yet more transportive function: the notion of travelling, not only over (to England, to Trafalgar Square, to . . .), but *back*. Time travel and its historicist baggage offer the literary scholar a presence, indeed a metaphysics of presence, that earlier movements in poststructuralist criticism would not have dared to proffer as a reward for academic labour. And that presence can be embodied, not only by a time period ('the Victorian era') or a vague but attractive collective representing that period ('the Victorians'), but also by a perhaps-representative individual, a biographical subject-to-be-captured ('Sir George Scharf').

Increasingly we became aware that our travels were motivated by what Helena has called 'the erotics of the archive', that animating fantasy of complete knowledge of a thing, person or event through scrupulous professional research (Michie, *Honeymoons*, p. 9). This desire goes by many names, including 'fever' and 'romance'. Jacques Derrida famously describes 'a compulsive, repetitive, and nostalgic desire for the archive, an irrepressible desire to return to the origin, a homesickness, a nostalgia for the return to the most archaic place of absolute commencement' (Derrida, p. 91.) Carolyn Steedman notes the feverish toll taken on the body of the archival researcher by an obligation to 'myriads of the dead, who all day long have pressed their concerns upon you' as if archive fever were a contagion passed from subject to researcher (p. 17). Suzanne Keen uses the phrase 'romances of the archive' as the title of her book on novels with archival settings like A. S. Byatt's *Possession*. For Keen 'in the face of postmodern skepticism, this kind of contemporary fiction claims that its world-making can answer questions about what really happened, though it does so without surrendering its power to invent' (p. 3). Plots of detection and sexual desire unfold in the archive under the sign of full (and carnal) knowledge. Fever is the symptomatic bridge between desire and disease, anticipation and obligation.

And here, of course, we come to the question of 'love', which is so important to our book's title and whose many valences we list in the preface to this book. We cheerfully admit at various points in this chapter and in the rest of this book to our own investments in archival desire and in archival romance. We are less easy with, but always interested in, the idea of love. We decided, however, that our uneasiness was part of the point: while desire can denote a search for sex or knowledge, or a variety of other objects and affects, it can also suggest a search for something more primal, more embarrassing and harder to define. Our journeys in and through the archives allowed us to think about what it meant to love our work, to love going to London, to love each other, to love Victorian literature, to love 'George'. We have used the term in all of these contexts – and perhaps also in others – and want to mark in our title and elsewhere the slipperiness, the power, the triteness and importance of the term as the motivating force behind our research. We also wanted to give that feeling a place and a structure: we experienced differently (and at different times) not just love but love among the archives.

Why, we wondered, not for the first time, is 'the archive' so often referenced in the singular, when, in fact, it represents so many places one can go?[16] Even the most abstract and theoretical accounts of knowledge and power must account for differences in relation to that power. On our own journey back, beginning with the album in the British Library, we moved on to more typical records and papers in the National Portrait Gallery, then to forms of archival tourism in London and present-day Turkey and, before coming to the end that this book represents, took a detour to Helena's dining-room table in Houston with a re-creation of one of the dinner parties recorded in George Scharf's album. These journeys through space – across town, up and down stairs, across a continent and back and forth from kitchen to dining-room – were also journeys to different kinds of archives that we have provisionally called the ephemeral, the institutional, the monumental and the visceral. Each archive, each location, comes with different expectations; each produces and can begin to answer different kinds of questions, to address itself to a different aspect of the biographical subject.

The ephemeral archive: the lives of objects

Objects from a given historical period activate a metonymic chain by which those looking at, holding or researching these objects can feel asymptotically closer to the historical reality from which the objects derive.[17] For us the menus we discovered in Scharf's album represented not only Scharf himself, not only the food represented on them, but something like (the erotics of the archive again!) the bodily experience of being a Victorian. Our own bodies became part of that chain as we lifted the album and carried it to our desks, often attracting the stares of our fellow researchers. Of course, for us, there was one more link in that chain, one more promise held out by the album. In these historicising times, literary scholars of the Victorian period, like those in other fields, can feel the professional pressure to 'do' history. To become – fantastically and for a moment – a Victorian under the weight of the album is also to become, or to renew one's identity as, a Victorianist.[18]

Our identities as archival researchers involved, over time, a series of often rote bodily acts. At first our main task was copying the materials, in the beginning by hand and then later by laptop. To type the details of menu after menu is very much like eating the meals described in them. Typing them all out brings to mind (if not to the body) the full effect of all those courses they used to eat at Victorian dinners – the minimum being a soup course followed by fish, then entrées, then relevés, then roasts, followed by entremets (desserts and savouries). We admired the straightforwardness of a dinner party given in December of 1877, in his bachelor's quarters, by George Scharf himself: turbot soup, then pork cutlets with tomatoes (the entrée), saddle of mutton (the relevé) and goose (the *rôti*), followed by mayonnaise of chicken and mince pies (the entremets), and ending up with *glacés* of raspberry, wine jelly and maybe lemon, though that last one was crossed out. (We speculated that Scharf changed his mind about the sorbet selection after he had filled out this particular menu card, and that he saved this one for his album, rather than placing it on the table because it had been marred (Fig. 1.4).)

Scharf's own menu would constitute only the bare outline of the dinners he was typically served at great country houses like Knole and Chevening, where the meals' richness would be multiplied by offering numerous choices for each of the six or seven courses. For example, at an October dinner at Blenheim Palace ten years earlier, Scharf had been served as an entrée not just pork cutlets but also calf sweetbreads and quenelles of hare; the saddle of mutton he was to choose as the relevé for his dinner party came with potato croquettes and roasted goose at Blenheim Palace; roasted goose was all Scharf was to serve for the *rôti*, but at Blenheim they had partridges and pheasants. At still grander dinners, the multiplicity of dishes would be augmented by elaborate sauces and accompaniments. On a good night at Knole in 1877 (and, as we shall see in Chapter 4, not every night at Knole was so good), the entrées included individual terrines of hare mixed with chopped black truffles and foie gras as well as chicken 'Piémontaise' prepared with white truffles; the next course was a *filet* of beef 'Providence', garnished with more truffles and more foie gras plus chicken quenelles and olives.

Poring over the menus we each found dishes that we had never eaten but which became, without passing our lips, instant favourites. Helena was drawn to the nursery-room simplicity of raspberry sandwiches, while Robyn liked the overprepared main dishes like

Fig. 1.4 Menu card from dinner hosted by GS in 1877.
©The British Library Board, 1887. c.14.

ballottines de volaille à la au jardinière [sic], which turns out to be poultry that has been boned, stuffed, rolled, poached, coated in aspic and sliced. We were both charmed by an all-dessert menu printed on the inside covers of a white card. On the left inside cover are 'Ices': 'Strawberry Cream. Mille Fruit. Raspberry Water. Lemon Water. Vanille Cream'. On the right are 'Desserts': 'Grapes. Savoy and Almond Cakes. Apples. Oranges. Norfolk Biffins. Almonds and Raisins. Pears. Tangerine Oranges. Cob Nuts [a type of hazelnut]. Crystallised Fruit. Preserves. Figs and Imperial Plums. Olives. Rout Cakes [sweet, rich, fruit-flavoured cakes – the kind *Emma*'s Mr Woodhouse doesn't want anyone to eat because they are unwholesome], &c'. Given such an array, how would one choose? Imaginatively, we ate them all.

This bodily experience of the archive – the feel and smell of the papers and inks, the fantasised exposure to the meats and sauces, soups and glacés – lends a sense of realist detail to the Victorianist's project. Touching menu cards that George Scharf handled, picturing events where such meals would be served, activates the archival metonymy linking the researcher at the reading room table to 'real history' felt on the pulse and guaranteed by the tongue. To be in the ephemeral archive is to accede to one of its dominant fantasies: that we can get beyond words, beyond traces, to things. Ephemeral objects are material links to the past, but they are also flimsy and fragile, easy to imagine as all-but-transparent screens for the real. The fragility of the objects can actually make them seem even more real – we were capturing these items before they disappeared; both archivists and librarians, we were now preservers of the past. We might even be said to be incorporating that past and preserving it inside us.

Of course, to talk about Scharf's album of menus as part of the ephemeral archive is to ignore (or repress) its location in that most privileged of official archives: the British Library, where layers of regulation to its access and use protect our original source (for the near future) from destruction. It does, however, capture the ungainly strangeness of the object's presence in the manuscript room among other, more dignified texts. The British Library can tell us nothing of the provenance of the album, other than that it was donated to the British Library in 1887; no one in manuscript or research services could explain why this piece of Scharf's 'papers' had floated free from his named archive at the National Portrait Gallery or even whether it was Scharf himself who donated it.

'Ephemeral archive' is of course a contradiction in terms; it is the archive of that which usually gets thrown away but for some reason is not.[19] But no logical contraction can erase the difference between paper and cardboard, the sense that something has been collected that might easily have been seen as waste. As we turn to the institutional archive, we see that it, too, contains what might be called ephemera but also that certain pieces of paper escape that archive to form other, more contingent collections.

The institutional archive: the NPG on paper and screen

At some point after transcribing all those meals, even the most gluttonous archival researcher might feel she has had enough. One last bite of raspberry sandwich and it was time to move on – but to where? One fantasy of the archive and the things in it involves movement forward as well as backward, the powerful activity of Freedgood's 'strong metonymy', which authorises a movement from things to their histories (pp. 11–17). If the archive allows for or demands strong metonymy, where were we to find the strength to decide the direction of our journey? If the fantasy of the archive is, in fact, transportation, where were we to go next? One obvious answer was to more traditional kinds of sources: biographies, letters, diaries. We have admitted that we knew nothing about George Scharf, but (comfortingly) it seems that this ignorance (or lack of interest) was shared by others. The Scharf entry in the *Dictionary of National Biography* is quite brief; the only lengthy treatment of any events in his life is, as we shall see later, in a book on his travels with Charles Fellows in Asia Minor (Slatter, pp. 11–17). The accumulation of detail about where he sat and what he ate and drank, along with the names of restaurants and clubs as they changed or remained the same over the crucial years of the mid-century, rubbed up in awkward ways against the nothingness that served as our response to his name and the brevity of the public record. It was time to get up from the dinner table.

Any archival researcher will follow us from this dilemma to the next step – from George Scharf's bits and pieces of cardboard to his collected 'Papers'. The Scharf papers are housed in the Heinz Archive and Library of the National Portrait Gallery in a building across a narrow alley from the edifice that would be the final home of the collection of portraits Scharf had been so instrumental in creating and that opened to the public only the year after his death.

The Scharf papers are part of an institutional archive in two ways. The first has to do with their status as a primary, named collection. While, of course, the more famous and the more scattered may have named archives of their papers in several places, all of these would be, in our sense, institutional. The Scharf papers are institutional in a second sense: his papers and the life they represent are inextricably and indicatively tied to the history of a particular institution. Scharf 'belongs' to the NPG and it to him; unlike the album, the papers in the NPG archives have found a logical institutional home.

After being handed our badges and being shown the reading room, we were given a 'handlist' to the Scharf papers. The term itself describes the relation of the researcher to the archivist, and the archivist to the material. The list was handed to us; our access was mediated by the young woman at the front desk. It would be she, and the many others that followed her that day and for the next fifteen years, who would find the material and then hand – indeed dole – it out according to the strict protocols of the library, which only allowed each researcher one item at a time and only a few items per visit. Hands in an archive are equivocal: they record and thus preserve information from the archive on paper or computers, but they can also damage the items they touch. Although we were not required to wear gloves in the Heinz Archive, we were acutely aware of our hands – and of the protective eyes of the archivists as we worked under their gaze.

The handlist from 2002 (this is the scanned version that has survived our various computer crashes in our own self-archiving project) is a three-page word-processed document with record numbers (ranging from 22–C-4 to 22–E-2) for each item listed. The items are divided into 'Official papers' and 'Personal and family papers'. The 'Official papers' are those having directly to do with Scharf's role as director of the NPG; papers relating to other professional projects, such as his book on the portraits of Mary, Queen of Scots, are listed under 'personal and family'. The lists interpolate particular genres recognisable from other archives: the official papers feature 'journals', 'account books' and a 'wall map' from Scharf's office. The official list bears a faint trace of Scharf's own organising and self-archiving system – and, indeed, of his voice: the listing of the 'Appointment book to view portraits' is followed by the parenthetical phrase (titled 'To call and see'). The personal list of items is much longer and includes 'family correspondence' as well as 'Diaries' of Scharf's father, mother and aunt. Doubly named as personal is one box labelled 'Personalia', containing among other things George Scharf Sr's palette and birth certificate. While most of the 'personal and family papers' are, in fact, papers, many are not: the collection also contains the 'camera lucida' Scharf used for copying engravings, for example, as well as his 'Order of the Bath Star and Badge', intact in their original presentation case. Reading across the categories of 'Personal' and 'Official', one can see an attempt to align genres with each: the markedly official 'Secretary's journals' are paralleled in position by the 'Diaries' on the personal side, although the objects preserved in the collection seem mostly to reside somewhere on the border in between.

One crucial effect of the handlist is to separate institutional ('official') traces of Scharf's life from his other activities and yet to provide the institutional archive as a context for both. This separation predictably broke down as we read with and against the official record and learned, for example, that Scharf (and later his mother and aunt, as well) lived in rooms above the NPG when it moved to Great George Street; that one of his assistants in the Gallery also acted as a servant in Scharf's lodgings; that Scharf became increasingly intimate with his boss and patron, Lord Stanhope; and, indeed, that Scharf himself had donated personal as well as NPG-related papers to the Gallery. Despite, or perhaps in part because of the way the 'Papers' are structured, the NPG and the institutional archive become the context for all elements of Scharf's life.

We talk in more detail in the next chapter about how we began our work in the institutional archive and how we were drawn, as literary critics and as seekers after (Scharf's) interiority, to the 'Diaries 1845–1895'. The years we spent with the diaries, one month's booklet at a time – a fifty-year period of Scharf's life and a fifteen-year period of our own – came to dominate our sense of the institutional archive. It was only later, starting in 2003, that we had time to look at the 'official' papers and to understand the porousness of the handlist's categories from which we had made our initial choice. Our visits to the archive in London and the rhythms of our item requests and our reading were determined in part by the binary structure of the archive itself.

And then, on or about 1 June 2010, everything changed.[20] The Scharf papers went digital. Our first inkling of this major restructuring came as an accident and a gift (see Chapter 2), but since then we have on many occasions worked with the digital archive and felt each time the effects of an epistemological sea change that reach down into the daily conduct of our research and writing. In some ways the change is empowering. To revisit some items we no longer have to make the journey back to the United Kingdom; although it is rare to be able to access the text of the precise item we need online, we have a fuller and more complicated picture of what the archive contains and can move with ease from entries for one item to entries for another. In some ways, however, the digital archive is even more tightly bound than is the material archive to the NPG as an institution.

The face of the NPG's website is turned towards persons imagined to be interested in seeing portraits. This orientation makes it very easy to find Sir George Scharf the portraitist and Sir George Scharf the sitter (in the case of self-portraits, these are, of course, the same). One only has to type 'George Scharf' into the search bar on the home page to be presented first with a choice between father and son and, then, between Sir George as sitter and as artist. Coincidentally, there are seventy-nine images in each category: most of the entries include thumbnails that can be enlarged or bought as prints. The website is less easy to navigate when looking for manuscripts; indeed, if we are on a computer without the appropriate bookmark or other saved link, we still, after countless visits to the site, have to proceed by trial and error through the layers of information that intervene between ourselves and the entries from the Scharf papers.

An anatomy of one attempt to find what was in the new digital version of 'Personalia' might illustrate some of the rewards and complexities of working with the digital archive. Clicking on a home-page link to 'Research' brings you to a list of links that includes 'Heinz Archive and Library' and, then, takes you to a list that includes 'Search the Archive Catalogue' and 'Archive Journeys'. Both options can eventually get you to the Scharf papers, although 'Archive Journeys' offers four preselected experiences, one of which is 'Sir George Scharf (1820–95): Father of the National Portrait Gallery and Victorian Socialite'. Like the handlist, the title of the Scharf 'archive journey' splits Scharf into two, embodying the divide not only between personal and professional but between the institution and the broader world – for example, the world of dinner parties and social engagements. The metaphor of paternity both domesticates Scharf and collapses his personal identity with that of the institution he helped to establish.

The site entices the user deeper into the archive journey with the

invitation to 'take a glimpse into the life and work of this remarkable man'. Like the tag lines that summon one to the other three
journeys, this one is framed in visual terms and is accompanied
by a thumbnail portrait, in this case, a cabinet-card photo of the
elderly Scharf from 1889, bending over a sketchbook. The viewer
who accepts the invitation to go further and deeper will enter the
home page of the George Scharf archive journey and find a timeline of Scharf's life that includes the various locations of the NPG
over the years and a link to 'Official Scharf,' comprising 'Father of
the Gallery' and 'Researcher', and to 'Private Scharf', including
'Victorian socialite' and 'Londoner', all illustrated by thumbnails
of selected Scharf portraits from the NPG collection. At the bottom
of this home page is a reference to the Scharf papers and a link to
the search engine for the archive catalogue, but not specifically to
the papers themselves.

If you follow the link to the archive catalogue you end up in the
same place you would find yourself if you had not been tempted
into taking the 'archive journey'. This page looks more like the
home page of an ordinary digital card catalogue: if you type 'George
Scharf' into the text box you get the NPG's entire collection of
library and manuscript items relating to Scharf. The fourth item
on the list is 'Papers of Sir George Scharf'. A quick glance shows
that the record numbers from the handlist have been incorporated
into a more coherent institutional idiom: while on the handlist the
Scharf archive numbers had no obvious external reference, all of
the numbers for the Scharf items (and for other items in the catalogue) now begin with the designation 'NPG'. The general record
number for Scharf papers is NPG/7 and the subcategories that
follow, designated as 'fonds', 'sub-fonds', 'sub-sub-fonds', 'series'
and 'files', include an additional number for each layer. Thus a
file item might be labelled 'NPG7/3/6/1/2'. The NPG has thus
marked the Scharf papers at every level of specificity.

The Scharf papers themselves are subdivided into three sections,
elaborating on the binary of the handlist: 'work for the National
Portrait Gallery', 'work for external bodies' and 'private papers and
personal effects'. The third option offers seven further choices,
including 'Diaries', 'Account Books', 'Correspondence' and, again,
'Personalia'. Clicking on 'Personalia' produces further subdivi-
sions: for example, 'clothes', 'personal souvenirs', 'trade cards' and
'playing cards'. 'Clothes' reveals only two items: 'Doily collar' and
'Waistcoat'. Opening 'Waistcoat', one finds two thumbnails, each

representing a colour photograph of an elaborately embroidered muslin front for an unfinished garment (Fig. 1.5).

It is almost irresistible, given the power of archival fantasies we have discussed above, not to see the journey through the multiple layers of the website as moving closer and closer to Scharf himself. It is hard not to understand the trajectory of the archival journey as moving down and in – as getting not only down to but inside of Scharf. As the record entries get increasingly specific, as we make the choices that will, we think, take us where we want to be, we are both rewarded and frustrated by the appearance of new categories, new choices: rewarded because of the very specificity of the items and frustrated because for every choice ('clothes') we must temporarily leave behind the, perhaps, equally enticing 'playing cards'. Given the complexity of the archival organisation and the fact that the back button does not always take you back just a single step, one must negotiate the fear of never being able to retrace one's steps, of undoing, revisiting or moving against the gravitational pull of the digital archive.

The final step, the last choice, sometimes but not always rewards the viewer with a visual guarantor of the reality of the archive – the thumbnail of the text or other object embodied in the entry at the lowest level. In the case of the waistcoat this promise, held out over time and from layer to layer, is fulfilled – at least for a moment – by not one but two thumbnails, which, when enlarged, reveal two halves of a waistcoat needle-worked with flowers, scrolls and lattices in pastel shades. It is perhaps fitting that this moment of arrival is undercut by the very obvious absence of the body and the person in question: the waistcoat is in pieces; it was never worn; it never, presumably, enfolded Scharf's body unless, perhaps, he tried it on and found that it could never, in fact, be made to fit. We speculate (how could we not?) that the waistcoat was too small for Scharf's expanding middle and that the act of enlargement produced by our clicking on the image could have no counterpart for the real, bodily, George Scharf. Anyone more focused on the older Scharf than on his middle-aged self might see the waistcoat as a present or a commission whose use – and, indeed, usefulness – must have been interrupted by the death of its owner.

These two possibilities repeat the binary logic of the archive. Although the handlist to the material archive is more obviously divided into two, the digital archive is on all levels made up of a series of yes/no decisions. As with all digital texts, this is as true on

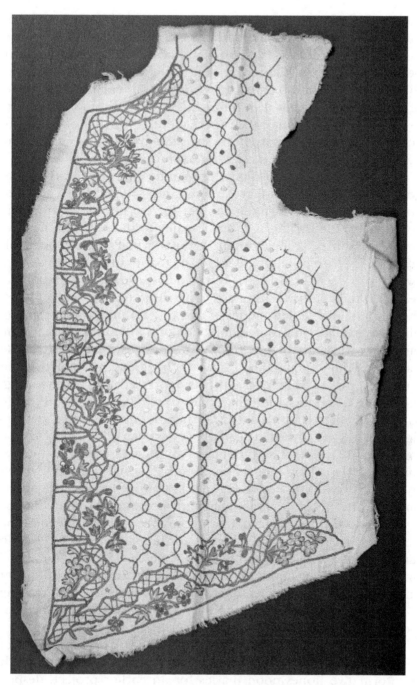

Fig. 1.5 Waistcoat from GS Personalia collection at Heinz Archive.
©National Portrait Gallery, London.

the level of programming language as it is on that of the website interface, where the choice to click or not to click produces and is produced by a cascade of decisions whose sheer number seems to belie their origin in the binary. The image of the waistcoat (even though it comes in two parts) does not look or feel like the product of yes/no choices, but it is. Since this is the institutional archive, users are guided through the process of discovery – the self-guided 'archive journey' that is *not* pre-packaged – by the needs and protocols of the 'home' institution, the home page.

Too often the field of digital humanities within literary studies gets reduced to a notion that the computer is no more nor less than an infinitely capacious filing cabinet for storing and sorting the contents of 'the archive'. As our journey to the waistcoat demonstrates, a digitised archive certainly grants virtual access to materials (though they are not in material form) that used to be very expensive to go and see. As Marcel O'Gorman has argued, however, digital research and composition ought to do more than collect archives; they should enable new modes of thinking unhindered by the two-dimensional limitations of writing. O'Gorman looks to digital composing as a means of incorporating what Jean-Jacques Lecercle has called 'the remainder', that which eludes rational thought and conventional discourse but gets expressed through punning, metaphor, anagrams and other kinds of troping. Our project is in some ways aligned with what O'Gorman identifies as that remainder, which is 'the other of academic or scholarly language' (p. 4): we know that what we say about our subject – especially when we find ourselves calling him simply 'George' – often evinces levels of irony and even levity that usually get left out of scholarly discourse and that our speculations about Scharf's experiences do not always stand up to the test of academic rigour. We have not heeded the ultimate call of the digital, however, for the same reason we would far rather have our hands on that waistcoat than look at thumbnail images of it on our laptop monitors. Our old attachment to paper and ink pulled us back, summer after summer, to that reading room across the alley from the NPG, where those fifty tidy boxes of George Scharf's daily diaries reside.

And here we come to the central place of the diary in the erotics of the archive. Despite years of Helena's having read disappointingly uninformative honeymoon diaries for an earlier project, despite Robyn's having shared with Helena those repeated disappointments, and despite our knowledge that 'diary' can mean many different things, both of us felt the unmistakable archival frisson when we saw those delicious boxes. And if the menus became quickly for us a metonymy for something that might be called Victorian life, the diaries became a metonymy for Scharf himself. For us – at least at first – the Scharf behind (or was it inside) the boxes of diaries was a subject, a person and (dare we say it?) a character.[21]

This fantasy persisted despite the fact that the 'personal diaries' of the handlist and digital archive are for the most part combinations of account books and something like retrospective almanacs. Every day Scharf faithfully wrote down every shilling he spent on paintbrushes and lozenges, haircuts and washing, seltzer and gin, tips to servants and gifts for friends, rail fares and cab fares and coach fares. Conscientiously he made a note every time he paid the rent on the villa where he practised his piano, renewed a subscription to a journal or gave his housekeeper her salary. And every day he wrote down the weather: 'fine and very pleasant', 'lovely afternoon', 'very wet day', 'wet chilly morning', 'very dull afternoon'. That last looked like a piece of editorialising on the events of the day but turned out, upon repetition, as in many British diaries, to mean that the sun was obscured by clouds.[22] One thing the diaries seem not to do is to tell any kind of story about the interiority of the subject who recorded them. Much as we might be tempted to imagine George Scharf indulging in the pathetic fallacy, even the 'very dull afternoon' does not tell us anything about George Scharf's feelings.[23]

Our fantasy of embodied subjectivity had, as our recourse to 'character' implies, everything to do with our literary training. We felt as literary critics that we needed a way into the diaries and, thus, into Scharf. It would have made sense to have started with the first diary and made our way through them year by year. Instead we acted on impulse or, perhaps, according to disciplinary intuition: we would look for the diary entry corresponding to what we assumed would be the date of Scharf's only appearance in the album as a host. Attracted, as we shall discuss later, to the exceptional rather than to the representative instance, we homed in on the description of Scharf's dinner party of 28 December 1877, the one where he had apparently substituted raspberry for lemon ice (see Fig. 1.4).

And we hit (literary) pay dirt. Here are the entries for the day of the party and the day before:

Friday, 28 December
Home dinner 7 o'clock
Franks, Dayne Bell. Collambull, Reid, Thoms. Burton, Taylor, & Worsley
[expenses & walk home]

Successful dinner:

	GS	
Taylor		Dick
Burton		Bell
Reid		Collambull
	Franks	

Very lively talk, Extra waiter (Midland).
All carving done off the table. The hired flowers & new table linen looked very nice. To bed after 1 o'clock

For fans of George Scharf, and there are at least two of them, it was some relief that he was able to pull off a 'successful dinner' and that the expenses of flowers and new table linen should, for this meticulous recorder of expenses, have been so obviously worth it. Transported back in time, we read back to the day before – to the expenditures and work involved in preparation:

Thursday, 27 December
[expenses include butcher, charwoman, cigars, 'extra to Ball (1 shilling 2 pence), Caviare {sic}, Flower & fruit shop & to Biscoes to order for next day's dinner table'.]
Beautifully bright day. Ice in the streets & ground hard.
Dark early in the morning.
I breakfasted late at 8:15 after a strange dream of preparations for being beheaded, & woke during the operation.
Walked to the Gallery & afterward, went northward and skirted the Horti[cultura]l Garden. Went down the Gloucester Road.
Played [piano] at villa till 7 o'clock & then walked home by Brompton Rd. Fine starlight night.
Rent at Onslow Villas for 4 weeks £1.
Gave Madame M. a leather frame almanack & a Whitaker.

Is there anything more central to subjectivity than the Dream? Only the Nightmare. For archivists who came with specifically literary training, the Nightmare was a chance to use our special interpretive skills. We were finally qualified. The tedious details of the diary could be brought together into a Reading.

The diary entry from the night before the dinner is full of delicious intimations of character. Scharf was clearly anxious, we concluded irresponsibly, about this unique experience of transformation from parasite to host. Derridian echoes aside, the night-mare of beheading was clearly both about castration and about that central responsibility of the host, the carving of the meat. For us, the album had defined Scharf as a guest; hosting a dinner party in his home was a sign of adult masculinity, a masculinity for which the never-married George was radically unprepared and to which he was even more radically resistant. The fact that he was dream-ing about *preparations* for being beheaded suggested the trauma of preparing for the dinner party and the definitional moment of carving. Indeed, an even closer reading of the entry for the day of the dinner itself gives new meaning to the comment in the diary: 'all carving done off the table'. With this comment we could either conclude that Scharf was simply choosing *service à la russe* rather than the older *service à la française* – where carving was done at the table, often by the lady of the house – or that he was too anxious about carving to do it in front of his friends. The former is, alas, more probable, although even the famous Victorian cookery-book writer and chef of the Reform Club, Alexis Soyer, alludes to 'the continual tribulation in carving at table, for appetites more or less colossal, and when all eyes are fixed upon you with anxious avidity' (p. xiv). It is possible to imagine that Scharf's carving anxiety went beyond the typical nervousness identified by Soyer; perhaps Scharf, who employed no butler, was rattled enough by his nightmare to have delegated the carving to one of the extra male servants he hired for the occasion, rather than taking up the knife himself. Both primary and secondary sources, then, added evidence for our reading of trauma.

It took us many years and another trip to the archive to discover that the dinner party on 28 December was not a unique event. As we read further in the diaries, records of more dinner par-ties at Scharf's home began to intrude on the uniqueness of this one. Always for men only, always including up to seven guests, the dinner parties Scharf gave at home happened, disappointingly for our theory, frequently. A look back into the album even revealed another menu and another seating plan from dinners at Scharf's home, neither of which warranted special mention in the diary. Like many eager archival researchers, we had overlooked evidence. Perhaps holding a dinner party was not a trauma for George Scharf. Perhaps, on the night he had that nightmare, it was just something he ate.

As our nightmare story reveals, we operated at first with the literary critics' perhaps naïve but understandable faith that writing could provide a wedge we could use to pry open our subject's consciousness, the element of the self that most interests us as readers of Victorian fiction. We have admitted in this section to a certain methodological irresponsibility in our initial relation to the diaries, and here the monitory figure of the historian, dressed perhaps in the most authentic of Victorian costumes, rears both head and episteme. We do not want to exaggerate the difference between literary scholars and historians. We have read books by historians like Natalie Davis who have combined speculative writing with more traditional historical narrative. We have enjoyed the metahistorical wit of scholars like Seth Koven and Carolyn Steedman, whose meditations on absence, evidence and fantasy have inspired and mirrored our own. We have admired full and, yes, highly 'literary' readings of texts by historians like Lara Kriegel. But we still maintain – and historians who have discussed the project with us have supported us in this contention – that our initial intuitions and fantasies about what archival material can do were different from those of most historians who might encounter the same material. Despite everything, in looking for narrative, we were in the first instance looking for exceptionality: for those things that made George Scharf different from other people, those things that made him individual, something like a character. We were also looking for the exceptional moment: the dream, the trauma, the unique dinner party that would operate for us in the idiom of the singular. As we thought through what to do with George Scharf in our long-term project, we were advised by our historian friends to think of him otherwise, as representative, as a figure who would tell us about bachelor life in Victorian London, about mid-century immigrant experience, about the complications of class identification among urban professionals. As we will elaborate later, we simultaneously did and did not take our friends' advice.

The monumental archive: a trip to Xanthus

So far the George Scharf we had constructed was, so to speak, a paper figure, patched together out of our encounters with menus, diaries and those objects that are collected, preserved and read in libraries and those buildings we call archives precisely because they contain papers. There are – perhaps we should say there were – other buildings associated with Scharf that do not contain papers and that are only obliquely part of what we might call his paper trail. That trail led us outside of the library and outside of England to what we might call Scharf's monumental archive: to the record, if we can call it that, of his engagement with the archeologist Charles Fellows; with the ancient archaeological site of Xanthus in present-day Turkey; and with the tombs, temples and stones he preserved for posterity by translating them onto paper before they were carried, stone by stone and ton by ton, from Asia Minor to the British Museum.

Scharf's Xanthus adventure moved us out of the British Library, first to the British Museum and then (Helena without Robyn) to Xanthus itself. Of course, it is only recently that the journey from the library to the museum would involve any travel; in George's days – and in our earlier days as researchers – the reading room of the British Library was part of the British Museum, the transition from paper to stone a less than monumental one. Helena recalls the always slightly startling pleasure of spending the morning looking at manuscripts of Victorian plays and taking brief breaks to wander around the Elgin Marbles, sometimes (well, always) with a stop for a scone or a sandwich in the café a few steps away from the antiquities. The relocation of the British Library has now for many years turned us into mere tourists when we go to the British Museum. This revisitation put us back to work. Armed with Enid Slatter's wonderful book *Xanthus*, we started, as many visitors to the British Museum do, with the enormous Nereid Monument, the most famous and the most spectacular of the spoils of Xanthus.

It is hard not to raise the ghost of the Elgin Marbles when thinking about what were once known collectively as the Xanthian Marbles. Slatter mourns towards the end of her book that the Xanthus pieces can no longer be visited as a group, and that unlike the Elgin Marbles there is no special room for them, nothing that marks a collective identity. Even when the Xanthian Marbles were exhibited together to admiring crowds in 1848 in the 'Lycian room', Fellows was disappointed. He had hoped that the marbles and casts would 'be shown in relation to each other and to the region as a whole, in a chronological sequence, ranging over six centuries, illustrative of the historical changes in Lycia' (Slatter, p. 329). He had the surprisingly modern idea of including as a visual context mock-ups of the rock tombs that even British ingenuity could not move from their original location. From the beginning then, the story of the Xanthian Marbles in England is one of frustration and insufficiency.

41

A decade or so after the publication of Slatter's book, we found the collection to be even more dispersed. Most disappointing to us was the disappearance from the area that contained most of the Xanthian Marbles of the famous Lion Tomb, described by Slatter as shaggy and perhaps unattractive to Victorian audiences, but rendered by Scharf in his characteristic curly line as (in our eyes) almost impossibly cute. Whole rooms that had housed some of the marbles were closed. Conversations with the docents led us on something of a wild lion chase; we were offered a lion's head from Ur, probably some two hundred years older than ours, and sent to the front courtyard to view the majestic lion from Knidos, probably some two hundred years younger. No member of the marble bestiary was attached to a tomb. Helena's younger son did an impromptu version of one of those museum treasure hunts designed to inspire children bored by antiquities with the thrill of the chase. We were all on a lion hunt. At some point, of course, we fell back into archival mode and called the curator. After some discussion it became clear that our – Scharf's, Fellows's – lion was in storage; although initially willing to let us down into the storage rooms, the curator discovered that the room in question had no electric lights and the lion was literally blocked from access by tons of stone. Daunted by the tonnage and by fantasies of being crushed in the dark, we agreed to end our research for the day.

What would a sighting of the real Lion Tomb have told us? How did the tomb get transformed into the archival fetish it became for us? Perhaps it was because, of all the archaeological drawings we had seen – at this point we had only seen reproductions in the Slatter book – the one of the lion on the Lion Tomb seemed most of a piece with Scharf's other drawings and most connected to Scharf. One sketch in particular of two views of the tomb gives us, on the right, a seated lion whose rounded lines and enormous head suggest a toddler rather than a predator (Fig. 1.6). The lion's paws – also enormous – are more puppylike than feline. No claws are visible, just four billowing pads. The lion looks even tamer in the profile of the other view, his cheeks puffed out as if he were about to whistle. On the side of the tomb a lion actually attacks a man, who is, in turn, stabbing it with a knife. Despite the violence of the action, the lion looks as if he is dancing with his human partner, as he peeps coyly over his shoulder perhaps for the viewer's approval of a particularly well-executed step. While we had no way of know-

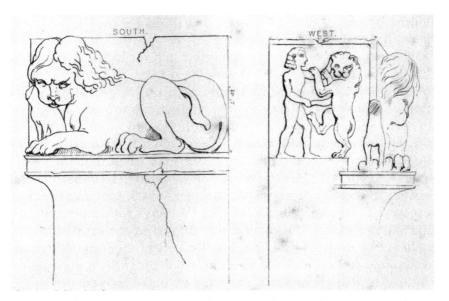

Fig. 1.6 GS sketches of lions on tomb at Xanthus. From Charles Fellows,
An Account of Discoveries in Lycia, p. f176.

ing how fierce the lions looked on the tomb, we found compelling
the idea that under Scharf's hands even the most terrifying crea-
tures became domesticated.

Was what we were looking for, then, something like Scharf's
hand or, to expand the metonymy, his fingerprints? We might fantasise for a moment about a biographical forensics where we could
envision identifying sweat from Scharf's fingers, charcoal from his
pencil, Scharf's DNA on the rough surface of a tomb. These were
and are, after all, things he touched, explored with his fingers,
perhaps fell over, unearthed, moved if they were small enough. On
one level, of course, the tombs at Xanthus were, for all intents and
purposes, impervious to that touch: in this lies their monumental-
ity. The controversial and self-serving British argument for their
removal – that the marbles would otherwise be destroyed by looters
– suggests of course that these enormous blocks of stone were more
ephemeral than we might think; we know that several large stones
fell, probably as a result of an earthquake, between Fellows's initial
visit to the site and the 1839 visit with Scharf. What we found ourselves doing in the search for Scharf's lion was fantasising about
a monumental archive that was somehow corporeal, an archive
whose more-than-human scale, nonetheless, offered back to us a

human presence. And, of course, that human scale was achieved through the mediation of paper.

What a difference it made actually to visit Xanthus, on a hundred-degree day two weeks later. Helena went without Robyn but with her research assistant, Basak Demhiran, who happened to be visiting her family in Turkey for the summer. Xanthus is an active archaeological site; probably most of the Lycian monuments have already been excavated, but the archaeologists have been working to unearth Etruscan and early Christian items. For their self-appointed guide, a seventy-five-year-old Turkish man who had been assisting at these excavations for some fifty years, the most exciting discoveries were the early Christian buildings with mosaic floors that had constantly to be recovered with dirt to protect them from looters. The original Xanthian Marbles served them quite literally as stepping stones; they followed the guide gingerly, notebooks in hand, as he leapt from tomb fragment to tomb fragment.

Although the excavation work had stopped for the day, the site was full of things, signs of professional activity. At the heart of it all, of course, were the gaping absences: the enormous stones that had once marked the site for Fellows, which were now thousands of miles away. One tomb was capped by a replica frieze from the early twentieth century – the others were just not there. Standing on a broken tomb looking past the Xanthus river that had itself changed its contours since Fellows's and Scharf's expeditions, Helena could only think of what was missing: Scharf's presence blown away on the hot wind.

What does it mean to look for a Victorian gentlemen in, on and through the monuments of ancient Lycia? Why travel to their original setting when, by definition, these monuments are exhibits elsewhere, missing from their origin? What trace of presence can we find or want to find in the monuments themselves, now removed first to the British Museum and then, in some cases, to the basement storage rooms of that museum? In some sense the archival project mirrors the original project of removal; as Michel De Certeau notes, the process of reading an archive is a process of thinking otherwise: 'The issue is not only one of bringing these "immense dormant sources of documentation" to life, of lending a voice to silence, or of lending currency to a possibility. It means changing something which had its own definite status and role into *something else* which functions differently' (p. 74). If Fellows and Scharf in moving the Xanthian marbles to the British Museum gave them another function, if in transferring them to paper and to England they became 'something else', this is, in fact, the characteristic, culturally powerful and ethically uneasy work of the archive.

The visceral archive: a Victorian dinner party

Our most entertaining attempt to come to terms with Scharf brought him much closer to home: Helena's home, that is, not Scharf's lodgings and certainly not Knole. The idea for this different kind of archival experience came not from Robyn or Helena but from a then-prospective graduate student at Rice University, where Helena teaches. During the graduate recruitment weekend for the entering class of 2009, Helena gave a workshop on the early stages of our archival project. She ended with the problem of what to do with Scharf, given that we did not want to write a biography. Joanna O'Leary, who had already confided to Helena her interests in food and Victorian literature, had a simple suggestion: 'Why don't you cook one of those dinners?'

The suggestion blossomed into a year-long project in which the Victorian Studies Seminar (VSS), composed of graduate students and faculty at Rice, read primary and secondary sources about Victorian food and planned a banquet for the end of the year that would be based on one of the Scharf menus. We imagined, in other words, a year of scholarship and paper to be followed by, to culminate in, to be rewarded by, a night of food and drink. Sophie Weeks, the graduate assistant for VSS, suggested starting an archive of our own by creating a website for the project on which we would include materials from Scharf and other Victorian sources as well as photographs of the banquet and blogs by the participants.[24] Robyn was to come from her home in Vermont, of course, to be the guest of honour (if that designation can include acting as cook, housecleaner, flower arranger and server). After much discussion about whether we could bear to eat turtles (if we could get them), about whether a saddle of lamb could be hung in a Houston kitchen in summer for three days (the answer is no), and about whether we could find dishes that would challenge us into a historical experience without being so complicated that we could not hope to make them as part of an eight-course meal, we chose as our base menu the one from the dinner Scharf ate at Knole on 25 August 1877.

Not every one of the fifteen diners who made their way from the consommé 'royale' through the obligatory (at Knole) Parmesan savouries – not to mention the four kinds of wine – had George Scharf always at the forefront of their minds. Even Robyn and Helena forgot for long stretches of time – while laying out with our own hands a different set of dishes for every course or otherwise acting in a most un-George-Scharf-like way – that the banquet had anything to do with the man who ate something somewhat similar 132 years before. Our bodies, to the extent that they stood in for Scharf's, were differently gendered, aged and classed. And even had we matched Scharf demographic for demographic, had we been male, fifty-seven, and of his peculiar – and to us incalculable – class status, having lived his history would have made a difference to our historical experiment. His body would have been used to the kinds of food, the amount of alcohol, the sounds and the silences of the Victorian table. He would have experienced as repetition what we experienced as unique. And yet, as Helena noted in her blog, George was a ghost at the feast. The modest and genteel consciousness we had constructed for him out of his unremarkable diaries lent a benign spirit to the event.

What precisely were we doing as, eschewing Victorian costume, we, nonetheless, strove for some approximation of authentic experience? The literature on historical re-enactment suggests that we were participating in history's 'affective turn', and that we might be doing something called public history.[25] The few accounts of re-enactment that see anything positive coming out of the practice suggest the possibility of political and ethical effects. While it is certainly the case that the banquet gave us all a deeper appreciation of the work of Victorian servants, we are not sure – and this is crucial – what the word 'deeper' might really mean. What seemed at least in retrospect (and perhaps in self-justification) useful was how the experience of the banquet allowed us (forced us, really) to inhabit at least two temporalities and at least two bodies at the same time: each dish was both the thing itself – good, bad, but always rich and oversauced – and an inadequate replication of another imaginary dish that lived beyond the reach of the tongue, the taste buds and the best silver forks we could get our hands on, produced in the 1920s at the height of the anti-Victorian-design reaction. The multiplicity of temporalities that confuses the Victorian/contemporary binary enriches what Katie King calls the 'bit of pastpresents', the useful juxtapositional work of re-enactment (p. 459).

All this cooking, eating, serving and cleaning, however, produced something else, something that we can call an archive for the twenty-first century. Most obviously, that archive lives in and is embodied by the pictures, video and text of our experience as it is uploaded onto a website. But the archive is also, as Derrida and Steedman note, a place of memory, in this case as perhaps in all cases, a bodily one. Eating saddle of lamb produces bodily memories for which the website is (only?) a glowing prosthesis. As we watched, three months after the banquet, the beautiful video of the evening created by Eun Young Koh, we heard in its music and saw in its images the taste of the food. This was (and is) not just a corporeal but a synaesthetic archive.

We have spoken so far as if the eating of the food had little to do with George Scharf. For Robyn and Helena, at least, the fantasy at the banquet was not so much being a Victorian, not so much being George as consuming him. We were not so much eating chicken 'Marengo' (topped with poached eggs and crab claws, crawfish being out of season) as absorbing George through the mouth and the skin. If it worked – and fantasies work simply by being fantasies – it was because in eating and drinking we could temporarily imagine the breakdown of barriers, the crossing of boundaries. And, of course, 'temporarily' is the key word. We have immortalised (for however long it lasts on the Internet) the event on our blog and in talk about the banquet with each other and with the other guests. But what is most likely to last for both of us, we think, is a piece of ephemera, another piece of paper: the box-shaped menu, in imitation of the one from Knole, designed by Elizabeth Womack and folded under her direction into the appropriate shape by a group of graduate students. Its background is yellow, where the background of the menu from Knole is white. Departing from the stately plainness of the original, ours is covered with blue toile-like birds, more eighteenth-century than Victorian, more post-modern imitation of 'Victorian' than either. Most wonderfully, one of the birds is cut out and stands up to serve as a latch for the box. Like George, we saved examples of this beautiful menu, although we did not put them into a scrapbook. We may be every bit as obsessive as George Scharf himself, but – busy twenty-first-century academics and working mothers that we are – we have neither the patience, the organisational drive nor the leisure to keep an album like George's for maintaining a material, metonymic link to the gastronomic experiences of our pasts. Instead, we commit the dinner party here to paper, the medium in which our archival adventures began and end.

George Scharf is dead, the scraps of our meal long consigned to compost and to Houston's complex ecology of waste management. The riverbank in Xanthus has been reconfigured, and tourists line the beaches where Fellows first landed. We have what we can keep of it all: our paper notes, the folded boxes and this book itself that will be consigned first to a library and then, perhaps, to an archive.

Writing George Scharf's 'life'

In telling the story of the visceral archive, we might seem to have come to the end of the story of 'George Scharf'. Once we had answered the question of what to do with Scharf by deciding to consume him, we wrote a temporary ending to a project that included a published article and a series of conference papers. While we took great pleasure from our co-authorship, part of that pleasure stemmed from the many different kinds of freedom associated with our work together: freedom to travel, to experiment with voice and, crucially and finally, freedom from having to turn everything we wrote into a book. Several years after our last bite of *poulet Marengo* in the manner of George Scharf, we decided to revisit our resolution not to write that book. Although the decision to continue felt momentous at the time, we both realised that it had in many ways already been made. We did not want to stop. We had more than enough material. We were, more importantly, haunted by the story of Scharf's life or, perhaps more accurately, by the possibility of turning his life into a story – or stories.

Perhaps the biggest barrier to writing a book up to that point had been the issue of genre. We knew – even though we were not sure what we meant by this – that we did not want to write what we always mentally capitalised as a Biography. Part of our recoil – and it was as visceral in its way as our reactions to Scharf's textualised meals – was entangled in the idiom of boredom we had initially attached to the institutional archive and to Scharf himself. Although we continued, affectionately, to call Scharf 'boring', we had long ceased to find him so. Boredom became projected instead onto an imagined biographical project: to write a Biography – or rather, to collect material for a Biography – would be, we felt, to submit to an exercise in tedium, to subject ourselves to the endless and apparently colourless detail of the archive. This fear of being bored was ironic, given that we had, over the years, so immersed ourselves in the minutiae of Scharf's life that we had needed to construct a 200–plus-page

Master Chronology, a document that – despite its vibrant colour coding – has to be one of the dullest pieces of writing in the world.[26]

Boredom is, of course, a somewhat shaky defence against intellectual inquiry. And this is precisely the point: it is a defence. Our association of Biography with boredom also contained more than a tinge of academic snobbishness. We agree with Martine Brownley's assertion that the genre has been undertheorised and that scholarship on biography has been relatively untouched by the poststructuralist challenges to its assumed foundational subject that have led to exciting developments in autobiography studies.[27] As avid readers of biography, however, we should have reminded ourselves of the astonishing richness and variety of contemporary biographical practice, much of which implicitly offers the critique that is only beginning to emerge in the scholarship. We say 'biographical practice' here, not only to emphasise the hundreds of day-to-day decisions made by biographers, but to avoid what we find to be the unduly rigid nominalisation of 'Biography' or 'Life'.

In order to write 'George Scharf' (how useful that placeholder could be!), we had to find at least a working name for the kind of book we were producing. Not a biography, not a 'life', not a historical novel: we were trying to write something less conventional, more fluid, more strange, something we were properly qualified, as literary critics rather than historians or creative writers, to compose. As with the case of the terms we considered for naming Scharf's identity, we find ourselves attracted to genre names that combine nouns and verbs: 'life-writing' is for us the most capacious of these terms, although its productive grammatical indeterminacy makes it hard to use as the subject of a sentence or – especially – in a book's title. We have split apart and pluralised 'life-writing' in our subtitle, 'Writing the Lives of George Scharf, Victorian Bachelor', to underline our conviction that not just Scharf but every biographical subject has many different lives that could be written. The gerund emphasises our belief that the writing of those many different lives never can be finished.

For a long time we tried out the idea of calling this book a 'vita', with its punning nod to Vita Sackville-West and to Knole, her ancestral home, which figures so prominently in Scharf's menu collection and in the final chapter of our book. *Vida* with a 'd' is also the name given to short biographies of Provençal troubadors; we liked this connection to Scharf's love of singing and to the place of music in his recorded memories of his own life. We also were drawn to the way 'vita' in the familiar academic locution of curriculum vitae stresses the professional current of a life, connecting, perhaps, our own working and writing lives to Scharf's. In the end we came to the conclusion that we were not really either inventing or prescribing a new genre, so a new generic name wasn't necessary. We have transferred the term 'vita' from the whole project to the timeline representing the events of George Scharf's life that precedes this introduction, incorporating moments big, small and in-between – a sample of the competing and complementary scales that make up any life.

Resigned to engaging in life-writing after all, we have drawn inspiration from a number of experimental biographies that interrogate the notion of a unitary self or blur the boundaries between biographer and subject, fact and fiction. One response to traditional renditions of selfhood has been to multiply the subject(s) of any given biography, as in Jan Marsh's *Pre-Raphaelite Sisterhood* and Juliet Barker's *The Brontës*; another, to use a place or an event as the focal point and biographical subject, as in Peter Ackroyd's *London: The Biography*. We found many wonderful examples of creative biography writing, but two in particular stand out for their methodological innovations.

One of our favourites among these experiments is the tantalisingly titled *The Immortal Dinner: A Famous Evening of Genius and Laughter in Literary London, 1817*, by Penelope Hughes-Hallett. It is centred on a dinner party given by the artist B. R. Haydon for John Keats, William Wordsworth and Charles Lamb, among others. Although the book starts out with a fairly conventional biographical chapter on the slightly less-than-famous Haydon, entitled 'The Host', other chapters include 'Crossing London', which traces the journeys the guests took from their own homes to Haydon's; 'Christ Entering Jerusalem', which is about the giant historical painting by Haydon that hung on the dining-room wall; and a series of chapters whose titles indicate topics of conversation as they were recorded by Haydon in his diaries. The book's structure is suspenseful; we watch the guests assemble over many pages before we hear them speak. Although *Immortal Dinner* is not a book that foregrounds the role of the biographer, one of its charms is a sort of metaleptic verbal contagion in which the author seems to mimic the expansive style of the dinner party raconteur.

Love Among the Archives is in many ways the mirror opposite of *Immortal Dinner*. Like Hughes-Hallett's book, it, too, features a group of talented London men with interests in the arts and follows them as they sit down to dine. *Love Among the Archives*, however, is structured not by suspense or singularity but by repetition; although some dinners are more important than others, the sheer number of opportunities to eat in this story undercuts their specialness: they are a fact of everyday life. Ordinariness has another register as well. Even Haydon was considered by his friends (and certainly by himself) to be a genius; a dinner party that included him and three of the most famous writers of the Romantic period whets the appetite for *bons mots* – and Haydon duly recorded them. By contrast, we know almost nothing of what was said at Scharf's dinner parties by himself or any of his guests. What we know in abundance is what they ate and where they sat. While some of Haydon's guests expressed themselves strongly in other contexts about potatoes, mutton or wine, it is as if *Immortal Dinner*'s conversation unfolded over empty plates and glasses. Finally, there is the question of the role of art in the two kinds of dining experiences; because of Haydon's preoccupation with his own masterpiece, Hughes-Hallett is able to devote an entire chapter to the artwork that served as background to and occasional topic of conversation. We know from Scharf's sketches and diary entries that his lodgings were filled with drawings, paintings and sculpture, but these are not present in his descriptions of the dinners themselves. Indeed, Scharf's accounts of the dinners – and they often surfaced as accountings of the cost of food and wine – make no mention of his guests' status in the world beyond the table. Almost without exception, the men around the table are diners, defined for the moment and beyond by what they eat. All this makes Scharf's dinner parties, unlike Haydon's, mortal. Our challenge has been to work up from mundane detail and not down from the loftier heights of Keats's poetry or Wordsworth's genius.

Another of our inspirations from the world of life-writing was Neil Bartlett's *Who Was That Man?: A Present for Mr Oscar Wilde*. The subtitle's unusual usage of 'Mr' to refer to a famous author and its identification of the book as a 'present' to him set the book up as an exchange between the author and its subject. Although it does not name itself as such, we think of *Who Was That Man?* as a queer biography, not only for its subject matter but for its form, with its collection of short pieces of prose varying in narrative level, person and addressee. The book even discusses the act of collection as having an important historical role in gay male life, placing itself as an example in that history. What we like best about Bartlett's piece of life-writing is the way it interrogates the foundational conditions of biography, including the fame that is both an assumption and an effect of much biographical writing. Bartlett asks the titular question, not because his biographical subject is obscure, but because, over time, Wilde has been so important to so many different readers with varying investments in him as a figure. When we asked ourselves the question, 'Who Was George Scharf?', it was, at least originally, more literal. Bartlett's work reminds us that the 'discovery' of Scharf's sexuality – if it had been there in the record for us to find – would not have mitigated the need for questions.

Though we do not claim to be inventing an altogether new genre of life-writing, we are making five significant departures from conventional biographical practice: we employ an unconventional temporality in writing Scharf's life, we foreground the master narratives that in spite of our best efforts seemed to keep forcing themselves upon the facts we uncovered, we give priority to many of the mundane details of daily living that would not typically make their way into a biography, we make the choice to emphasise the partial nature of this set of stories about Scharf's life and we subject Scharf's own prose to an unusually close kind of close reading. By using the form of our text to disrupt biography's most persistent formal conventions, we hope to resist – although we cannot always avoid – the most banal and progressivist versions of writing a life.

Our first experiment with biographical practice is the triple temporality we deploy in *Love Among the Archives*. Our approach keeps three temporal planes simultaneously in play: story time, discourse time and something that we will call 'archive time'. Story time governs our chronological reconstruction of what happened in the life of Scharf. To be a proper story, a narrative needs to be the recounting of a sequence of events connected by causation. Our sources mention many events, and they often occur in sequence, but connective tissue is often missing. Even when Scharf as diarist articulates a cause-and-effect relation among events, we read him sceptically, symptomatically and imaginatively. This means that, in our narrative, causation is usually a speculation or improvisation. We freely acknowledge that we are constructing a storyworld, which is not at all the same thing as writing history. Still, we offer our account of George Scharf's professional and social lives as a way to observe some of the things Victorianists are doing when 'history' is what we want to get out of the archive. Rather than making the linear temporality of Scharf's life the organising principle for the chapters, we have presented his chronologically ordered experiences in the form of the 'vita', or timeline, which precedes this book's preface.

Discourse time is something we observe in Scharf's own writing of diaries and letters. Discourse time for Scharf operates along three separate but coinciding tracks: that of the letter or daily entry, that of the memorial anniversary annotation, and that of his annual summaries of the preceding year. When we cite a piece of Scharf's own prose, we keep in mind the level of discourse time in which he writes it, with a special interest in his reiterative narratives, little stories he records over and over in anniversary notations and year-end summaries, like the day he 'ceased to shave' or his mother's funeral. Anniversary time is recursive time; Scharf is always looking back to look forward. The structure of our book mimics, to a certain extent, the recursion and repetition of Scharf's diaries: we license ourselves to bring back quotations and evidence from chapter to chapter, assigning additional meaning and weight with each encounter.

Archive time is the temporality within which we made our discoveries, a chronology spanning more than fifteen years of uncovering some fact about George Scharf in his album, sketchbooks, correspondence or diaries; mulling over questions suggested by that fact; and going back to the archive to seek answers to those questions only to open up more puzzles to solve. Archive time structures each chapter, which we narrate in the spirit of detective stories. Of course, as individuals, the two of us experienced the project differently, came to different conclusions at different times, changed our separate minds about what had happened in Scharf's life and sometimes argued each other into changing them back. We know our choice to write the book in the first-person plural maintains a fiction of perfectly dual focalisation, as if the order in which we came to know the story we are telling were exactly the same for both of us. Because this ontological togetherness is only a fiction, we have at crucial moments in the text used our first names where we still disagree or simply got to the same place at different moments.

If individual chapters embed archive time into their structure, the book as a whole traces the arc of our interest and discovery. The first chapter on Scharf's sexuality presents the material that first allowed us to imagine a book. Trained not only as Victorianists with an interest in the marriage plot but also as feminist critics and as theorists of gender and sexuality, we were attracted to the complexity of Scharf's relation to sexuality as the possible sub-ject of a full-length study. Issues of class and social status came later, becoming more urgent, more interesting – and sexier – as we moved back and forth between and within archives. The final image of Chapter 4, of George in bed at Chevening, is far removed from the George of our speculations in Chapter 2: this bedroom scene reflects a shift in or rather opening up of our interests over the course of archive time to include class, bodily pain, hospitality, portrait identification and generational history. Scharf's body, still (but in some ways differently) gendered is profoundly different from the one we imagined while working on our first chapter, and we try to register that difference through the structure of the book.

Our focus on archive time adds a layer of self-reflexivity to this book that might be its most obvious departure from typical bio-graphical practice. Writing the story of our archival discoveries means writing about our own scholarly and personal preconcep-tions, desires, reactions, interpretations and reinterpretations as we became aware of them in the process of finding out more about George Scharf. Particularly in this introductory chapter and in Chapter 2 on the marriage plot our attention is almost evenly divided between Scharf's life story and the story of our trying to assemble it. The personas emerging from the narrative of our archi-val adventure are caricatures of ourselves as English professors, meant neither to ascribe any psychological depth to the Helena and Robyn who speak our narrative discourse nor to suggest that there is anything special or unique about the personas behind our narrating voice. We hope the meta-archival commentary in the first half of the book will serve to render us 'relatable', as students like to say, rather than to establish us as exceptional characters. *Love Among the Archives* is not a book about us. The last two chapters increasingly shift the focus from our experience of the archive to the materials we found there, though the self-reflexivity of our project is present to the end. We are always trying to extrapolate from the unremarkable life of George Scharf to larger historical, theoretical and methodological observations we hope will be useful to those who think and write about other, more exceptional lives, especially when those lives are Victorian.

Our second innovation also subverts the temporality that ordi-narily governs life-writing. Just as archive time usually structures the order in which we reveal information about Scharf's life, master plots that we have internalised from reading nineteenth-century fiction shape each of our chapters. As we will explain in detail, the facts we know about what happened to George Scharf seemed at first to come to us pre-packaged as scenes from Victorian novels, often not very exciting ones. When we were still new to the Scharf archive, realist detail in a Victorian setting called out for insertion into a marriage plot, a family romance, even a sensation novel. Given a conglomeration of names, dates and incidents, we could not help trying to place them in the context of those narrative structures that have persistently shaped British and US culture since the nineteenth century (not to mention our own thinking about our personal and professional lives). The more we tried to fit the disparate facts of Scharf's life into any of these familiar narrative trajectories, the more those facts would thwart us. Not surprisingly, we learned that neither Scharf's love life, nor his family life, nor his professional ascent conformed to the patterns predicted by Victorian fiction. And yet, as we see it, the marriage plot, the family romance and the plot of professional success persist into the twenty-first century as canonical narrative forms within the field of Victorian studies, framing the way scholars think about mid-nineteenth-century British gender, sexuality and class. We try to play Scharf's story against the master plots that framed our expectations for what ought to have happened to the hero of our piece. To a great extent this has been the impetus for our trying out new identity categories that generally belong only to minor characters in Victorian plots but that do fit our protagonist.

Our third innovation, which has to do with the texture of our research and writing, we call 'somatic life-writing'. This practice involves what we see as a quasi-Victorian attention to realist detail, especially to the minutiae of lived experience. *Love Among the Archives* is the only example we know of somatic life-writing. Biography is supposed to subordinate the diurnal and the physiological to the larger arc of the historically significant. In a regular biography some events in the subject's life signify, and some do not. In mining Scharf's diaries for knowledge about exactly what went into (or, indeed, when Scharf gives Too Much Information about his various digestive complaints, out of) his body, about his ever-increasing weight, about his sensitivities to the weather and his propensities for falling down in the street, we are trafficking in what Robyn has elsewhere called the subnarratable.[28] In any given genre, the subnarratable consists of those things that 'go without saying', that are considered by tacit convention to be too obvious or too trivial to relate. We are lowering the threshold of the subnarratable in order to model the degree of immersion this kind of life-writing has required. For us, the answers to 'Who Was George Scharf?' encompass not just an account of his contributions to the history of portraiture or museums, or even of his relationships with friends and family members, but also a sense of what it might have felt like to be George Scharf, across the spectrum of physical and emotional sensations his diaries can let us glimpse.

One could argue that the fourth innovation is a matter of necessity. While all biographies, all pieces of life-writing, are partial, both in the sense of having a bias and of being incomplete, *Love Among the Archives*, as the first extended piece of life-writing about its subject, cannot hope to capture all facets of Scharf's life and career. Art historians or scholars of museum history might be shocked at how little we say about Scharf's key roles in the history of portrait identification or in the development of cataloguing and display. There has been little written, in fact, about nineteenth-century techniques of portrait identification generally: we would love to see such a history written and to learn more about Scharf's place in a field that has so quickly turned to quasi-forensic techniques. Our book does offer glimpses of Scharf's technical practices, of his reliance on colour and clothing for the identification of portraits and of his perhaps strategic and perhaps intuitive investment, so appropriate to the development of the NPG collection, in the sitter at the expense of the artist.

Scharf's innovations in terms of the history of exhibition and display have perhaps been more influential. For example, according to Elizabeth A. Pergam, Scharf's arrangement of portraits for the Manchester Art Treasures Exhibition of 1857, before he became NPG director, were highly innovative. Scharf chose to exhibit paintings from different countries and different national traditions chronologically, often on opposite walls, so visitors could compare, say, the development of Italian and German schools of painting (Pergam, p. 64). While it is tempting to see Scharf's aesthetics of display as linked to the broader and, perhaps, deeper habit of temporally inflected thinking so central to our own accounts of Scharf, we do not spend much time in this book looking at his several key contributions to the history of display.[29]

The partiality of our picture of Scharf has, of course, something to do with the limits of our expertise – and of the background information available to us. It also results from our focus on the available personal letters and diaries: both date from the mid-1850s (George's mid-thirties) onward. Although we have looked at many kinds of materials from his early life (and from the lives of his family), most of the information we have comes from the middle to the end of his career; our George is middle-aged, growing in girth and reputation, working to write his own life according to his own culturally inspired narratives of success.

And finally, our fifth innovation is born of our literary-critical training. As our example of the nightmare suggests, we try to avoid what undergraduates might call 'reading too much into' the prose we find in Scharf's diaries and letters. Nevertheless, we subject Scharf's prose to something we think of as 'strong close reading'. We try to construe our subject's statements in every way we can imagine, looking not just at his diction and syntax but also at orthography as signs of his state of mind and of the emotions he so seldom articulates. We are subjecting non-literary and even non-rhetorical texts to an intensely rhetorical reading, taking into account erasures, crossings-out, underlinings, repeated lines, diagrams, monikers and shifts in verb tense and mood. Sometimes what we read between his diary's lines seems to be all the content we can find.

We should say a word about some choices we have made in the actual writing of *Writing the Lives of George Scharf.* The first has to do with the name of our subject. Common usage would dictate calling him 'Scharf', except when the necessity of differentiating him from his relatives, especially his father, would require the use of 'George Jr'. We found ourselves establishing a flexible pattern dictated by the three masterplots that structure our book's chapters: in Chapter 2, shaped by the 'Marriage Plot,' we call him 'George'; in Chapter 3, the 'Family Romance', he is 'George Jr'; and in Chapter 4, the 'professional plot', he is 'Scharf'. When it comes to naming our subject, we are admittedly not perfectly consistent in any practice except one: we never call him 'Sir George', because his knighthood came so late in life. In the institutional archive the 'Sir' is what distinguishes him from his far less successful father; we mean no disrespect when we diminish that difference by simplifying it to 'George Jr' and 'George Sr'.

The commitments of our life-writing practice involve keeping a series of temporalities simultaneously in play. We have sometimes struggled to embody these temporalities – and the relationships between them – in the available menu of English tenses. As Helena has argued elsewhere, the linearity of English syntax makes certain kinds of layering or simultaneity difficult to represent at the level of the sentence (Michie, 'Victorian(ist) "Whiles"', p. 278). While we adhere for the most part to the literary protocol of using the present tense for the textual and some form of past tense for the historical, the addition of another layer – the unfolding of our own discoveries in archive time – makes for some complex sentences and paragraphs. If we could have kept it up, we would probably have written the entire book in the continuous present that characterises (one of) the narratives of Dickens's *Bleak House.*

As we have indicated, each of this book's chapters both reflects and reflects upon a master plot from Victorian literature and culture. We begin with the romance plot in part to preserve the order of our own explorations of Scharf's texts, in part because of our sense of that plot's hegemonic cultural power, and in part because sexuality is so central to twenty-first-century ideas about subjectivity and identity. Our next two chapters take up the parallel powers of the *Bildungsroman* as a life-shaping plot: we found it helpful to focus, first, on the part of that romance that requires individuation from the family and, then, on its imbrication in narratives of professional success. Throughout the book we try to maintain and scrupulously to recount a double relation to these narratives: while we see them as deeply problematic, we also try to be aware of our own investments in the plots (in all senses) that shaped Scharf's culture and continue – we would argue – to shape our own.

Chapter 2, 'Reading for romance: the marriage plot', is structured as a meta-archival narrative that follows our at-first unconscious attempts to build a love story out of the flotsam of this Victorian bachelor's life. In the face of the silence of the archive about any physical relationship George Scharf ever had with another person, we trace our initial efforts to identify his possible objects of desire. We tell of our increasing awareness of the importance of his homosocial private circle and our eventual realisation that there was someone, after all, who stood out from the crowd of George's male friends as a person meriting special mention in his diaries and, therefore, in our story of his life. Following the paths of our separate revelations about the role Jack Pattisson played in George Scharf's emotional life, we relate the story of hunting for Jack in George's diaries and in letters collected at the National Portrait Gallery.

On the way to Jack, we interrogate our own investments in the marriage and romance plot and ask ourselves to what extent the cultural hegemony of the marriage plot can be challenged. We describe the thought processes that led to our decision to retain 'marriage plot' as the chapter's master term when it became clear that George's desires – and our desires for him – did not involve women or marriage. Throughout the chapter we explore the problem of the archive's relation to sex and, in particular, to sexual secrecy. It is here that we discuss different ways of reading (in) the archive that might make sex more visible in, say, diary entries about money, gifts or weather. Our chapter ends with the story of Jack's replacement in George's domestic circle by George's friend and colleague Freeman O'Donoghue, eventually to become the author of the first *Dictionary of National Biography* entry about Scharf. This relationship, in many ways a less intense reiteration of the one with Jack, establishes a new kind of intimacy dependent on ill-health and a new form of life-writing involving the listing of bodily symptoms. As George ages – we think – out of a romance plot, we are challenged to find new ways of reading and writing.

Chapter 3, 'Reading for differentiation: the family romance', juxtaposes George Scharf Jr's life with the domestic plot of the Victorian *Bildungsroman,* in which the protagonist moves up and away from his family of origin to find himself in a more exalted position in the world than the one from which he started. This version of our story begins with the classic triangle of psychoanalysis: the father, the mother and the son. The first section looks at how the relationship between father and son both is and is not contained within a narrative of differentiation; we show how the differentiation plot necessitates projecting the father as a failure, and how the evidence for that failure is overdetermined by plot and undersupported by evidence. The second section looks at how George Jr's literal and figurative moving away from his father allowed the son to set up an idealised household with his mother in the building of the National Portrait Gallery and to incorporate – again with sometimes remarkable literalness – his mother into the space of his professional life. The third section takes a step away from the charged dynamics of the nuclear family and from the idiom of interpersonal affect to reframe the Scharf family as a business, and George Jr both as the head of that business and as its product. This section focuses on 1856, a year of financial crisis within the family, and on the attempts of various family members to understand, mitigate and control that crisis. We hear in this section the self-effacing voice of the aunt, always an afterthought both in the Scharf family and in psychodynamic narratives. We also move in this section to a different kind of archival procedure and to a fuller reading of accounting than was possible in Chapter 2. The brief final section moves further outside the psychodynamic triangle to the strange and, indeed, mysterious figure of George Jr's less fortunate younger brother, Henry. We end by asking whether the story of differentiation is literally a story of the individual; can it have two heroes or does its development depend on the death of the brother as much as it does on the death of the father?

The fourth and final chapter, 'Reading for success: the professional plot', takes up from a different point of view the story of Scharf's class and professional ascendance by focusing on Scharf's work in two great country houses: Knole, the home of the Sackvilles, and Chevening, the home of the Stanhope family. Alert to the stories and genres that fantasies about country houses have produced, from inheritance plots to sensation and Gothic novels, we offer case studies of two aspects of Scharf's working life: his ambiguous position and activities at Knole in the 1870s and 1880s and his complicated relationship with Lord Stanhope, his superior at the NPG who often served as Scharf's host. The generic intertext for this chapter is the sensation novel, with its emphasis on inheritance and on belonging and un-belonging that gets played out in country houses and estates. In the chapter's first section we explore the meaning of Knole to Scharf and within the national imaginary; we ask ourselves what precisely Scharf was doing at Knole, what he got out of his long association with the house and with the then-impoverished and litigious representatives of the Sackville family who were living there. This first case study traces Scharf's professional and social activities at Knole and the various identities – as guest, consultant, employee and quasi-family member – that defined him during his sojourns there. The second case study moves us a few miles from Knole to that other salient country house, Chevening, home of the Stanhope family. We start with the apparent fact of Scharf's intimacy with that family and ask ourselves how this immigrant son became such a familiar if not familial figure in this aristocratic house. The answer can be traced in part through Scharf's correspondence with Stanhope in their respective roles as director and chairman of the board of the NPG. We are able to follow the development of that relationship through the archive – although always working around its gaps and mysteries. Here we turn from the written to the visual record of Scharf's time at Chevening, looking especially closely at his intimate sketches of Stanhope family life. We end the book not with Scharf's death but with the death of the earl he called his 'best friend', and with Scharf's rhetorical positioning of himself as witness and mourner.

2

Reading for romance: the marriage plot

S O FAR WE HAVE structured the story of this project around an originary narrative and, indeed, a moment of origin – our encounter with George Scharf's album of menus and invitations that served as our introduction to him (see Fig. 1.1). Certainly that origin shaped our initial sense of George as a guest, a diner out.

If we had not always had before us the glowing after-image of the menus, the gilded names of country houses and the calling cards of the rich and famous, we would perhaps have read the diaries differently: we might have read George not only or primarily as a guest but also as a host. Although, as we describe in the introduction, we found traces of Scharf as a host in the album and in the nightmare of hospitality we construed from those traces, the album resolutely and snobbishly tied him to country estates and their social rituals. The diaries, however, show Scharf as an almost obsessive giver of dinners, small and large, and as the centre of what one guest called 'The Ashley Place Circle', a group of male friends defined by the address of the lodgings Scharf rented for the last two and a half decades of his life. The diaries provide lists – sometimes, on special occasions in the form of seating charts – itemising a series of regular guests who were usually young, mostly untitled and invariably male. The diaries allow us to see, as the album does not, the importance of home and of the process of planning, budgeting for and producing (through his cook, who was also his maid-of-all-work) a series of dinners, elaborate and high-calorie by our modern standards, but fundamentally different in style and in substance from those he ate as a guest at great houses.

Derrida reminds us, of course, that the role of guest and host are mutually constitutive; both are obviously aspects of the story that we hoped would become a life, if not a *Life* of George Scharf (Derrida, p. 18). But the shift in focus in our reading of the diaries from guest to host, from entries about country houses to entries about London lodgings, allowed us to tell a set of stories about Scharf completely different from the ones the album had inspired. Although the identity of 'dinner guest' emphasised, we thought, the importance to our project of George's body – its massive size, its desires and its pleasures – we found that the turn homeward to host allowed us to think about George's body and desires in yet another way. This chapter is one among our many stories about George; it is a meta-archival story of how we came to see him differently as we reread the diaries to find the dinners and social engagements that he had not chosen to archive in the album.

In telling the story of George as host, we could, of course, begin with the earliest diaries or, indeed, with the earliest information we have about him; most life-writing does begin with or before the birth of the protagonist. This is a story worth telling, and we will tell much of it in the next chapter. But as we have said in the introduction, we are also interested throughout this book in thinking about problems of life-writing, archival research and temporality and in finding a formal structure for our book that allows these questions to be articulated. We decided, therefore, to organise the present chapter according to the chronology of our discoveries, or what we call 'archival time' as it unfolds in conversation with discourse time and story time. We stage this conversation to demonstrate the many ways in which George's story becomes our story, his romance plot indicatively an expression of our investments. The chapter thus unfolds recursively, as we tell of our going back to reread documents in the archive or to re-examine facts and assumptions that change dramatically when placed in the context of new revelations about George's circumstances and the culture that shaped them.

When we saw the diaries catalogued as 'personal' at the NPG – at that early moment in archival time when the staff at the Heinz Archive and Library first turned call slips into things for us – those things seemed perfectly to embody the romance of the archive (Figs 2.1, 2.2, 2.3). First, they came as all archival objects should, in boxes. These were not the innocuous acid-free boxes provided by twenty-first-century libraries and archives but real Victorian boxes, one for each year, each containing twelve miniature books, one

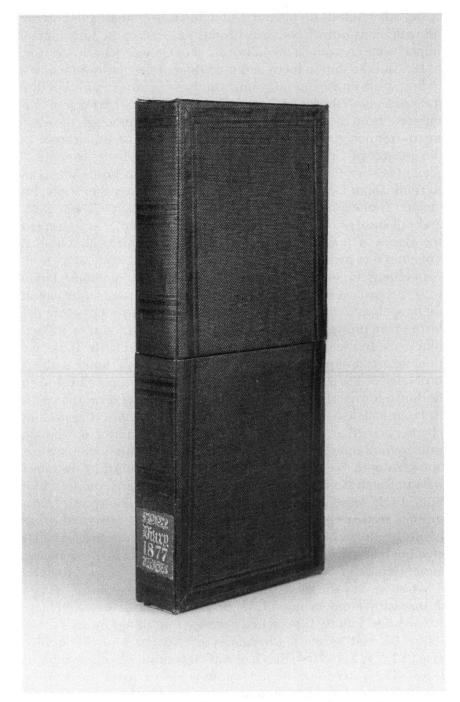

Fig. 2.1 Boxed diaries for 1877. ©National Portrait Gallery, London.

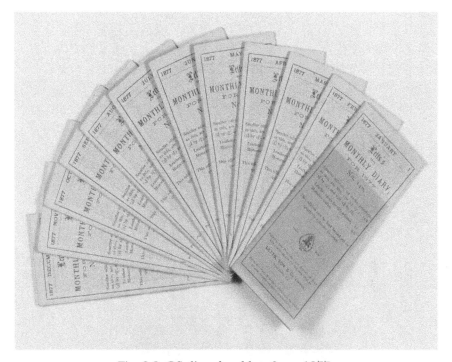

Fig. 2.2 GS diary booklets from 1877.
©National Portrait Gallery, London.

for every month of the fifty years between 1845 and 1895. Like the album, these boxes were interactive: we revelled in the joy of taking out an individual palm-sized book and slipping, say, November 1856 back where it belonged, between October and December. We held in our hands order, precision and a compelling mix of transparency and secrecy. We thought we had a plot in the unambiguous progression of time and character in the meticulous and mostly legible handwriting that seemed at first to fill almost every page. Together, the fifty boxes and the six hundred individual booklets looked as though they might make, add up to, a life.

As we came in for a closer look, paced by the rhythm of the archive (we were only allowed to have two boxes and thus two years in our hands at a time), we met initially with disappointment. For the first few years of the diaries,[1] there were many blank days; although the later diaries were conscientiously kept up, they were strangely off-putting: a typical entry would start with notations about the weather, then list a few (often illegible) names of friends

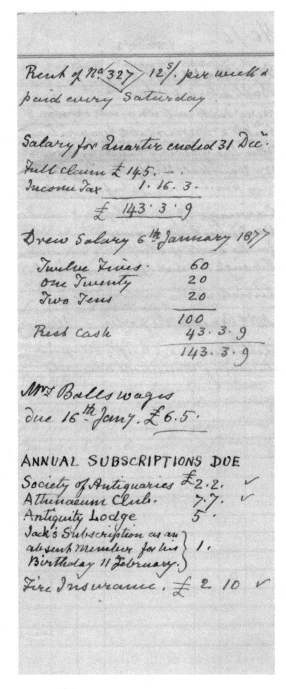

Fig. 2.3 Sample page from GS diary from January 1877.
©National Portrait Gallery, London.

met for dinner and end with a meticulous accounting of all the shillings Scharf spent on claret, gloves, notepaper, or railway fares. There were exceptions to the almost uniform tediousness of the entries: an account of the dream of being beheaded that we have discussed in detail in the previous chapter, a series of very moving entries on the deaths of his mother and his friend Lord Stanhope and those comparatively detailed year-end summaries from the late 1850s through to the 1870s that offered us a skeleton on which to hang narrative. Although Helena, in particular, having read honeymoon diaries for her *Victorian Honeymoons* project, was used to the collapse of the genre's archival promise – a process we call archival deflation – we had continually to recalibrate our expectations with the emergence from the stacks of a new year's worth of boxed books and to renegotiate our relationship with the style, persona and temporalities of the diaries. Although quitting the project was always theoretically possible, our framing of this option ('abandoning George') tells you something – perhaps all you need to know – about our investments in sticking to it. Part of what kept us going (and we are dutifully ashamed at the banality of this) was our lurking conviction that everyone, no matter how unremarkable, has a story you can find if you just pay close enough attention. Even more banally, we suspected that it might be a love story.

Looking for love in all the wrong places

To turn into a love story a set of diaries written in midlife by a biographical subject who was given to accounting rather than narrative, who never married and who never once mentions sex or romance except – briefly and elliptically – as the somewhat baffling concern of other people, might seem to require a great deal of work. It is, however, work that our culture has already done for us through the ubiquitous and hegemonic marriage plot. Marriage is not only the name and end point of a plot in the literary sense, but it is also a cultural imperative shaping the way we make sense of a life. It names certain kinds of novels, but it is at work in almost all of them. It can be seen in the pressure on individuals to marry, in the equation of marriage and adulthood and in the way in recent history gay rights – and gay existence – has become legible in mainstream culture only with the emergence of the issue of gay marriage.[2]

Our sense of the power of the marriage plot to override differences of gender, sexual orientation and attitudes towards sex prompted us to retain for a long while the term 'marriage plot' as a working title for this chapter and as the name for the constellation of archival, personal, literary and, perhaps, just plain voyeuristic desires that led us to try to find a sexual identity – and partners – for George. As it became clear to us that he was not interested in either women or marriage, we were faced with a series of choices. We could keep 'marriage plot' as a sign of its cultural power but, thus, risk minimising the cultural, legal and narrative differences between the expression of heterosexual and homosexual desire in the Victorian period and in our own time. We could use the presumably more capacious 'romance plot', in which the differences would still be unmarked, but which, for better and for worse, would not posit heterosexuality as the privileged possibility for narrative. We could call George's plot a 'queer plot', thus signalling its defamiliarising of both objects of desire and the epistemologies that make those objects visible, but we would then emplot queerness in a way that undermines the term's radical possibilities.[3] We could break with historicism and chronology and call the plot of this chapter – the plot of George's desires and our desires for what we imagined his to be – the 'gay love plot'. It was difficult to discard the term 'marriage plot' because it is so difficult to discard what it describes, but we finally decided to use 'romance plot' for our own early and uninformed investments in George's love life, and reserve 'marriage plot' for those moments when the plotting involves compulsory heterosexuality.

We found it all too easy to turn George into the hero of a romance plot. The first unconscious step in that project was our eagerness to identify candidates for George's sexual interest, a task made both tempting and daunting in a diary that included so many names without descriptions. It is part of what we think of as George's snobbishness to name-drop, that is, literally to drop a name onto the page without context. When he is talking about titled acquaintances, the effect suggests name-dropping in the metaphorical sense: he writes as if he had always known the aristocrats whose names stud his pages.

In a way, the process of identifying names in the diary became a process of elimination from the master narrative of marriage and romance. 'Miss Bayley', a name that came up frequently in connection with visits to Wimbledon in the 1860s, turned out to be too elderly to be (in our incorporated Victorian idiom) 'suitable'. A 'Mrs Faber' (why not an eligible widow?) turned out, sadly, to be the mother of one of Scharf's hostesses and, thus, to have other reasons for her frequent appearances as a companion at dinner and on walks in the country. The decorated place card of a 'Miss A. Birdwhistle' (invited, perhaps, as his particular partner at table?) made its way into Scharf's album in place of his own card as the souvenir of one dinner party, but he made no mention of her in the diary for the day of the dinner party, and we never ran across her name again. The intriguingly named 'underbutler' at Knole, who came to George for advice during a dispute between the servants and Lord Sackville and whom George tipped generously, was a promising starter. Alas, once the crisis at Knole was over, he was never mentioned again.

As we identified and then discarded potential love interests, we became aware that, in senses both profound and shallow, we did not know what we were doing. What might it mean to determine a relationship was or was not sexual? Although biographers have had to cope with this issue for a long time, mostly but not exclusively in relation to the question of same-sex relationships (Was Henry James gay? Did Thomas Hardy ever consummate his marriage? How sexual were Boston marriages?), there is no evidentiary protocol, no manual called something useful like *How to Determine Whether Sex (or Some Approximation) Took Place between Two or More People When They Don't Explicitly Say So*. If that helpful book remains unwritten, some biographical subjects seem eager to help by acceding to the archival fantasy of the Secret Code for Sex. Victoria Sackville West, whose life touches our project through her residence at Knole after George's death, marked with an *X* in her diary each time she had intercourse with her husband in the early years of their marriage (Alsop, p. 104). Clara and Robert Schumann wrote what must rank as the all-time most tantalising genre of the marriage-plot archive, a joint 'Marriage Diary' in which a mysterious 'f-shaped mark' seems to stand for the occasions when they had sex with each other (see Lebrecht).

Another version of the fantasy of combined secrecy and legibility is the discovery of an actual separate, sexually candid document or set of documents in an otherwise recalcitrant archive. As we were writing this chapter, Wendy Moffat published *A Great Unrecorded History*, her wonderful *New Life of E. M. Forster* that focuses specifically on Forster's sexuality. Quite a bit of the new material for Moffat's book comes from two kinds of sources: Forster's private diary, locked during much of his life and restricted to readers until its 'opening' in 2008, and a series of scattered documents in various public and private archives. Moffat explains that some of these documents 'have been coaxed out into the world from remarkable hiding places – a vast oak cupboard in a London sitting-room, a shoebox humbly nestled among mouse turds in a New England barn' (Moffat, p. 20). The cupboard, the shoebox and the locked diary are standard containers in and of the powerful fantasy we are invoking. Without benefit of the secret mark or the no-longer-secret archive, most attempts to locate 'sex' or 'sexuality' (including Helena's attempt in *Victorian Honeymoons*) are improvisations; many (like ours here) are textual, even literary in methodology: an affair of that slippery process that goes under the triumphal name of 'close reading', or what undergraduates often call 'going too far'.[4]

Not surprisingly, in this as in other contexts, we found ourselves in a specifically literary mode. At first we were reading the diary as if it were a Trollope novel, where we might find significant glances, obsessive recollections, subtle but powerful moments of physical touch or other even more overtly erotic content. Frustrated in that attempt, we tried to reread the diary as if it were Kazuo Ishiguro's *The Remains of the Day*, where the gaps between the narrator-protagonist's remarks and his silences contain worlds of unspoken passion. Here we were looking for frequency of mention, textual disturbances such as blots or unusual underlinings and emotionally charged diction. This proved to be a more instructive rubric for at least partly comprehending Scharf's emotional life, as the diaries are much more like Ishiguro's novel than they are like any of Trollope's, in that the moments of affective event are seldom articulated and do not follow the telos of desire-complication-consummation for which we were looking.

These missed encounters with the romance plot tell us several things about the questions ingrained in us by our lifelong reading practices. First, of course, we are always asking, 'What is the protagonist's sexuality and how does it become emplotted?' Second, 'Who might qualify as a plausible object of desire for this protagonist?' We found that we had a somewhat narrow and embarrassingly intuitive sense of who might be eligible. What after all, does the idea that Miss Bayley was 'too elderly' mean? When we eventually tracked down the perhaps sixty-year-old Sarah Bayley, we found that Elizabeth Barrett Browning was convinced that she was having some sort of sexual relationship with a John Kenyon, who, incidentally, left money to

Miss Bayley, to the Barrett Brownings and to George Scharf in his will.[5] Another question we are always asking as readers of Victorian novels is, 'How can we place the protagonist on the spectrum of sexualities?' We concluded that sexuality for us was predictably and problematically entangled in ideas of identity and identification: not only of George's possible love objects, but of George Scharf as subject, an issue we address at the end of this chapter.

A world of men

Having discarded Miss Bayley, the underbutler and others as possible love objects, we turned our gaze (and our desire for plot and character) to other persons more fully present, if still sketchily described in George's diaries. Together, these people – names at first and, then, with more research, in some cases more fully fleshed out individuals – comprised a shifting group of male friends, many of whom were significantly younger than George, who showed up regularly in the diaries as guests at Scharf's intimate dinners at home, and who sometimes spent the night in one or other of his London lodgings over the span of twenty years. These men can be distinguished from other kinds of 'friends' – Scharf uses the same word in an older sense to describe patrons and connections, as we will see in Chapter 4 – by their age and their status (none of them, for example, owned country homes). Perhaps most importantly, however, their relationships seem to unfold in and centre on London and on George's homes. Scharf himself, in a year-end summary to the 1862 diary (the earliest to have full entries) produces a taxonomy of almost exclusively male friendship:

> It is very gratifying to find all my views well understood & my pursuits so thoroughly supported by Ld. Stanhope, the Duke of Marlborough and Lord Derby. Charles Lewes[6] is chief among my younger friends, Mr Crabb Robinson & Miss Bayley are my best and steadiest old friends. Wigram and Lawrence are my firmest of my own standing. Pattisson is younger in years but my equal in cordial spirits. (D 31 December 1862; underline in original)

This entry, for all its distinctions, moves quite efficiently from titled supporters to the youngest and (at the time) least distinguished of his friends. Slippage occurs, as it does with many of us, between age and longevity of friendship in the phrase 'my best and oldest friends', two temporalities that compete in the Scharf diaries.

Centred in the entry are those 'firmest' friends of Scharf's 'own standing', a standing that is going to be subject to change in year-end summaries of professional triumphs to follow. By the 1860s and 1870s a group of male friends solidifies in the diary. Some names fall away, while others are exchanged for more intimate forms of address (Pattisson becomes 'Jack', 'Mr Cr. Robinson' becomes 'Robinson' or 'Crabb', etc.).

Over the course of the diaries, we noted that the recurring names of certain male friends include Sir Augustus Wollaston Franks, an independently wealthy antiquary six years younger than George, whom Scharf knew through his lifelong work at the British Museum; Sir Richard 'Dick' Worsley, sixteen years George's junior and a cousin of Samuel Butler, the novelist; William Frederick 'Beau' Beauford, who was twenty-two years younger than Scharf and whose son, Frank Somerville Beauford, was eventually to marry a baronet's daughter;[7] and Henry Crabb Robinson, born in 1775, much older even than George and like him a perpetual bachelor. Robinson is probably George's only intimate friend with a name that would be recognisable today – through his 1869 *Diaries, Reminiscences, and Correspondence*, where he chronicles his friendships with the great English Romantic poets. And there is Jacob Luard Pattisson, or Jack (about whom much more to follow). All of these friends, with the exceptions of Pattisson and Robinson, were university men, and Franks and Worsley, at least, came from a much higher social echelon than did the Scharfs; though there is less readily available biographical information about Beauford, his son's marriage suggests he, too, was of a higher class than George. These are the people Scharf envisioned as his peers, and his sense of their equal status must have hinged on their shared knowledge of and enthusiasm for antiquities, architecture and art. That an autodidact like George Scharf could function as an intellectual equal with men from much more privileged backgrounds is one of the many signs of his exceptional abilities we cannot ignore. A sketch George made that has been preserved in several versions in the National Portrait Gallery and catalogued as 'Sir George Scharf and friends' captures Scharf with Franks, Worsley and Beauford (Fig. 2.4). Each looking in a different direction, with only George's avatar glancing at the viewer, the men seem caught up in their respective worlds of reading or smoking, yet the balance of figures on the sketch's horizontal plane and vertical alignment confirms them as a group, gesturing to a masculine world of activity both individual and aggregate.

Fig. 2.4 'Sir George Scharf and Friends'
(1873 sketch by GS of William Frederick Beauford,
Sir Augustus Wollaston Franks, Richard Worsley and himself).
©National Portrait Gallery, London.

In our tracing of these friendships, and in trying to assess their meaning to George, we were faced with a characteristic obstacle. These men are never, as it were, introduced into the diaries: they appear without context or identifiers, even at first mention.[8] And, with a few minor and one major exception we will discuss later, they are never represented in emotional terms. Instead, these men almost always appear according to what we came to understand as the generic conventions of George's diaries: as names on seating charts of dinner parties, as items listed in anniversary entries marking the passage of time and as recipients of gifts or as lenders or debtors in the accounts following almost every entry. To learn more about their relationships with George, we found that we had to read *with* the grain of the diaries and against the teleology of Victorian fictional plots: in other words, we had to follow food, recursive time and (especially) money.

George's relationships to his male friends – like those with his titled connections and his family[9] – were obviously mediated by food. He hosted many dinner parties, whether formal or casual, sometimes spending more than he could comfortably afford on wines, oysters and caviar to entertain these men. Those among them who consistently loaned George money when his income fell short of his manner of living might have noticed a discrepancy between his style of entertaining and his inability to live from paycheck to paycheck, but if they criticised his modest extravagances, there is no record of it in the diaries. During the prime of his social life, George entertained single men and grieved when their marriages impaired their availability.[10]

Entries noting that one or more of the friends 'dined' at Scharf's lodgings are often followed by a menu for the night. This might be true even if only one friend was present as on 4 October 1870:

Beauford dined & spent the evening with me
Giblet soup
Boiled cod & oysters
Shoulder of mutton
Salimi [sic] of partridges
Patte [sic] foie gras
Anchovy toast
Pears, apple fritters
Sherry & claret

An entry describing a larger dinner on 15 September 1877 also includes a chart like the one for the 'nightmare dinner'; Scharf's own seat at the head of the table is identified by the characteristically rounded 'GS', with which he also signed his sketches. The entry suggests the centrality of George's home to the comings and goings of a group of men: 'Home dinner. Davis arrived at 10:00. Lively party. Soup, salmon, fillet of veal, Gosling, plum & apple tart. Cheeses. Sherry claret & champagne. Dick [Worsley] slept in my study & Michaels returned with Franks to the British Museum'. Entries like this one are common throughout the 1870s: male friends are listed and identified by the time and place of their arrival and departure, and meals are lovingly detailed. We use the word 'lovingly' here in part as a synonym for 'attentively', but also as a marker of an archival problem: so much about food, so little about the friends who ate it. So little about what friendship – individual or group – might have meant. It would be easy to have recourse here to a discourse of sublimation. Scharf talks about food because for some reason he can't or won't talk about something 'deeper'. Even without making specific arguments about the relation of food and love or food and sex, we can posit food as a substitute or a distraction.

While this is a tempting idea (and a novelistic if not a novel one), it does not completely account for what food and people have in common in Scharf's diaries in particular: the names of each are almost always items on a list. His diary entries can, in fact, be read as almost endless series of lists: food, friends, expenditures and portraits. (The last reminds us of the nature of much of his professional work, producing catalogues of portrait collections or items of ancient art.) What, if anything, can we make of a mind for which the list is the central idiom? Is this a scientific mind, where multiple items are divided into categories? Is this a realist mind, in which detail and repetition are crucial to representation? Is this somehow a Victorian mind? Or is the mind that makes lists refusing to linger on the single object, hiding it in plain sight, like Poe's purloined letter or an individual piece of bric-à-brac in a Victorian parlour? And what does it mean anyway to look to a diary, the way we are trying to do, as an index of a mind?

If male friendships in the diary are linked intimately to the discourse of food, they are also crucial in the temporality of the diaries – in how George registers the passage of time. Although we would classify everything he writes in them as falling under discourse time, Scharf's diaries work with and unfold within multiple and competing temporalities. The most obvious in these, as in any set of diaries, is the quotidian, accretive rhythm of the daily entry that moves the diaries forward from January to December of a given year. While this forward movement has much in common with the structure of a Victorian plot, George's diaries depend as much on repetition as they do on an idea of progress. Progress is enshrined retrospectively in the diaries in their almost ubiquitous year-end summaries written on the last day of the old year or sometimes the first of the new. Scharf's practice of ending a year by reviewing its personal and professional landmarks – in fact, by listing them – allowed him to mark his progress from year to year, to write, every winter for twenty years, another instalment in a progressivist serial.[11] A typical case is the year-end summary for 1859, written from the home of the Duke and Duchess of Marlborough on the first day of 1860:

To Woodstock Church with the Duke and Duchess of Marlborough & family. A new rector preached his first sermon and a very good one on the fishing nets of the church. In the afternoon Mr Steel preached in the Chapel upon the passage of life & life is a repeated tale. Sensible and very clearly delivered. The occupation & locality which ring the new year upon me were perhaps to indicate a pleasing event both in the past year & my future life. My position in the Portrait Gallery is excellent & the confidence of the Trustees unreserved. Lord & Lady Stanhope several times invited me to Chevening & especially on the occasion of Ld. Mahon's coming of age [t]heir friendship was strikingly shewn. Lord Lansdowne invited me to dinner at his house in town & to Bowood during the past week. My Mother & Aunt, different from last Christmas & my birthday, at same time have kept very well and happy. Their health seems excellent. Lord Overstone has continued his proofs of friendship. So likewise Field Enfield, Miss Bayley. Lawrence & Crabb Robinson. My Presentation at Court was also an Event.

This entry, bookended by references to the aristocracy, moves characteristically through the ranks of friends; the transition from Lord Overstone to Field Enfield and the ever-singular Miss Bayley suggests what we know to be true, that Miss Bayley at least proved her friendship in part by gifts and loans. The names of those friends of Scharf's 'standing', Lawrence and Crabb Robinson, are merely items in a list and in a stand-alone sentence. Scharf's presentation at court, a capitalised 'Event',[12] overshadows, in this case, the continuous presence of Scharf's old (young) friends. Even the year-end summaries, then, are caught between temporalities of stability and progress; the lists of friends change only slightly from year to year, although, at the end of the decade we find that there has, in fact, been significant change. Life is, indeed, a 'repeated tale'.

The language of the year-end summaries is often more emotional than that of the daily entries. It is here, for example, that we were able to read about George's early financial embarrassments and his pride in his new career landmarks. His year-end summaries also traditionally express gratitude to old friends and mention new ones. On 30 December 1863, Scharf writes:

In reviewing the year I remember to have lost a friend in Lord Lansdowne. I have great reason to be thankful for the continued good health of my Mother & Aunt & for the favour and friendly interest of Lord & Lady Stanhope & the Duke & Duchess of Marlborough. Introductions to and invitations from the Archbp. of Canterbury [. . .] Keeping up with old friends like Mrs Kenyon [?] & John Murray has been pleasant. Pattisson I feel still more truly attached to and Franks has become intimate with me & we find points of common interest especially my chronology of art now in hand. Young Charles Cordell in whom I felt much deep interest seems likely to be a passing acquaintance & poor Lockyer's loss of his wife and subsequent insanity have clouded the latter part of the year.[13]

Most of George's year-end summaries begin, as does this one, with titled 'friends' in the Victorian sense of connections and end with 'friends' in that more modern, more intimate sense. The mention, in the predictable place towards the end of this summary, of his younger friends is notable not so much in its intensity as in its imbrication in the idiom of progress that usually only marks his professional ascent. (Not surprising, given George's penchant for listing and chronicling, rather than analysing or synthesising, the work he mentions takes the form of a 'chronology' of art.)[14]

The year-end summaries are only one way in which male friendship is inserted into the temporalities of the diary; as we have said, Scharf was a great recorder of anniversaries of all sorts: birthdays, certainly, but also anniversaries of the deaths of his mother, father and aunt Mary; of the arrival of his father in England (which was to share a date with his mother's funeral); and of events in his own life like the early trip to Xanthus with Sir Charles Fellows or his several bouts of scarlet fever. During the 1860s and 1870s Scharf noted birthdays of his close male friends, often with a comment about the disparity between their ages and his own. On his own fiftieth birthday, for example, he notes, without context, that 'Carpenter is my senior by 4 months' (D 16 December 1870). On 3 March 1870, he writes in his diary that it is 'Rae's birthday. Born 1835, aged 35', adding that Rae is '15 years my junior'. Thus the calculus of male friendship is inserted into the larger projects of accounting and remembering.

Keeping track of time is, of course, a form of accounting that in Scharf's diaries runs alongside the keeping of accounts in the financial sense. The economic picture, which we discuss in more detail in the next chapter, is a complex one, since Scharf is both a borrower and a lender, as well as a giver and a recipient of gifts of money, food and household objects. His December summary, 1856, finds him in debt, a condition that friends of all kinds help to resolve over the course of the twelve months:

> Few years have contained so many varieties for me as 1856, anxieties support & losses characterise it. My excellent friends C. H. [Tewman?] and J. Kenyon are gone. My lectures at home [London] brought many friends round me. Mrs Fraser & daughter. Oxford lectures & at Leeds also in Passion week. Charles Kean's seeking my aid for the Winter's Tale.

Roger's sale, sketching his house. My financial embarrassments, kind help from Franks and Enfield. Loans & presents from friends. Leaving Torrington Square. Expenses of moving & repairs. Honourable expedition to Edinburgh at expense of the Archbishop [. . .] My illness. Great incidental expenses.

Manchester exhibition. Kind friends. New life, numerous introductions & good prospects for future. Mother and aunt well as ever, especially the latter thank God.

Note from Henry of apology, reconciliation, etc. I sent him a present of books and prints. Mr Kenyon's legacy of 500£ and other helps from him, from Miss Bayley, Crabb Robinson, Enfield & Lord Overstone have combined to maintain my position & feel on a surer basis. (D 31 December)

This is the only one among his year-end summaries to include such detailed references to money. Even so, Scharf's 'embarrassments' are inserted into a progressivist and ameliorative narrative that depends on the 'kind help' of many people. The year's diary records hard work, but the lecturing, sketching and designing of costumes and sets that are part of a nascent professional plot are ultimately insufficient: he must rely on gifts from his friends – living and dead – even to 'maintain' his 'position'. While in Chapter 3 we consider the role of George Scharf Sr in this debt and gift economy, we would like to stress here how George Jr must turn from family to friends: family members in this economy take from George, and friends give to him. Although on our first reading of this summary we did not know whether George paid for the gift of books and prints he sent to his brother, Henry (as it turns out, he did not), clearly it is the gifts from friends that allow George to become a giver in turn.

George was not to return to the financial abjection of 1856, in part because in 1857 he began to receive a regular quarterly salary as director of the National Portrait Gallery. Far into the 1870s, however, long after he was established as a national expert on portraiture, long after he began to attend royal levees and to appear in the national press as a guest of the titled, he continued to accrue debt and to accept small loans and gifts – usually twenty to twenty-five pounds – from his male friends, particularly the apparently well-heeled Franks and Worsley. There is something charmingly candid about his entry for 29 July 1876: 'Dick [Worsley] sent a cheque for £25 as a Present. I know of no one else like him except for Franks.' The entry suggests – even and perhaps especially, given the idiom of appreciation – that male friends are interchangeable at least to the extent that they occupy similar positions in a network of debt and accounting.

But by the 1870s Scharf found himself in the position to give to friends as well as to receive from them. Early in 1870 he notes, 'Beauford dined with me. Gave him a Salviati opal glass with serpent round the stem' (D 27 January 1870). A few days later Scharf describes a similar social event: 'Charlie Stuart & Jack had supper with me. Gave Charlie a pair of Woodstock gloves, his size being 7¼' (D 10 February 1870). The next day was 'Jack's 29ᵗʰ birthday', and Scharf gave him 'four pairs of white kid gloves, and 1 pair of Woodstocks' (D 11 February 1870).

It is at this point in our archival accounting that we began to see something of a surplus, a subtle pattern that we thought we might be overreading. While George clearly gave presents to many of his younger male friends, those to Jack Pattisson were embedded in a slightly different discourse. Although Charlie Stuart got one pair of Woodstock gloves (very practical, because they were wash-and-wear), Jack got four pairs of more luxurious kid gloves *plus* a pair of Woodstocks.[15] George also apparently knew Jack's glove size, since he did not write it down. In these months full of activity within this gift network, Jack gave George 'an oak cigar box' as a 'present for my new residence' (18 January 1870). Scharf unaccountably entered the box among items on his list of expenses for the day – in our reading, a striking category error.

How does one account for friendship, for love or, for that matter, for archival hunches? It was the reading of lists of gifts and expenses that initially made Helena feel that Jack had a special place in the diaries and in George's life. For better or for worse, accurate or not, our immersion in accounting had allowed us to see matters that were of interest to if generically at odds with the romance plot. It allowed us to see the importance and the singularity of Jack (Fig. 2.5).

We don't know Jack about George

The last sentence of the previous section sets a particular narrative in motion: as we mentioned earlier, we are calling it, with ruthless anachronism, the 'gay love plot'. It is also, however, a narrative of archival discovery anchored by the 'we' who had a hunch about Jack at two distinct moments in our research project. The truth

Fig. 2.5 Jack Pattisson c. 1862. ©National Portrait Gallery, London.

about the latter story, the meta-archival one, is that it is really two stories – Robyn's and Helena's. Each of us came to a sense of Jack's importance at different times in our reading, even though we discussed the 'evidence' for the gay love plot on many occasions. The story you have just read is Helena's. It is a story of accounting, and accounting for, of adding up numbers even if they do not – as they never did with George – quite add up. Robyn's story of noticing Jack starts in a different place and a different time, in September 2009 (archival time) and 31 December 1867 (story time).

Robyn's ah-ha! moment came not from the lists of expenses and gifts but from the diaries' temporal architecture. In a year-end summary for 1867, she read, 'By Pattisson being so constantly at our house of an evening I have found a pleasure in home that I rarely felt before' (D 31 December 1867). Ordinarily the strongest terms in which Scharf writes of his male friends are 'interest' (as in the 'deep interest' he felt for Charles Cordell) or 'attachment'. 'Pleasure' is beyond the bounds of his normal diction; 'pleasure

Fig. 2.6 Jack Pattisson at work in GS's home, August 1869.
©Trustees of the British Museum.

in home' makes Jack a member of the family or, more accurately, given the double edge of the familial idiom, a member of the household (Fig. 2.6). George also characteristically uses the temporal to index the emotional: 'constantly' means 'very frequently' and also 'faithfully'.

And Jack was faithful. We first noticed the ubiquity of 'faithful Jack' during and after the final illness of George's mother, an event we had originally identified as one of the few emotionally charged moments of personal revelation, the potential site of something worth telling, as we will do in Chapter 3. For now we simply remark that on 2 January 1869, the day before his mother died, Scharf noted he had lunched with her for the '*last time*' (emphasis in the original); and then, 'Afterwards when Jack & I came up before 5 o'clock, Mrs Parlett [Mrs Scharf's attendant] said she was much changed & we had best not go into the room.' Jack was again – or still – in the house the next day, when George came back downstairs after his last glimpse of his dying mother, into 'my library where Jack was sitting'. When Mrs Parlett came into the library at two o'clock that afternoon to announce his mother's death, Scharf wrote, 'We were much shocked & at once went up into the room and found her very blue in the position as [sic] I had left her' (D 3 January 1869). Two days later, George reports that 'Lewsey's men came at breakfast time & fastened the coffin lid down. Neither Jack nor myself desired to she see her when moved from the place or position in which she had expired' (D 5 January 1869). In such intimate scenes, the force of the 'we' in a phrase like 'we were much shocked' or 'neither Jack nor myself desired' is powerful. Knowing as we did that George had only one brother whose name was Henry, and not yet having mastered the long list of George's male friends, we could not on a first reading guess what this 'Jack's' role in the Scharfs' family life might be. Henry was nowhere to be seen at Mrs Scharf's funeral on 6 January 1869, where, as George writes, he

> and faithful Jack followed the remains of my dearest Mother to the grave. After the ceremony was over we walked homewards, Jack to the Admiralty and I to South Kensington Museum. Saw the armour & miniatures there on loan from the Meyrick collection. Came back through the parks & saw the Albert Memorial in progress and the new Hall of Science rising to the South of it. Jack rejoined me at home before lunch.

As was not at all uncommon according to the diaries leading up to those sad days, 'Jack spent the evening with me' (D 6 January 1869). For the next two weeks Jack disappears from the diary, returning eventually on 16 January from an unexplained visit 'to Ashcott and Berkeley Castle'. The first time we encountered these diary passages we lost track of Jack in those days after Mrs Scharf's funeral, turning away from him with the impression that he was some sort of family retainer, as the term 'faithful' implies.

We did not entirely forget about Jack, however. The name 'Jack Pattisson' came up often enough in our exploratory readings of Scharf's diaries to have caught Robyn's attention once again while she was transcribing another, earlier, of Scharf's year-end summaries. We had been looking for – and had found – extended lists of the high-born friends and acquaintances who had shown favour to Scharf over the preceding year, like the entry we have already mentioned from December 1862. Somehow Pattisson makes his way into the long first paragraph of the summary, wedged between the prince consort and Lord and Lady Stanhope in a position that would usually be reserved, according to the protocols of these year-end summaries, for aristocrats: 'Pattisson my young friend continues steadily attached to me and is in reality a pleasant ally in point of attention to my Mother & Aunt. He helped me very efficiently in taking the Elderlies to the International Exhibitions.' At the end of that same year-end summary, in a passage we quoted above, we found a rare allusion to George's writing process, a moment of self-consciousness bringing story time together with discourse time:

> It is very gratifying to find all my views well understood & my pursuits so thoroughly supported by Ld. Stanhope, the Duke of Marlborough and Lord Derby. Charles Lewes is chief among my younger friends, Mr Crabb Robinson & Miss Bayley are my best and steadiest old friends. Wigram and Lawrence are my firmest of my own standing. Pattisson [emphasis in the original] is younger in years but my equal in cordial spirits. The year is out I can only record thankfully for the past. As I wrote Pattisson the clock struck twelve & I therefore close 1862. May 1863 prove a worthy successor and may God direct my ways to do always that which is righteous in His sight. Amen. (31 December 1862)

Now, this was unusual. 'As I wrote Pattisson the clock struck twelve.' There is something romantic, maybe even a little obsessive, about George's noting the coincidence of the act of writing that name and the change to the new year. The underscore, infrequent in Scharf's orthography, marked the name 'Pattisson' as somehow special. Robyn would return to this moment, and to this rare scene of writing, to contextualise her own sense of the importance of Jack in George's life.

Coming to the reluctant realisation that we were not likely to find an explicit record of a love affair anywhere in Scharf's diaries, we resolved to identify Jack, a process that would admittedly have been easier if we had read more carefully the three-page, typed handlist for the George Scharf papers at the National Portrait Gallery, which contained a somewhat cryptic entry for a correspondence between a Jacob Luard Pattisson and George, an oversight that is doubtless our worst archival blunder. In seeking Jack outside the handlist, however, we were playing to Google's strength: family-originated genealogy. Using Jack's birthday (a gift from the Scharfian gift economy), we found one Jacob Luard Pattisson, born in 1841, whose life story is outlined on a website tracing the 'Zimapanners', all the people who had owned, lived in or had a financial interest in a certain house in Cornwall now called Zimapan.[16] 'Jacob' turns out to be our Jack, George's Jack. We found on that website some details that took us aback. Most disappointing, given our quest for

George's gay love story, was the discovery that, 'at the age of 31, Jacob L. Pattisson married an MP's daughter, Ellen Jane Miller, 26, on 1 October 1872 at Trinity Church, St Marylebone, London' (see Peter King Smith, 'Secretary to Lord of the Admiralty'). This meant that less than four years after the intimacy we had observed between George and Jack at Mrs Scharf's deathbed, Jack was already settled into what looked like the ending of a marriage plot of his own.

More encouraging was the tantalising detail that 'in 1881, Pattisson was lodging at 1 Warwick Street, Westminster, London, in the household of Henry M. Williams, a telegraph clerk. There was no sign of his wife Ellen'.[17] If Jack had mysteriously acquired a wife, he appeared just as mysteriously to have lost her and to have substituted a man for her as a living companion. However – equally mysteriously – the wife shows up again later in the family historian's account: 'By 1891, Jacob Luard Pattisson, aged 50, had moved to 28 Devonshire Place, Eastbourne, East Sussex, where he lived in lodgings with his 45–year-old wife Ellen Jane, commuting by train from Eastbourne to his post at the Treasury in London' (see Peter King Smith, 'Secretary to Lord of the Admiralty').

So far in the process of accounting for Jack, we had felt a certain pride of ownership, as if George's (imagined) secret were ours as well. In a web search for images of George's rooms at the NPG, however, we came across evidence of others who had noted Jack's presence in George's life, albeit only to dismiss the possibility of the story we were trying to construct. A web search turned up a beautifully illustrated article of uncertain provenance, written by Catherine Karusseit and containing reproductions of Scharf's highly detailed sketches of his living space at Great George Street. The accompanying essay examines Scharf's sketches of his domestic space in the context of the gendered decorating of Victorian homes. Karusseit comments on the sketch of Jack Pattisson working at a table in Scharf's library, raising the possibility that Scharf's and Pattisson's relationship might have been a 'homosexual' one, given Scharf's description of Jack as his 'most preferred friend' (see Karusseit). Citing John Tosh's assertion that Victorian bachelors often formed intimate friendships having at least some overt signs of homosexual feeling, she minimises the possibility of a love affair between George and Jack by pointing out that the 'use of elaborate language in letters between friends, regardless of their sexuality, was characteristic of the period' (Karusseit. Compare Tosh, p. 110). Of course that's true. If Pattisson shows up as 'dear Jack', 'dear old

Jack' and even 'dearest Jack' in George's diary during the 1870s, that does not indicate anything beyond friendship. But, on the other hand, it might. We had, of course, heard the 'inflated language' defence of heterosexuality before. By that token, until J. A. Symonds became a case study in Krafft Ebing's 1866 *Psychopathia Sexualis*, no man – and certainly no woman – had ever been romantically or sexually involved with anyone of the same gender. We held out to each other the possibility that the diaries for the years before Jack's marriage would tell us something more about the nature of George and Jack's relationship.

Our unflagging hope of finding a gay love plot in the diaries after all sent Robyn back into the archives for a few days in the spring of 2011 with a specific mission – to reexamine at every mention of Jack from his first in the diary to the fateful date of his marriage. As she read and transcribed every 'Jack sighting' within that time span, Robyn experienced all the affects associated with Victorian novel reading – the accelerated pulse that comes with suspense, the flush of pleasure brought by desires fulfilled and the stinging tears of shocked disappointment – except for closure. Reading the diaries this time 'for the plot', as Peter Brooks might say, she constructed a story that George's diaries do not tell, because the diaries narrate nothing: they only list events without much sense of causality or of any relation at all between isolated events beyond the temporal patterns we have already mentioned. Faced in archival time with not much more than a list of unconnected occurrences, Robyn put together a story for George that also became the story of her own responses to George's text. This is that story.

Although the date of Jack's employment at the National Portrait Gallery is not mentioned in the Zimapan House history, we gathered from Scharf's diaries that at some point in the early 1860s Jack became George's unpaid assistant at the NPG while simultaneously working as a clerk at the Admiralty. In 1862 Scharf was forty-two years old and Pattisson, twenty-one (Fig. 2.7). Though George was old enough to be Jack's father, he never refers to Jack's attachment to himself as 'filial'. George prefers the language of fraternity, or 'brotherliness', in his descriptions of their relationship, reserving 'filial' for Jack's relation to George's mother, though Jack's own mother was alive and well at the time. When George was present, Jack would play card games and word scrambles with Mrs Scharf, to her continual delight. During George's frequent extended absences at the great country homes, Jack would look in on Mrs Scharf every

Fig. 2.7 GS in 1861. ©National Portrait Gallery, London.

evening. Certainly Jack played the role of a younger brother in this, as he was to do during the final illness, death and funeral of Mrs Scharf in 1869.

Mrs Pattisson and Mrs Scharf were eventually to visit each other, and the families established cordial relations. Jack came from more prosperous stock than George did, having grown up, the second of sixteen children, in Witham House, a grand eighteenth-century townhouse on Newland Street in Witham, Essex.[18] The family included ten sons, several of whom were eventually to become friends of George's. Jack's father, Jacob Howell Pattisson, was an attorney who had inherited his own father's fortune when his older brother died in a boating accident, and he had risen to gentry status by marrying Jack's mother, Charlotte Luard. If Jack's family was once richer than George's, however, they were not more respectable. Before Jack reached his majority, his father – who had amassed a crippling £60,000 debt – disappeared for two months, leaving Jack's mother to relocate with all their children and a small independent income to Tonbridge in Kent.[19] Bankrupted, Pattisson the elder returned to his family but was unable to attain the professional respectability he had once enjoyed. If the family was no longer wealthy, they were still middle-class. According to *Who's Who, 1907,* Jack did not go to university but was educated at Felstead School.[20] We think Jack's attendance at what *Wikipedia* describes as having been by 1851 'a regular public school of the modern English type' might tell us something about the character of his early sexual experiences, though the inference is based only on British boarding schools' reputation for initiating boys into same-sex erotic practices.[21] Gay sex is among the many things Jack had the opportunity to learn at school, unlike George, the self-educated man who never moved away from home.

George's home was to become the space where he and Jack, after George had taken him on as a volunteer assistant, would become intimate friends. In his summary for 1864 George noted, 'The fact of Pattisson coming here almost every evening to do such work as I could give him under the head of "clerical assistance" has done me a great deal of good & kept me very steadily at home' (D 31 December 1864). The quotation marks around 'clerical assistance' call into question the absolute necessity of Jack's nightly presence at Great George Street, and while the drawing George made of Jack working at George's library table suggests there was at least some such work to do, the responsibilities Jack undertook included such non-professional jobs as being entrusted with money for buying cigars every three months or so.

Although Jack was not on salary while he was working for George or entertaining George's mother in the evenings, he was the beneficiary of George's largesse in other ways. The two men frequently attended the theatre or opera together, with George always paying for the tickets and the cab. George also paid for Jack's rail travel to visit his family members at Tonbridge or to meet one of his brothers' ships coming in at Portsmouth, gave him gifts of cash on his birthdays and tipped him on Valentine's Day in the same way he did his two house servants, but at double the rate. When George received a windfall, like the £150 cheque he got as a gift in 1869 from Lord Derby or the £500 legacy he inherited from Miss Bayley later that year, he would give Jack a small portion of it 'in friendly share', though he did not share these funds with anyone else. Their connection was, among other things, an economic one, with all the largesse going in one direction, making this friendship unique in George's circle.

Reading with the grain of accounting, Robyn found our first clue that George and Jack might have formed a household. Four months after George's mother's death we find this recorded expense: 'To Jack for cab for his things, £1 1d.' (D 7 April 1869). The removal in a cab of Jack's 'things' is the only direct reference to his relocation, but from that day in April until the middle of May, George's daily noting of who 'dined with me' in Great George Street changes to 'dined with us'. Even after Jack took a job in Ireland as the assistant to Lord Dufferin, he continued coming 'home' to George's lodgings. On 13 May 1869, George gave Jack ten pounds for his fare to Ireland, five pounds of which Jack repaid 'as soon as he came home again'. Despite Jack's new posting, George expressed confidence that their relationship would not suffer.

> Dear Jack starts this morning for Ireland to stay a month with Lord Dufferin on trial as his Private Secretary. In giving up his duties at this Gallery I shall feel his loss very severely. But we shall, I quite trust, be as fast friends as ever, & my consolation is the conviction that separation is not estrangement. I hope to see him very often indeed. (D 15 May 1869)

Although Jack was supposed to have stayed in Ireland a month, he returned after two weeks, 'much pleased with his visit and disposed to continue with Lord Dufferin' (D 3 June 1869), and George, true to form, planned a dinner party on 4 June, to welcome Jack 'home'. For his 'successful little dinner party of six', featuring 'turbot & pigeons', George's seating chart places Jack at the foot of the table across from George himself at the head. George gives him the place of honour while at the same time affirming Jack's special connection to his host, mimicking perhaps the position of husband and wife, master and mistress of a household. If we look at the record of the dinner in the visual idiom with which George was most comfortable, we see the two men brought together by the use of initials.

Over the course of that summer 'dear Jack' became George's 'dearest Jack'. When it was time for George to relocate, Jack went with him to look at lodgings for let in South Kensington, near the new location of the NPG. They were constantly together until 'Dearest Jack's' final departure for Ireland:

> Dearest Jack came late in the evening to a hurried supper before going home to pack & starting for Ireland the next morning. I was very sorry to lose him again after so constantly being together. He is more brotherly than ever. (D 11 August 1869)

Up to this point in the diaries no one else besides Miss Bayley, Scharf's mother and his old auntie earns the epithets of 'dear' or 'dearest'. The description 'more brotherly than ever' recalls George's insistence on picturing the much-younger Jack as belonging to his own generation and sounded to us, deep in the gay love plot, like protesting too much. Certainly George's actions during Jack's absence were as affectionately extravagant as the language he used in the diary. Having inherited a piano from Miss Bayley, George actually sent his own piano to Jack in Ireland as a gift. Reading this detail through the connotations attached to the piano Jane Fairfax in Jane Austen's *Emma* supposedly receives from Mr Dixon, Robyn thought it a not insignificant clue. The possibilities the piano represented for the romantic nature of George's attachment to Jack continued, in archival time, to shimmer.

The next two years followed the pattern of 1869, with Jack returning from Clandeboye in Ireland for brief visits ('Jack sleeps here for the present') and spending the summers in London socialising and sitting up late smoking and chatting with George (D 17 January 1871). Unlike other friends who are noted as spending the night from time to time, Jack 'has the housekeys as before' (D 5 March 1872). In April and May of 1872 Jack is once again (or, perhaps, still) living at George's place. We deduce this from such comments in the diary like 'found Jack at home when I got back soon after 10' (D 29 April 1872), 'Jack came later and slept here' (D 13 May 1872), 'Jack came in at ½ before 12' (D 14 May 1872) and the intriguingly faint pencilled phrase, standing uncharacteristically alone on an otherwise blank diary page, 'Home Jack' (D 7 May 1872). When Jack 'came in in the evening and enjoyed a cold steak supper', there is no indication of where he is coming from (D 11 May 1872). If George knew where Jack was spending his early evenings, he didn't tell us.

Robyn was nervous as she approached what she knew to be the important date somewhere in 1872 when George would find out about Jack's impending marriage. The dreaded moment arrived when she turned the page to 23 May. Interestingly this was not the moment of contemporaneous writing she had been looking for, because George was up to his temporal tricks again, resisting linear plots. In a retrospective entry, he writes, 'Jack told me afterwards that on this day, ~~evening~~ at Warwick Square he made his engagement.' It is the entry two days later, on 25 May, that reports the announcement in real time: George writes, 'Jack breakfasted with me & I continued my sketch of him. On returning from Kensington at 4 o'clock received a message from him that he was engaged to be married.' Caught between two temporalities of knowing, George inserts Jack's engagement into the genre of the anniversary, and Robyn was to read the words of the narrating George before she was able to get to what we thought of as the moment itself, when the experiencing George learned the truth. She was incensed. What kind of cad tells his best friend and domestic partner that he is engaged to be married by leaving him a note? She had to feel the outrage on George's behalf, because George makes no comment. Because he says so little about his own feelings on 25 May, we are inclined to read them into – or out of – his silences and erasures. The day after he received Jack's message, George wrote nothing in his diary except 'at Panshanger',[22] no details of expenses on the trip or notes about the work he was doing that day. In the retrospective entry – when did he write it? – the striking out of 'evening' is as unusual in Scharf's diary as the almost-blank page. We recalled that George struck out a word in his narration of the moment he learned of his mother's death, another moment of barely suppressed high emotion.

Even more unusual is the inkblot we discovered in the record of a still more disturbing development two days after George learned Jack was to be married. Among the accounting notes, Scharf writes, 'To dear old [old is blotted] Jack towards [the 't' is written over an 'f'] his Canadian outfit £5' (D 27 May 1872). Jack and his bride were to emigrate to Canada, and Jack was to make his first trip there in just ten days (Fig. 2.8). Robyn found this development distressing, particularly since George had not mentioned Jack's imminent departure on whatever day he had learned about it. 'Dear old Jack came in late' on 10 June, the night before he left for Canada. 'Our parting was comfortable,' George writes, 'as he promised to stay with me when he comes back in September.' George's 'dear Jack', his 'dearest Jack', had been transformed in the matter of a few days into 'dear old Jack', a locution with less erotic force and more of what feels to us like a somewhat forced brotherly affection.

Robyn read with an increased sense of urgency as Jack went to Canada by himself and then returned, as promised, for his wedding. It's 'dear old Jack' who comes back to George in the most intimate scene recorded in this period of the diaries: 'Dear old Jack came home early & woke me up at 7 in the morning. He knocked & rang at my door & I went out in my nightshirt & let him in' (D 18 September 1872). The detail of the nightshirt says so much, and yet so little. Not having seen his dear (old) Jack

Fig. 2.8 Jack Pattisson outfitted for Canada, 1872.
©National Portrait Gallery, London.

for four months, George in his impatience hurries from his bed to the apartment door to let him in. Incompletely covered by his nightshirt, George ... does what? Embraces Jack and kisses him passionately on the mouth? Shakes his hand with fraternal heartiness? Jack comes through the door and ... goes where? Into the dining-room or library to wait for George to get dressed and for the housekeeper, Mrs Lee, to come in and make his breakfast? Back up to George's room and George's bed? Once again, Robyn met a dead-end she could break through only with her own desire for some kind of imagined consummation.

'Don't be shocked!'

If Robyn's desires at this point were for fulfilment within the plot of George's life, Helena's investments, equally strong, were for archival consummation. Like many a researcher in the archive, she began to fantasise about finding a document: not just any document but the 'message' that George had received from Jack announcing his engagement. Helena had no faith that this document could be found. The term 'message', for one thing, suggested something especially ephemeral; perhaps George had quickly read two scrawled lines or even a telegram and had thrown it, crumpled, into the fire. Helena pictured the scene with some internal embarrassment about the series of archival clichés she found herself invoking. As an experienced researcher with two archival projects under her belt, she should have known there would be no smoking gun.

Which is why, when she idly googled 'Jack Pattisson' for perhaps the twentieth time in three years, she didn't feel any particular excitement when she noticed that George Scharf's papers from the NPG were now online. Which is why, when she saw the file of George's correspondence with Jack from 1872, she did not expect much. Which is why, when she clicked on a little 'thumbnail' sample of what was in the file (only a few of the letters had thumbnails), she did not immediately notice what she was seeing. The words with which the letter in the thumbnail began – 'Don't be shocked!' – could have been addressed directly to her (Fig. 2.9). Although the letterhead was from George's lodgings at 8 Ashley Place, the handwriting was not his. 'Don't be shocked,' she read again. 'I am engaged to be married!' It is not too much to say that at that moment, *for* a moment, Helena became George, the shock jumping from screen backwards in time to letter paper and to a body that loved food – even more than she did – and Jack even more, perhaps, than food. She was George, reading the note from Jack on his own letterhead. Perhaps George stopped after the sentence to put the paper down, to adjust his glasses, to wipe his eyes. Helena turned away from the screen, conscious that this was both the consummation of a moment of one kind of archival desire – to know, to see, to read – and the death of another, that is, to put it plainly, the desire for George to be happy in the plot Robyn and she had created for him. This is how Jack began the letter:

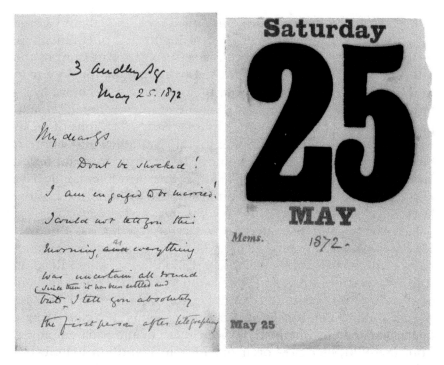

Fig. 2.9 'Don't be shocked!' Letter from Pattisson to GS, 25 May 1872.
©National Portrait Gallery, London.

I could not tell you this morning, as everything was uncertain all round
but since then it has been settled and I tell you absolutely the first person
after telegraphing to my mother who knows not a word either.
My young woman is one Nellie Miller daughter of my old Tooting friend
and now of Chislehurst. Her Father was the Colchester M.P. in Milbank
St and not the Candle Man [???]. He has been dead some time.
We have been fast friends for about 10 years and I believe both understood what it would end in as indeed both families <u>now</u> declare they did.
Unfortunately she is anything but pretty – but <u>of course!</u> very nice – very
petite, and fair – (Jack to George, 25 May 1872; JP 72)

The shock to Helena came not only from the news but from the
temporality in which it was inserted. Jack is mentioning Nellie's
name to George for the first time, and yet the mutual attraction and
its assumed result had been 'understood' for ten years. George, like
Gwendolyn Harleth at the end of *Daniel Deronda*, learns he is living
in another temporality, a plot other than the one in which the
romantic hero lives. Jack has been living in a conventional marriage

plot. In trying to minimise this epistemic shock, Jack aligns George with his own mother, who is also, according to Jack, out of the loop: in the instant when the telegram is sent to Mrs Pattisson, in the interval of the few hours that Jack's note lies waiting for George to find when he comes home at four o'clock, George becomes Jack's father, a role he was to inhabit when he eventually organised and paid for much of the wedding. The very first paragraphs of Jack's story are, of course, belied by temporal contradiction: George is 'absolutely the first person' to know, but already with important and numerous exceptions: Jack's mother and the Miller family have known the secret for ten years and obviously are informed of the latest development.

Jack cannot minimise the news, at least not in the first sentence. He can, however, minimise Nellie, who is 'anything but pretty', and, in an oddly specific moment of description, 'very petite'. Reading it for the second, third and fourth times, Helena could not help contrasting Nellie's size to George's, a contrast set up by Jack's use of past and present, background and foreground. If Nellie is small, Jack's world of confidants is extensive; it includes his employer, Lord Dufferin, now the governor of Canada, and Lord Dufferin's wife. Jack's letter continues:

> Lord and Lady D. have written to me most kindly – They were the only possible obstacle, but as they took it so well, everything else has gone straight – I propose to get leave to come back for her after Xmas – She has about £500 a year of her own & will have more – This of course enables the affair to proceed as otherwise I could not have kept a wife. (ibid.)

In invoking Lord Dufferin, Jack makes it clear that even his professional life is not in George's keeping. George knows, of course, that Jack will be moving to Canada and who his employer is to be, but this letter reframes 'Lord D' as an authority in multiple domains, the final arbiter in the marital as well as the professional realm.

If Jack's first paragraph suggests the epistemic vertigo of the multiplot novel as practised by George Eliot, Jack's marital accounting suggests something created by Jane Austen or Trollope or even – think Richard Carstone – Dickens. Like George's own accounting, and that of his family, it is used as much to elide as to confront economic reality: if Nellie has '£500 a year', can Jack really be said to be 'keeping' her? As the marriage grew closer, we found that the Millers seemed to be trying to prevent it; while we could not determine the source of their objection, it could well have been financial. Jack's numbers cannot help but make the story of the marriage a financial one, linking Nellie to Lord Dufferin in a plot of economic advancement.

Jack closes his letter with a request for a 'blessing' and a meeting between George and a now unnamed Nellie:

> I cannot come to Kensington to see you now, so I send this to wait your return, and I will come round on Monday before going to Franks. Keep it absolutely to yourself please at present. but [sic] send us your blessing, and spare me a minute on Tuesday to introduce her before she leaves London.
> Ever yours affectionately,
> J.L.P. (ibid.)

The difficult work of this difficult letter is to transform 'shock' into 'blessing' and to place George firmly in the paternal position. Jack, however, adds a postscript that suggests he is not easy with what he has said so far. In the margin of the letter, below his signature, and at an angle to the rest of the writing, Jack adds the following, unpunctuated: 'Your kind present this morning all but made me tell you but it was a promise on both sides to be silent till Lord D approved that I could not say [sic] what I was longing to' (ibid.). The present – a copy of a book on Freemasonry, one of those all-male enclaves George and Jack had for several years shared, carefully noted in the expense ledger of George's diary – returns the story to Ashley Place and to the gift economy that solidified George's relations with his younger male friends. The gift, a reminder of the exchanges upon which their relationship was based, disrupts for a moment – at least rhetorically – the other, heterosexual economy in which the letter is enmeshed.

The shock of finding Jack's letter blinded Helena temporarily to the other thumbnails on the screen, and to what else the archivist at the NPG might have found and selected to illustrate this file in the collection.[23] After fifteen years of working in archives that told only one side of, say, a honeymoon story, she had no hope that the next thumbnail would be George's response. But it was.

My dearest Jack,
At any other time the news which you now send would have affected me very differently. At present I am naturally surprised, but with <u>unmitigated pleasure</u>. In former times I should have dreaded your marrying because I should have naturally seen so much less of you, but now that

circumstances are taking you away from us, I can only hail with gratitude that which cannot fail to increase your happiness & it is the very thing for you to do. I need not tell you how very heartily I ~~will~~ wish you [then, added with a caret above the line] joy ~~you~~ & all possible prosperity and congratulate you ~~thoroughly~~ warmly.

I am just off to Panshanger & shall look eagerly for a glimpse of you on Monday. I may not be back till latish or just in time for Franks' dinner.

I fully appreciate your great kindness & friendship in writing so promptly to me. As what I write henceforth will be seen by <u>two</u> pairs of eyes, I must take pains and write better. You know that I feel more than I could ever hope to express – so no more at present.

Ever yours affectionately,

George Scharf

Of course any time on Tuesday we will have a Meeting, 3 making the Quorum! (George to Jack, 25 May 1872; JP 72; emphases in the original)

Still stuck in her identification with George as the reader of Jack's news, it was with a difficulty that might or might not have mirrored George's that Helena imagined him as a writer, as writing a response to Jack's announcement. Scanning the scanned letter on her screen, her gaze came to rest on the underlined words 'unmitigated pleasure'. George had archived this pleasure, at least rhetorically, by the second sentence. But the first sentence, before the emphatic expression of delight, offers a' shadow story – and, typically, a shadow temporality. 'At any other time', the sentence tells us, George 'would' have felt differently; there would have been no unmitigated pleasure, perhaps no pleasure at all. The second sentence, grammatically speaking, undoes the first, but how much residue is there, how much trace of the former time, which would have been characterised, we learn later, by 'dread' at the news? Indeed, the second, happy, sentence is surrounded by the syntax of other times, other emotional universes. The temporality of the first sentence reasserts itself in the third: 'In former times,' he says, 'I should have dreaded your marrying, because I should have naturally seen so much less of you.' 'Dreaded' is a strong word here, balancing and, perhaps, in its turn erasing 'pleasure'.

If the first few sentences oscillate between pleasure and dread, between what George says he feels now and what he might have felt at another time, the rest of the letter follows something of an arc, something of a plot, something of a marriage plot. When George counterfactually imagines Jack married but still in London, he pictures 'naturally' seeing far less of his friend. This is the story of the marriage plot, of men like George's old friend Charlie Cordell marrying and slipping away from their masculine community; it is a story that presents itself as nature. There are small signs that George might be struggling with (or against) this plot; by describing himself as 'naturally surprised', George asserts for a moment another kind of nature centred on his feelings and his claims.

By the end of the letter the plot reaches a resolution; George can no longer imagine Jack without Nellie. The slightly coy joke about 'two pairs of eyes' imagines what Helena has called 'the conjugal gaze' at work, in which the vision of man and wife are perfectly aligned (*Victorian Honeymoons*, p. 12). Perhaps there is some marker of resistance here; George does not imagine (yet) that the two pairs of eyes have merged into one, that Nellie is (quite) flesh of Jack's flesh. She will be from now on, however, always reading, always watching. Jack and George will never experience the 'alone together' of marriage. 'I must take pains and write better' is both a cliché and a sign of painful labour; he must write differently (better) to Jack, and the pains he takes are as real as his 'unmitigated pleasure'.

But what of the other 'two pairs of eyes' reading, as it were, over Jack's – and George's – shoulders: the eyes of two literary critics who found through a series of encounters both deliberate and accidental documents they dared not hope existed? It was when we finally had long, detailed and affectively charged documents in front of us that we truly began to feel at home in the archive. These were texts that demanded to be read in the way that we had been trained to read. George's own return to Ashley Place to find Jack's note reminds us, however, that homecomings are problematic and home a fraught place. Sometimes we think we are reading too much, going too far, becoming parodies of literary critics. In our very disciplinarity we might have become undisciplined. As with George, our only option is to keep two parallel stories in mind at the same time.

'Jackiana', or, giving Jack away

Having read and perhaps overread the letters available to us online, we had to wait three months to see the whole file at the NPG. September seemed very far away as we reread the online description of the file and mourned the fact that there were not thumbnails for each individual item. This capacious description read to us like the plot summary of a novel we would have to wait to read:

> A series of letters from one of Scharf's closest friends and personal assistant, Jacob Luard Pattisson, who at that time was personal assistant to the 1st Marquess of Dufferin, then Governor General of Canada. Pattisson's letters include accounts of his travel on SS 'Prussian' with the Governor and his wife, and details of their stay in Ottawa and The Citadelle in Quebec City, Canada. The letters from Pattisson also contain information on his marriage to Ellen Miller and their subsequent travels and stay in Clandeboye, Ireland and Ottawa, Canada. Some of the letters include rough sketches of figures and drawings of architectural features.
>
> The letters also include correspondence from members of the Pattisson family and Scharf's friends, mostly relating to arrangements for Jacob's wedding and bachelor party. This material also includes the draft of a speech Scharf gave, and details of the seating arrangement at the bachelor party.
>
> Also includes letters from Ellen Miller regarding her marriage to Pattisson, their later travels and photograph of herself.

If archival fantasies about diaries centre on ideas of self-revelation, those about letters offer the promise of revealing the nature of a relationship at a particular moment in time. While we were fully aware that the 'correspondence' might contain omissions, lies and prevarication, and although we knew from archival experience and from literary theory that letters do get lost in the mail, we nonetheless found ourselves vulnerable, once again, to archival deflation. Intrigued in particular by the idea of Nellie's writing to George 'regarding her marriage to Pattisson', we tried to conceal our impatience from the archivist who had understandably structured our visit according to the exigencies of staffing and other readers. It was on our third day of this last visit that we finally were handed NPG7/3/5/1/1, the full file of 'Correspondence with Jacob Luard ('Jack') Pattisson, 1872'. The contents were both disorienting and familiar: familiar because we had seen three of the items online; disorienting, because there were so many items, each encased in a folder of clear, slippery plastic. It was literally hard to hold on to the pieces of George's and Jack's lives as they poured out of the master file. Much to our dismay (and to that of the archivist), individual items took on a life and an order of their own, some actually slipping to the floor.

As we gathered up the rogue folders, we came across something that was not, strictly speaking, 'Correspondence', not a letter but a

Fig. 2.10 'Jackiana' label from file of GS correspondence
at Heinz Archive.
©National Portrait Gallery, London.

piece of paper inscribed in what was recognisably George's callig-
raphy: 'Jackiana 1872' (Fig. 2.10). It was a label for a collection, a
mark of George's self-archiving. We were reading *his* file, his collection that he had named after Jack.[24]

Our eyes were also drawn to another object in bigger and darker
font that had appeared on the thumbnail but was more easily iden-
tifiable once we saw it on paper: the 'Don't be shocked!' letter
shared a folder with a small square piece of paper bearing the
printed date of 25 May, the date of the letter itself. Apparently
George had immortalised the date he learned of Jack's engagement by removing the page for the day from a calendar.[25] For us
this bolder type, entering the archive from yet another chrono-
technology, signalled a new kind of expressiveness: black letter for
a black-letter day. We tried to imagine the impulse that would lead
to this particular form of marking: the cutting (or careful tearing)
of the page and its insertion (who knows exactly where) into a pile,
a file, a box of letters.

Once we had sorted the letters, we were able to construct a time-line of events between Jack's announcement of his engagement on 25 May and his wedding on 1 October. The order of crucial events was a little confusing because Jack changed his plans on several occasions. From 25 May to 11 June, Jack spent most of the time at Nellie's house in Chislehurst; he left for Canada on 11 June, stopping in Ireland at Clandeboye, Lord Dufferin's imposing country home, where Jack and Nellie were later to spend their honeymoon. Jack and Nellie had planned to spend the first part of their honeymoon in Devonshire with Nellie's family, but it seems that they went directly to Clandeboye. The newlyweds left the British Isles for Canada in mid-October.

Soon after writing the original message to George, Jack arranged the promised meeting of his friend and his fiancée. On 3 June, Jack sent George a letter with a carefully drawn map of the route from the train station to Nellie's parents' home. While there is no record of what Nellie and George thought about each other in this initial encounter, Jack and Nellie were very soon consolidated in a new way as a couple: Jack asked Nellie to write to George requesting that he arrange a dinner for Jack in London. Jack was apparently aware that using Nellie as an amanuensis might not sit well with George. Once again, he has recourse to the discourse of shock:

> I was so uncertain this morning that I asked Nellie to write to you which I hope you weren't shocked at – But since then I have told the chief [Dufferin] that I cannot get away till Monday evening and so now I want you to give me a little dinner say at 5 if you will on Monday instead of Sunday & then I can have Sunday quietly here and it will give me more time to talk to you. (7 June 1872; JP 72)

Nellie's letter to George begins with an assertion of what we can only call the conjugal metonymy, whereby Nellie is joined to Jack not only as a potential reader of George's letters but also as a writer of her husband's: 'Jack has begged me to write to you for him, because he is so dreadfully busy & is afraid he may not have time to do it himself.' She ends the letter with a joking reference to the visit: 'I hope, notwithstanding the unsteady state of your driver on Monday that you managed to catch your train, it was a great pleasure to me to see so old a friend of Jack's of whom I have always heard so much' (ibid.). Consciously or not, Nellie positions herself as closer to Jack than is George; she also indicates the unevenness of their knowledge of each other: she has 'heard so much' of George while he has heard, until very recently, nothing of her. The term 'so old a friend' is, perhaps, unfortunate under the circumstance, as a reminder both of George's age and of the length of time he was kept in ignorance of Nellie's existence. We hear, at a distance, the clash of temporalities.

For the length of Jack's absence in Canada, Nellie clearly understood herself as Jack's primary correspondent, passing on information about Jack that George already knew from Jack's letters to him. She waited on several occasions to write to George until she had news from Jack, but we know that Jack had written in the meantime to George. Jack also wrote as an intermediary between George and Nellie, tellingly in the context of George's planned wedding gift of furs. On 8 July, Nellie wrote to George, thanking him 'for so very kindly wishing to give me a sealskin coat' and for suggesting that she try on some furs when she came to London. Six weeks later it seems there had been some confusion about the gift. Jack, on the eve of his return to England, writes:

> Many thanks for your letter of 7th Aug from Chevening which reached me last Sunday 18th. It is 'too kind' of you to take so much trouble about the sealskin. I told Nellie that if any of her friends had presented her with furs not to be afraid of telling you before it was chosen as I know you would not feel hurt if such were the case, but I am afraid I have only muddled her. However no one has given her any, but on the contrary she has been looking forward to yours and I shall feel it all the more friendly of you making your present in such a graceful & useful shape. If she has said anything about waiting, please understand that she did not comprehend me, and that I am looking forward to the sealskin as much as she is. (n.d., August 1872; JP 72)

George's role as a benefactor is compromised here, while Nellie is portrayed as a 'muddled' and uncomprehending player in this newly and awkwardly triangulated gift economy.

George's pseudo-parental role was re-established in the lead-up to the wedding and in the wedding itself. George gave the engagement supper; the correspondence file includes drafts of his invitations to many of Jack and George's old friends. In one such invitation letter to W. F. Beauford, George uses, for the first time in our reading, a variant of the term 'bachelor', capitalised and collected into the aggregate noun 'Bachelorhood'.

Dear Beau –
I hope you will be in London by Monday night, the 30th to come here to
a 7 o'clock feed – as usual in freedom from ceremony – but especially to
meet Jack on the occasion of his deserting the ranks of Bachelorhood. It
is also Dick Worsley's birthday – so we may combine the two. I am asking
Dick by the same post, dinner only six in number, but I could not write
till Jack approved my plan. He does so cordially. Yours,
with love, GS
(20 September 1872; JP 72)

Since we have very few examples of earlier letters from George to
his London friends, it is hard to say whether the informal, masculine tone (the carefully planned dinner is a 'feed') is peculiar to this
occasion. It is also impossible to say whether or how often George
used the term 'bachelor' as an identity category in talking or writing to his friends during this period of his life. George does use the
term repeatedly in letters around the time of Jack's wedding, and
he is answered in the same idiom. Beau, for example, responds to
the invitation by saying:

I shall be delighted to come to you next Monday to celebrate the double
event of Dick's birthday and Jack's desertion of the noble order of
Bachelors (some might move as an amendment that the word 'unfortunate' or 'benighted' be substituted for that of 'noble' but it is a matter of
taste). (23 August 1872; JP 72)[26]

Jack's bachelor dinner produced its own archival traces: a seating chart, more ornate than usual, that included an elaborately
rendered date in the middle of the rectangle representing the table
and a draft of George's wedding toast. The latter poses in perhaps
the starkest (and most painful) terms the problem of reading for
absence. The draft is full of deletions, including a crucial one that
we note below. The toast begins with a moment of what could be
purely conventional resistance:

Speechifying I abhor!
Speechifying & ceremony have never yet been known in these rooms. I
had intended not to have said one word upon the present occasion but
the presence of two additional friends, whom we most gladly welcome
among us, will justify a very brief departure from the general custom.
(30 September 1872; JP 72)

In deciding to 'speechify', George notes a break from the usual
practices in his 'rooms' and from those countless social events that

have brought many of the men at the table together as a group before. He vows to speak 'simply'.

> Even now I will simply say:
> Before we leave the table let us drink to the health and prosperity of our dear friend and brother J.L.P. so shortly destined to leave us.
> He is now about to enter upon a new sphere, one which we are fondly encouraged to believe is a state of unclouded happiness & a perpetual exaltation of the spirits!
> May he find it so and may our best expectations even be exceeded. (ibid.)

It is, of course, impossible to determine the degree – if any – of irony in this hyperbole. George often has recourse to clichés in his diaries; the exigencies of the moment may (or may not) account for the conventionality of his description of marriage.

The final paragraph of the speech is a little more complicated because of the existence of two versions on the page. The edited version, which he presumably used, reads: 'Let us even encourage a hope that some fortunate unlooked for circumstance may occur to reduce the long term of their absence.' Although perhaps somewhat plaintive, this version properly refers to both Nellie and Jack. George has, however, crossed out something that sounds sadder and more personal: 'Let us even encourage a hope that some fortunate unlooked for circumstance may occur *to bring us all together again before the expiration of the dreary time that* [. . .]' (our italics). The 'us all', spoken to the table of male friends, might or might not include Nellie. George has crossed out 'expiration of the dreary time', probably because it is hardly celebratory, hardly compatible with the 'state of unclouded happiness & a perpetual exaltation of the spirits!' he has attributed to married couples earlier in the speech. George seems aware that the 'dreary time', the story-time temporality of dreary waiting for their return, belongs to him and not to the bride and groom.

In giving the wedding speech, George was functioning as something like a best man. His role in the actual wedding, however, was closer to the paternal one that Jack's 'Don't be shocked' letter began to structure for his 'old [. . .] friend'. George paid for 'a nice carriage with footman & postilions' to convey Jack, Jack's brother and himself from George's home in Ashley Place up to Trinity Church in Marylebone. During the ceremony George shared a pew with Jack's parents and at the wedding breakfast was seated next to the bride's mother. In multiple senses, George's function was to give Jack away.

We do not know how George viewed his efforts in support of Jack's wedding or, for that matter, how he represented those efforts to Jack. Jack seems from his letters to have been both grateful for and guilty about George's support. Jack's first honeymoon letter to George is hyperbolic in its thanks:

> Here we are all safe and sound – but before I give you any account of our voyage and adventures I must send you my best and warmest and heartiest thanks for all your kindness and hospitality to me and mine, and for all your consideration and self denial during the last fortnight. What I would have done without you I cannot think, and I never can be sufficiently grateful and at the same time sufficiently penitent for having accepted so much at your hands and for repaying it by making your house such a bear garden with all my people & papers. But your last kindness has gone beyond all, and I gladly write to you the first letter of thanks of the many I feel due from me. How you could have done so much & stood so much for me during this time is more than I can sometimes bear to think of, but I am sure you will feel how much I have appreciated all your affectionate sympathy and assistance, and so has indeed the little woman herself. I hope you will not suffer from the reaction – you must send me a line as soon as you can to say how you have been getting on since the 1st. (4 October 1872; JP 72)

We have not been able positively to identify George's 'last kindness' (see below), but it is clear from the letter that George did more than host a dinner and pay for a carriage. It is hard not to read 'self-denial' in emotional as well as in logistical terms.

Getting used to it

It would be easy to see Jack as the comfortable inhabitant of the marriage plot negotiating with his friend outside its parameters, but Jack's postmarital letters offer a more complicated picture. Helena has argued that the Victorian honeymoon was often a time of difficult erotic reorientation, even for those whose sexuality might seem to correspond more closely than did Jack's with the requirements of compulsory heterosexuality (Michie, *Victorian Honeymoons*, pp. 56–98). Jack's letter from Clandeboye shows some of the work of producing that conjugality, although in these efforts he is not much different from those whose same-sex relationships were less complicated. Helena, always alert to the often difficult cultural work of the Victorian honeymoon, found it hard to decide whether Jack was experiencing any special degree of disorientation.

The first part of Jack's honeymoon letter is quite typical of such communications, invoking the scene of leave-taking (especially for the bride) and orthographically reproducing the discomfort of representing the wedding night (in this case indicated by a long dash):

> I thought the wedding went very well all things considered, and that for a wedding it was tolerably lively – at the last I found myself unable to say goodbye [. . .] as the bride was breaking down after her parting with her mother and she wanted to be hurried away – we got to the Station in comfortable time, and found our carriage engaged all right and the luggage & maid all duly in the train. So we just walked into our seats and soon seemed to be at Rugby – There too everything was comfortable, and the rooms suitable & convenient. They gave us a nice little dinner and – we turned up to breakfast next morning in sufficient time to catch the Irish express at 12 o'clock, reaching Fleetwood at 5. The day was rather wet till 12 o'clock but after that very fine – at Fleetwood another nice little dinner was waiting but Nellie declared herself done up, and the little flask had to be resorted to – The effect of its contents and a bottle of soda together with a couple of wings of chicken which by my newly acquired authority I ordered her to eat, however soon put matters straight and she went on board and slept like a top until we arrived at Belfast at 6:30 yesterday morning. (4 October 1872; JP 72)

Familiar to Helena from her reading of other honeymoon letters was the repeated use of the word 'comfortable' in a context of what must have been some unease (Michie, *Honeymoons*, p. 15). The two 'nice little' dinners suggest a snugness very much in keeping with the Scharfian idiom. In the middle of all this comfort, however, Nellie is 'done up' and has to 'resort' to the flask that George has given Jack (perhaps this was the 'last kindness'?). Jack insists that Nellie eat chicken wings, orders her to eat them, orders for her. From the vantage point of his 'new authority', ordering takes into itself a new meaning; he sends her to bed to sleep through this second honeymoon night. George's 'beautiful little flask', as Jack calls it at the end of the letter, converts Nellie back into 'her old self', an interesting phrase given that the honeymoon had so much transformative work to do, and that Nellie herself, although little, was not, according to Jack, beautiful.

The end of the honeymoon seems to have required Jack to juxtapose the new world of conjugality and the older, homosocial world of Ashley Place. Jack writes to George on 16 October to tell him he is departing from Clandeboye and to thank him again, this time in Nellie's name as well as in his own:

> One of the pleasantest parts of all this business is the extremely cordial manner in which the Ashley Place circle have sympathised with the poor fellow and except that the little woman says that where so many bachelors were to be found not much good could result, I know how much she has also felt all the kindness which has emanated from No. 8. (JP 72)

Jack echoes George's new language of bachelorhood as a (half-) joking contrast to his new situation. Defined by place, by 8 Ashley Place, and by his role as host, George is othered by the marriage plot that has – at least for now – turned Jack into a spokesperson for his wife.

Reading in our typical novelistic way, we expected that the story of Jack and George would be over now that Jack had played the hero of the heterosexual marriage plot. We were taken aback, however, by what we found in Jack's letters to George from Canada. Jack and Nellie's first year as newlyweds suggests that Jack's reorientation was not, after all, complete despite the drastic change in environment. For a while, all looked to be proceeding according to the exigencies of the marriage (and reproductive) plot. About two months after the wedding day, Jack wrote to George, 'Nellie has taken to her sofa and is not fit for much from which you may draw your own conclusions.' The marriage plot makes Jack's euphemisms legible: Nellie was pregnant and therefore not available for sex. The Victorian version of the marriage plot presents the lack of sex (after the first few months of marriage) as evidence of its own success. Jack and Nellie themselves concluded that she was pregnant but by April of 1873 still did not know when the baby was due. On 21 April Jack told George that Nellie was anxious to be moved into a new house 'to feel settled for the coming event, but I am sorry to say she still keeps very weak and good for nothing'. The unsettled feeling came from a removal from Ottawa to Quebec, but also from the elusiveness of her due date:

> A certain halfway event which you reckon upon is no safe guide for the final catastrophe, and she is still very much bothered because none of the learned can agree when it will happen. The Montreal Doctor who was not aware that we were only married in Oct fixed the date [. . .] for an early period in June which rather made every one blush. (JP 73)

Helena's experience with the reproductive calculus of Victorian pregnancy and our shared (and complacent) sense of the ignorance of Victorian gynaecology interfered with our understanding that something was not quite right. We knew that Victorians sometimes used foetal kicking or even the usually third-trimester Braxton Hicks contractions as a confirmation of pregnancy: the confusion and belatedness of Nellie's case simply signalled to us the exoticism of Victorian reproductive knowledge. Taking for granted the temporalities of the marriage and reproductive plots, we fully expected the confusion to be resolved in nine months. But by July, when signs of illness had been present for the full term of pregnancy, Nellie was still 'on her back' and anticipating her confinement, 'as jolly as ever', though 'her nerves never really yet [had] recovered from all the bother of [their] engagement' (5 July 1873; JP 73). At the end of the month a baffled Jack wrote to George:

> At last the Doctors have been able to settle our doubts and fears by saying that they and all of us have been entirely mistaken and that there is no small baby on the road at all. They have been they say deceived in an extraordinary way but as we relied upon them and all the monthly nurses and married ladies who were called in at various times we don't feel so vexed at ourselves as we might though the poor little woman herself is terribly disappointed. I hope however that there is no disease of any sort but simply want of strength, but I never knew before that appearances could be so deceitful to the cognoscenti. However so it is and we must make the best of it. (29 July 1873; JP 73)

George's next letter from Jack is dated six weeks later (18 September 1873; JP 73) and thanks George 'for several letters', which had evidently gone unanswered. Jack's embarrassment about having 'reckon[ed] our chickens before they were hatched' expresses itself in terms almost identical to those he had used before: 'so many of the learned were deceived that we can console ourselves a little'. Jack can now 'give a much better report of the wife', as Nellie 'has been able to go out and show herself in society and return her calls since coming back to Quebec – absolutely for the first time since we have been married'. 'Not that she is very strong or ever will be', Jack adds, confidently.

If Nellie's symptoms were mysterious, our own were quite obvious. We were practising an archival form of Victorianist diagnosis-at-a-distance, the syndrome that allows contemporary scholars to say that Charlotte Brontë died of hyperemesis gravidarum or Jane Austen of bovine tuberculosis (or Bright's disease or arsenic poisoning). Nellie's symptoms (as reported awkwardly by Jack) offered numerous possibilities: a miscarriage with lingering effects? A hysterical pregnancy? Fibroid tumours mistaken for a baby? A foetus that somehow got resorbed into the mother's system, leaving its hormonal effects intact? Bad Victorian medicine? Jack and Nellie's sexual ignorance? The frontrunner (for us) was for a long while anorexia. Unlike George, Nellie appears not to have been much of an eater. We recalled with interest Jack's honeymoon letter about ordering 'a couple of wings of chicken' for Nellie as a remedy for her feeling 'done up'. There might, then, be another dimension to Jack's apparently conventional use of 'little woman' or 'little wife' as a substitute for Nellie's name.

How the false pregnancy happened is unknowable, but clearly Jack's descriptions of her condition indicate that for the whole first year of their marriage his little wife was not available for sex. It cannot have been lost on George that Jack had been telling him that he was living celibately. Jack's marriage plot had in some ways deferred its own closure, so much so that when the Pattissons returned to England just two years after being posted to Canada (rather than the expected term of six years), Jack once again began frequenting the bachelor gatherings at George's apartment. George's ardour, however, seems to have abated, as does the married Jack's availability for overnight stays at 8 Ashley Place. Gradually over the next twenty years, between Jack's return to London and George's death, the diary refers less often to 'Jack' than to 'Jack Pattisson' and eventually just 'Pattisson', placing Jack nominally in the same category as Worsley and Franks and all the other surnamed regulars in Scharf's homosocial circle.

Piano Wars

Romance plots end, but in real life – whether one is a protagonist or a researcher – they do not end neatly. Jack's reappearances in George's life as an occasional visitor and ultimately as George's executor reminded us of the insufficiencies of traditional literary closure. And yet, the romance plot retains its power to shape the meaning of events, even retrospectively. After finding Jack, our sense of earlier archival moments and preoccupations was reshaped by the currents of Scharf's romantic life; wading back, as it were, against those currents, we found that earlier landmarks had changed their contours. In her first pass through the diaries, Robyn had noted a pattern of entries we referred to collectively as 'Piano Wars': moments when our otherwise mild and gentlemanly biographical subject had apparently descended into fits of retaliatory rage when disturbed by the loud piano playing of a downstairs neighbour. For Helena, these moments of high affect hinted at the kind of characterological depth whose existence she had intuited but could not always locate. For Robyn, who shares George's love of music, German and German music, these episodes were doubly disturbing. She could sympathise with George's rising level of irritation at these ugly intrusions into his domestic comfort zone, but his uncouth behaviour, so unbecoming in a protagonist, made her uneasy. The Piano Wars were our first indication that Sir George Scharf was not living in a space that was at all comparable to the great houses we knew he had been visiting. For both of us, the mysteries of the Piano Wars were intricately connected to George's relation to domestic spaces.

Although we had had to 'read into' the archive to find discursive signs of George's distress over the loss of Jack, we needed only to read the surface of George's 1872 diaries to find him acting out his dismay through the Piano Wars. With too much solitary time on his hands in 8 Ashley Place, the flat Jack had helped him find in 1869 and that had been for a short time their joint home, George began to conceive a bitter hatred for the woman downstairs, whose noisy piano playing continually disturbed his solitude. The Piano Wars lasted for at least a decade, and we fancied that references to his outrage were the trace of George's heartbreak long after he stopped making overt references to missing 'dearest Jack' (D 11 August 1869; George to Jack, 25 May 1872; JP 72). What he usually called the 'music below' joined the daily details about expenses, food and the weather that formed the litany of George's diaries throughout the 1870s and into the 1880s. The Piano Wars disturbed George's rest, wrecked his evening enjoyments and devastated his feeling of being comfortably at home.

Although the Piano Wars got started before the crucial date of 25 May 1872, it got worse. The problem for George was not just that the piano playing downstairs was loud. He suffered aesthetic pain from the badness of the daily (and nightly) performances. Just after Jack's wedding in October 1872, when the loud playing occurs George begins to note a new retaliatory practice of 'walking Masonically' – which we take to mean pacing or maybe even stomping back and forth uninterrupted for periods of up to two hours – in the wee hours of the night. By this time he has begun obsessively noting the details of the bad performances downstairs:

109

Loud dance music began below at ½ past 7. Quadrilles of old school Herz [presumably something like 'Quadrilles 'Les Elégantes' arranged for juvenile performers on the Piano Forte' by Henri Herz, 1803–8]. Stopped suddenly after a very short time. Began again at ¼ before 9 with a gavotte & then an Italian overture after which apparently Chopin's Funeral March. I played from 9:30–12, & walked from 2–3. (D 9 January 1873)

The playing downstairs got worse, almost as though the downstairs neighbour, resenting the late-night 'Masonic' walking, was playing badly on purpose. The Piano Wars came to a crisis in May that puts George in the most undignified light in which we have ever seen him:

Piano playing began below directly after 10 o'clock and lasted nearly an hour. Scales, Exercises & a hideous chromatic hacking passage piece as on Friday. [Then he lists some expenses, then whom he met at dinner, then]: Walked in my room after 12.30. The woman from below began to ring my kitchen bell & then the visitor's bell, & then both together. Upon which she was told to go on & that I should walk 20 minutes after she had left off pulling my bell. She called me an infamous name & said that I ought to be ashamed of myself. I saw her going down from my door, dressed in red. After I had ceased walking, she came up and rang the bells one after the other & both at the same time; upon which I promised her half an hour more, & gave it her. I left off at 2.45. & fell asleep at 3 o'clock. She will learn in time not to force hideous music upon her neighbours when wishing to be quiet in the morning at breakfast, or when everybody else is quiet in the house of an evening. Kettley & Tebbutt dined with me. Small piano playing below from 9 to 9:30. (D 6 May 1873)

In 1876 the Piano Wars were still raging on (D 14 June 1876, D 30 June 1876). They did not abate until well into the 1880s.

As Robyn transcribed the details of George's rising fury, she was not quite as uncomfortable as poor George, but she was nevertheless discomfited. She wanted George to be better than this, even though good behaviour has never been requisite for the hero of a romance plot. Thinking about failed romance plots in broader literary terms, she tried to see George's obsessive fixation on the Piano Wars as a much more mundane example of the madness so frequently observed in English literature's tragically jilted or bereaved lovers, from Shakespeare's Ophelia, to Sir Walter Scott's bride of Lammermoor, to the hermit in Tom Stoppard's *Arcadia*. Fortunately, George prevented our story from slipping into tragedy (or maybe it would have just been bathos) by finding a new love object.

Romance plot redux

Romance plots in Victorian novels, and even in our divorce-prone culture, rely for their power on ideals of monogamy and singularity. Of course, even in Victorian novels there are second-chance marriage plots, and some of the most engaging romance plots in our time involve multiple marriages.[27] But even, and perhaps especially, if we look at the stories of the most-often-married (say, Elizabeth Taylor or even Robyn Warhol, known to some wags as 'Robyn Warhol Housley Warhol Warhol-Streeter Warhol Warhol-Down Warhol Warhol-Kriff'), the investment each time is in singularity, in getting it right. 'This,' in celebrity marriage speak and in our own attempts at accommodating serial monogamy to the marriage plot, 'is the One.' Insofar as our story of George had Jack as an endpoint, it was not just a teleological story but also a monogamous one. If the gender of the beloved was at odds with Victorian norms, his singularity made it legible in terms of the same literary and cultural romance plots that make agitation for gay marriage so compelling for many and the equally pertinent right of gay divorce an embarrassing afterthought.

But George had a second young man. Under 'Private Scharf' on the NPG's webpage is an antique photograph of a corpulent, bald, bearded and aged George seated at a rolltop desk on which a younger man is leaning (Fig. 2.11). The site names the young man but says nothing about his connection to Scharf. In the photograph George appears to be poring over a stack of papers cascading from the open desktop onto his lap, his head bent in concentration, one side of his face supported by his right hand, propped up on the desk by his elbow. While George looks down at the papers he holds in his other hand, the younger man stares coolly at the camera. The receding hairline of the man's slicked-back and carefully parted hair shows that he is not *that* much younger than George, certainly not as much younger as young Jack had been, but the aggressive bushiness and dark colour of his waxed mustache marks him as not much more than middle-aged.[28] A sepia-tone portrait with curved edges and a flashy signature at the bottom, the picture is apparently a cabinet card, with all the awkwardness of a stiffly held studio pose. The first time we saw the picture, it presented no questions for us, but only an answer: that's not Jack. This man's being not-Jack made us skim quickly over the caption identifying him as Freeman M. O'Donoghue and click ahead to the next Scharf portrait, entirely

Fig. 2.11 GS and Freeman 'Donny' O'Donoghue, 1886.
©National Portrait Gallery, London.

missing the important detail that in this picture the bare skin of
one man's hand appears to be touching the bare skin of the other's
wrist. Sitting for a photograph in the 1880s was not the work of an
instant. This is a portrait of physical intimacy.

George would have met O'Donoghue in the Print Room at the
British Museum, where O'Donoghue had worked as a cataloguer
since 1865, when he was seventeen years old. By the end of the
1870s, O'Donoghue was included in the dinners at 8 Ashley Place
about once a month, and in 1880 George noted on 8 March that
O'Donoghue came 'soon after 4 o'clock to begin helping me to
work at the artist part of the N.P.G. catalogue. He dined & staid
till 11 o'clock'. Soon O'Donoghue was dining at George's most
evenings, whether or not there was other company. On 9 April,
a month after O'Donoghue began coming to work on the catalogue, George noted that the woman in the apartment below him
was once again noisily practising the piano in the evening, but
that 'O'Donoghue went to sleep on the sofa and slept through

the noise'. On 17 April and for a while thereafter George paid his housekeeper three shillings 'for extra O'Donoghue trouble'. On Saturday, 8 May 1880, George came home to find that O'Donoghue had dined in his absence and was just leaving, but on George's return 'he came back for a while'. Jack, again on the scene though less frequently so, came to lunch on 9 May, and two weeks later, on 23 May 1880, 'Jack Pattisson came in and took cold dinner with us'. 'Us', having made the deictic shift from 'the Elderlies and me' to 'Mother and me' to 'Jack and me', now meant 'O'Donoghue and me'. Jack was back in the homosocial circle, but his place at George's was being taken over by the fellow whom George was, by November of 1880, calling 'Donny'.

Donny was paid only a little for the work he did for George, and, like Jack, Donny enjoyed George's generosity in other forms. On 26 May 1880, George took Donny on an expedition to Windsor ('O'D was greatly pleased'), paying £1 1s 6d for the trip, and on 9 June George and Donny went to Hampton Court together, then 'we came home at night after ½ past 9'. On 18 October 1881 George paid for an outing for Donny and himself to the Crystal Palace. Throughout the subsequent years, Donny dined at George's several times a week 'as usual'. Unlike Jack, though, Donny was not perfect. On 21 February 1884, 'Donny dined with me. He made a rude remark & I resented it before he went away'. Six days later, 'Donny dined with me. More subdued than usual; but no reference to the previous [...] mistake & I did not expect any from his nature'. Does 'no reference' mean no defensive recurrence of the rudeness? No apology? No awkward reminder of the offence? George doesn't say. He does say, however, on 23 July 1884, that he and Donny went 'to the Health Exhibition', where 'the fountains with coloured lights were very pretty. Chinese music amusing. But I felt flurried & fatigued. Donny is not a good manager or companion in a crowd'. In the hundreds of references to Jack throughout the diaries, even when Jack broke the news of his engagement and (we think) broke George's heart, George never wrote a negative word about *him*.

But George never took Jack on holiday with him. He took Donny at least twice, once to Brighton in October of 1884 and then again to Margate in July of 1885. It was during their holiday in Margate that the cabinet-card portrait of George and Donny was taken. George's pose at the desk turns out to reflect a painful stiffness in his neck that had begun the year before. The two men's touching hands turn out to reflect a closeness that was never to be interrupted by this younger man's marriage. Still unmarried at the end of his own life, O'Donoghue was as confirmed a bachelor as Scharf, and he continued spending his evenings at 8 Ashley Place, eating dinner, working on catalogues and playing cribbage through the long decade of George's final physical decline. Donny was at Ashley Place so much that Scharf's housekeeper of the late 1880s, Mrs Carter, objected to his presence. 'When I paid [Mrs Carter] her wages on the 9th punctually I got no thanks but rather abuse with objections to wait on Mr Donny', wrote George with many angry-looking blots of ink on a blank page at the beginning of March of 1888. On 9 March he elaborated: 'After paying Mrs Carter her wages instead of thanking me she made loud complaints of having "two families" to wait on looking upon Donny as a stranger when I told her that he was in the light of a brother to me. She said that she never engaged to wait upon any but myself & was very incoherent and strangely disrespectful. I fear that I must look about elsewhere'. The constant presence on the domestic scene of this professional associate must have struck a respectable woman like Mrs Carter as queer enough to make her behaviour 'strangely disrespectful'.

If there was something going on between George and Donny, something palpable enough to make its way into a photograph or to offend the housekeeper, it was not enough to cause us to abandon our investment in Jack as the hero of George's romance plot. Our loyalty to Jack was in some ways stronger – and more irrational – than George's. Part of this might have to do with a Victorian-novel-fed fantasy of monogamy or even a more modernist penchant for narrative anticlimax. Or perhaps our reluctance to embrace Donny came from another key element of the romance plot: its insistence on youth and on the youthful body. While George was by no means young during the long Jack years, by the time Donny entered his life and home George was repeatedly, sometimes repellently, and almost always tediously ill. Donny was present daily during George's last weeks, continually a witness to, for instance, the water that 'oozed steadily out of puncture holes' George's doctor made in his swollen left foot (D 30 January 1885). There is no doubt that Donny was, towards the end, George's nurse and caretaker. While such a relationship might include an erotic relationship, George's body enters – and lingers in – the late diaries through symptoms that seem to belong to other narratives – retrospective diagnosis to name one particularly compelling one. Contemporary gay male culture in the AIDS era has much to tell us about the erotics of care;

as we read the last diaries we strove to apply those lessons to the complexities of George's relationship with Donny.

In a sense, George's legacy comes to us through both Donny and Jack. Jack and Donny, along with Richard Worsley, served as executors of Scharf's will, and Jack's firm served as solicitors. It was Donny who wrote the original *Dictionary of National Biography* (*DNB*) entry on Scharf, two years after his death, in which he includes the information that Scharf 'went much into society, and throughout life enjoyed the esteem and affection of a wide circle of friends'.[29] This information is missing from the most recent *DNB* entry by Peter Jackson, in part, perhaps, because the more professionalised contemporary version of the dictionary tends to gloss over the social in favour of the professional. Donny's version offers us a glimpse of the diner-out, an extra man whose value to his friends was perhaps not so very extra after all.

After plot: illegible romance

In identifying George Scharf's relationships with Jack and Donny, we have inevitably 'outed' him. The outing of someone less-than-famous is, of course, different from the outing of those who are already 'out' in a different sense, those around whom may have grown biographical protections. We think of the reaction to the suggestion by Maynard Solomon that Franz Schubert may have been homosexual: the shock and even hostility in the world of music history, the parsing and reparsing of the word 'peacock' in his letters, the special issue of *Nineteenth-Century Music* devoted to what difference his proposed homosexuality might make (see Solomon and, also, Steblin). We think of the reaction to the idea that Jane Austen might be gay in the controversy over Terry Castle's having identified Austen's strongest affectionate ties as 'homosocial'.[30] We think of the hesitation of most scholars (Clayton is an exception here) to think of the sixth ('Bachelor') Duke of Devonshire's lifelong affection for Joseph Paxton as sexual.[31] While speaking explicitly about Scharf's sexuality might – or might not – offend the few people who know of the importance of his work, we have been spared the work of outing an icon. The 'So what?' question remains, however, perhaps intensified by the fact that Scharf is so little known. If someone not known – therefore, not known to be heterosexual, someone in whom very few people have a personal investment – turns out to be homosexual, what difference does it make?

And here we brush up once again against the question – and the problem – of Scharf's representativeness. Historians of sexuality know quite a bit about gay male life in London in the later years of the nineteenth century. Scholars have moved beyond the Wilde trials to look at more ordinary homosexual lives. We know something now about where late-Victorian homosexual men gathered, about what words they used for themselves and for their sexual encounters, about what male prostitutes cost in various parts of the city and about patterns of arrest and conviction for sodomy before and after the passage of the Labouchere Amendment in 1885.[32] We know the names of some (not too many, really) Victorian homosexual men, mostly those who got into legal trouble or who were brave enough to write about their experiences or to advocate for their rights. We know a lot about Oscar Wilde. Most, although not all, of what we know is about casual sexual encounters or cross-class relationships. We don't know much about homosexual relationships between professional men or about their domestic arrangements. While Matt Cook describes bachelor apartments in London's city centre where married men set up alternative households, there is very little written about unmarried men with primary and visible (if not always explicit) commitments to each other.[33] We don't know much about the respectable middle-aged, the middle-class, or the middlebrow homosexuals. George offers one window into this world, even if the view is a little murky.

Of course, we cannot be certain that George's life was as decorous as it seems. Against the romance plot, we have the possibility of a sexual antiplot: a series of brief relationships that did not unfold over time and provide the landmarks of plot and character. Perhaps George participated in the public, if coded, world of male casual sex and simply did not write about it. Unlike Irish nationalist and free spirit Roger Casement (Matt Cook, p. 25), George did not include payment for such sexual acts in his accounting, but we have said repeatedly that his accounts don't add up. We don't want to discount the possibility that George had a sexual life beyond the diaries and that the diaries in their very meticulousness were a defence against being known. Nor do we want entirely to exclude the possibility that George saw his relationships with Jack and Donny – his two so-called brothers – as platonic. What George saw and what we see are not, however, necessarily congruent. Our too-close readings of the diaries and correspondence lead us away from the queer antinarrative ('of course he had secret, random gay sex') and the antiqueer narrative ('of course Victorian men had intimate relationships that were asexual') and back to the romance plot, where we began. We mean to honour the seriousness of George's two long-term, stigmatised and ultimately illegal relationships, along with the other illegible romances that were flourishing, then as now, outside the straitjacket of the marriage and romance plots.

3

Reading for differentiation: the family romance plot

D ESPITE GEORGE SCHARF'S PROFESSIONAL success and eventual social status, most people who have heard the name are thinking of his father. It is George Scharf Sr's urban sketches – tracking street by street and demolished house by demolished house the emergence of Regency London and of the city we know today – that were brought together in the 1980s as an exhibition and a book, both entitled *George Scharf's London*. If George Jr does not get to possess, in the contemporary imagination, the city in which he, too, lived and worked, he did in his own time manage to surpass his father in reputation and class, to leave behind the slightly pathetic figure, the chronically underemployed immigrant debtor who shared – that is to say, anticipated – his name. The remarkable story of George Jr's class and professional ascendancy, marked by increasing signs of public respect, achieved its apotheosis in the nominal change that shortly preceded his death: the not-quite-posthumous creation of 'Sir George Scharf', the addition of 'Sir' to the name of the son, marked the distance between the two men for posterity.

The official record, in which George Scharf Jr becomes, after his father's death, the singular 'George Scharf', and close to his own death becomes 'Sir', tells a shapely story of filial differentiation, a story so culturally powerful that it has produced theories and disciplines as well as the more intimate stories many people tell about their own lives. The hero of this official story is the 'George Scharf' whose name, eventually shorn of its 'Jr', appears in the London *Times* in (admittedly at the end of) lists of guests at royal levees and

118

as the signature to letters to the editor. This is the George Scharf who writes articles for the *Athenaeum* and who is addressed with increasing intimacy by Lord Stanhope as the two men collaborate at the National Portrait Gallery. This is also the George Scharf who makes annual appearances in the diaries' year-end summaries, which, as we have seen, individually and in aggregate provide the structure for his triumphal narrative.

If we look beyond the official story, however, we find a messier, more intimate and more recursive story – or, more accurately, a set of competing stories that get one kind of energy from the master narrative of differentiation and another from the anxiety, anger and shame attached to local moments of failure to progress according to its exigencies. These moments, which tend to come not from George Jr's diaries, with their carefully crafted temporal structure, but from his family letters and from the diaries of his close relatives, complicated, for us, our sense of George Jr's triumph. While the broad outline – the seductive arc – of differentiation remained in place, the switch from one archive to another allowed us to see the cost of producing and living out a master-narrative of progress and differentiation, not only for George Jr's family but, perhaps, for George Jr himself.

Coming to terms with this new set of stories required yet another kind of archival reading, or more accurately of rereading. Although we had looked quite carefully at the diaries of George Jr's mother, aunt and father early in the project, we had set them aside when our own narrative impulses were hijacked by the mystery of George Jr's sexuality. We were more than willing to leave the family diaries behind for the sexier story, in part because even more than George Jr's own they were, at least initially, generically inscrutable. The women's diaries, in particular, made George Jr's look intimate, personal and confessional. The earlier diaries of Elizabeth Scharf, George Jr's mother, are actually catalogued in the Scharf papers as account books; they are sporadically kept, and entries sometimes appear in the wrong month. Both she and George Jr's aunt, Mary Hicks, virtually abandon the first-person that to us remained stubbornly constitutive of the genre of the diary: most of their entries catalogue not the women's own daily activities but those of George Jr: 'George had a smoking party', writes Mrs Scharf on 20 April 1855; 'George went to Manchester', writes Miss Hicks on 8 August 1856 (ESD, MH).

The father's diaries are more complete and more heterogeneous:

those from the early 1840s double as detailed records of his piece-work as a scientific illustrator for Charles Darwin and Robert Owen, among others; two typical entries begin with the words 'Drawing teeth' and 'Drawing crocodile', with notations about the time he spent on each project and how much he charged for its completion. In some ways the diaries are quite organised, especially the ones from the 1840s. Entries featuring particular people or subjects are often underlined and have a related decorative letter in the margin. Thus entries about George Jr usually have a 'G' in the margin and those about his brother, Henry, an 'H'. Somewhat less obviously, George Sr accompanies a description of a panorama with a 'P' (GSS 25 February 1840) and a description of a 'fine young Negro' whom he 'took [. . .] home with me for G to draw' with an 'N' (GSS 17 March 1841; underlining in original). Although 'G's are frequent in the early diaries, they are only one letter among many: there is no sense that the life the father describes is dominated or defined by the son.

The 1845 diary represents an abrupt change in genre: as George Sr describes a journey to his native Bavaria to visit his dying brother, the daily planner becomes a travel diary with its generic markers of scenic description and locatively inspired moments of introspection. The George Sr of this diary is both tourist and returning son, the beauties of the German landscape integrated into a romantic sense of homeland. If he records drawing in this context, it is as a vocational act inspired by landscape and his emotional interest in his countrymen and women. Even when he speaks of England in this diary, there are signs of what Victorians might have seen as a German sensibility (and syntax). '[O]h what a sudden change!' he writes, 'like by enchantment, I, to be transmitted into another Country, and into what a Country, my own Dear Vaterland! Oh those, in whose Country I have found a second home, who have let me find a living, a comfort, a happiness [. . .] and to crown all, a Dear little Wife to share that happiness' (GSS 22 October 1845; punctuation original). Both the early and later diaries are written in closer accord with traditional English usage; this particular diary also breaks with his own conventions of reserve.

The father's diaries from 1852 to 1859, all contained in one bound volume, are a slightly more sober affair; they echo the women's diaries of the same period by subordinating the diarist's 'I' to the filial third-person; George Sr, too, begins many of his entries of this last diary with the name 'George'. As we shall see, the tone of busy contentment disappears for long stretches in this diary, and the relative precision of his earlier notational practices breaks down. Like those of his wife and sister-in-law, George Sr's diaries, as we shall see in detail below, also function – with varying degrees of success – as account books, and as attempts to comprehend the family's complex (and often discouraging) financial situation. The lists of expenditures, familiar to us from George Jr's diaries, are supplemented by records of intrafamily debt and by expressions of anxiety about money.

Another important source for the Scharf family story are the letters George Jr wrote to his mother in the 1850s as his career began to take off. Many of them are quick notes, headed by a day instead of a date, to inform his mother of changes in his plans, which almost always involve staying longer at the home of a rich or titled connection. The letters also include instructions to his father (to be relayed by his mother) about matters of business: the purchase of drawing materials, the partial payment of a debt to a printer or supplier, a request that money for George Jr's travel expenses be sent immediately. Like the family diaries, these letters betray a fundamental anxiety about money; George Jr's worry over small sums competes in the letters with signs of the more familiar master-narrative of progress as he recounts increasing intimacy with the places that appear on the letterhead of many of his notes.

Coming to terms with the protocols of the Scharf family papers was not easy. We were at this point at home with and in George Jr's diaries, with their familiar rhythms, omissions and small snobberies. We knew his range of allusions; we were skilled at deciphering even his later, more crabbed, handwriting. Now our task was to put together a story across texts that shared few of the generic markers of even our evermore reduced expectations for personal revelation: the family diaries were filled with blank pages, shifted in tone and genre and sometimes contradicted each other as to fact. They were hard on the eye, and the syntax of the entries was often confusing. They were in some sense highly affective, but the affect was for the most part a sustained (and ultimately contagious) anxiety. The letters were really notes, often without the archival anchor of dates. Unlike Jack's letters to George Jr, they were not part of the latter's meticulous self-archiving project; we had to provide the shape – and often the chronology – for this incidental archive. What became clear, however, as we read and reread these items side by side was that they were as much challenges to the idea of the master-narrative of progress and differentiation as George Jr's diaries were to the master-narrative of romance.

If the marriage plot is a literary and cultural narrative with its own set of imperatives, so too is the plot of progress and differentiation. This one is not quite so easy to name, although we see its shaping cultural power at work in many registers. This plot is, we argue, resolutely male and middle-class. Historically, it emerges as a story of first-generation immigration and second-generation assimilation, or as a progressivist account of increasing opportunities for middle-class men. Psychodynamically, it is an Oedipal plot centred on the ejection of the father and the incorporation of the mother; it is also a plot of family romance, in which the son, convinced of his own specialness within the family, looks for substitute parents of a higher class while at the same time regressing to infantile relations with his own parents. In the register of literature, this is also the plot of *Bildung*, of identity formation through education, work and progress. Finally, in the idiom of popular culture, this narrative has recently emerged in the form of anxieties about adult children's 'failure to launch', or to leave their parents' homes.[1] All these versions of the differentiation plot have at their centre a talented son at pains to move beyond the limitations of his father's experience, and they offer a bird's-eye view of the son's journey that overlooks local instances of resistance or failure. While psychodynamic versions, in particular, acknowledge the psychic costs of enacting the plot, all these accounts privilege movements forward, up and away, often telling the story retrospectively.

This chapter attempts to acknowledge the power of the differentiation plot in all its registers and to interrupt that plot in terms of scale and temporality. By focusing on the very small – the few shillings as opposed to broader economic achievements or movements – and the temporally specific – the days and nights of intrafamilial negotiation as opposed to the triumphal end product – we hope to see the story of George Jr as many stories. If, as Susan Suleiman notes, the story of the individual is almost always told from the child position, we attempt, using admittedly incomplete records, to hear the voice of the grown-ups, even if those voices ultimately merge in the talismanic identity of the successful son (p. 356).

Our story begins with the father and with the complex temporal and psychic relationship we see between father and son as the son simultaneously identifies with and differentiates himself from this all-too-similar father. We show how the differentiation plot necessitates projecting the father as a failure, and how the evidence for that failure in the Scharfs' case is overdetermined by plot and undersupported by evidence. We spend some considerable time on the mystery of the father's ejection from the Scharf household just as George Jr began to record important professional successes, and we end the section on the father with the canonical moment of the father's death and with George Jr's strange and contradictory acts of mourning and dismissal. We then turn to the story of George Jr's relationship with his mother and to the idyllic household George Jr formed with, first, the mother and aunt and, then, after the aunt's death, with the mother alone; we look at the blurring of the lines between work and private life in the construction of that household and at the son's desire to incorporate especially his mother into the space and rhythms of his work.

After what is essentially a psychodynamic beginning, in which George Jr is seen in terms of his parallel relationships with his father and mother, we let the messiness, contradiction and eclecticism of the Scharf family archive lead us away from family and to the idea of household. 'Household' allows us to hear, however faintly, the self-effacing voice of George's aunt, Mary, who moved with the Scharfs from lodging to lodging. It also allows us to see the family not only as a group of biologically related people but as a system and as a series of places that individuals entered and exited through ejection, immigration, ambition and death. Finally, the term allows us to look at and to try to make sense of the Scharfs' financial situation and their anxious and ultimately failed attempts to understand themselves as an economic unit. If the previous chapter read George Jr's daily accounting for signs of romance, the third section of this chapter looks at the many different kinds of accounts kept by the mother, the father, the son and the aunt to identify and complicate the story of *Bildung* with a less progressivist narrative of financial and emotional entanglement. Both narratives are present in the story we tell of a single year, 1856–7, that looks, at least retrospectively, like a turning point in George Jr's relationship with his family and career.

The chapter's final section turns briefly to a figure marginal to, but in some sense definitional of, the Scharf household: George Jr's less fortunate younger brother, Henry. An elusive figure in the archive, Henry appears only fleetingly in his family members' diaries, having emigrated to America for unstated reasons and, thirty years later, having disappeared from the face of the earth. Taking

a cue from our informal approach to the Scharfs' joint accounting as a household system, we gathered what facts we could about
Henry's life and tried subjecting the Scharfs to a more technical family-systems-theory analysis, which led us to a story in which
Henry's fate, though still mysterious, was not at all surprising.[2] For
all its seeming determinism, Family Systems Theory turns out to
be useful to us as metabiographers, in that it shifts the focus from
the individual subject to his position in a series of family relationships. Depending as it does on such fragmentary material, Henry's
story is even more provisional in our text than George's. Here we
recognise that we sometimes resort to what Robyn has called disnarration, telling a story of what might have happened in the absence
of facts about what did.[3] Writing Henry's life story felt, at first, like
a detour from writing the life of George Jr, but the more we ana-
lysed Henry's place in the family system, the more clearly we could
account for his older brother's attitude towards him as well as for
George Jr's evident difficulties with differentiation.

Left behind: George Sr

To begin with George Scharf Sr is to begin with some of the earliest moments in the records of the family and with what we came
to understand as a primal story repeated often in the diaries of
both father and son. Appropriately enough in a book that attends
so closely to eating, this is a story about cakes (although not, alas,
about consuming them). On 6 January 1816 George Scharf Sr
arrived in London from Bavaria. This is a date that he remembers
and records every year in his diaries. George Jr begins to note this
anniversary in his own diaries only after the death of both his father
and his mother, at which point it takes on added meaning as the
date of his mother's funeral. In telling the encapsulated story of
his father's first day in London, George Jr adds a detail he must
have learned from his father: that, as a new immigrant to London,
George Sr found himself staring at crowds looking at 'white cakes'
in a shop window in Piccadilly (see, for example, D 6 January 1869).
These would have been Twelfth-cakes, elaborately decorated con-
fections offered by pastry shops for Twelfth Night celebrations.

The cakes are inserted into a complex set of temporalities. The
first time George Jr mentions the cake story is on 6 January 1869, the
actual day of his mother's funeral. The entry begins with the present day, without verbs and thus without tenses 'Funeral at 9 o'clock

a.m. in Brompton Cemetery'. The anniversary idiom allows him to move back a year to happier times: the entry recalls 'this night last year', when he 'was dancing at the servant's ball at Blenheim [. . .] open[ing] the Ball with Lady Cordelia', and moves further back, past the beginnings of his own life, to '[t]his day in 1816' when 'my father arrived in London at Whitehorse Piccadilly & was surprised at the crowds of people looking at white cake in the shop windows'. Finally, the entry returns to the moment of writing: 'The present day I have seen the last of my dearest mother' (D 6 January 1869).

George Jr's summary of the day of his mother's funeral brings to life a series of themes associated with his father. As an immigrant, George Sr was always, perhaps, on the outside looking in. Fixed into the position of outsider, George Sr joins the ranks of Victorian street urchins, pressing their collective noses against what would become, with the passage of years, increasingly lavish displays in increasingly large plate-glass windows. But George Scharf Sr's story is a little different. He is, characteristically, at least in his son's doubly retrospective account, not merely looking at the cakes – the luxurious sign of the good English life – but at the people looking at them. It was this urban eye that would enable George Sr's most enduring sketches and paintings of Regency London streets and street life.[4] Also present in the primal cake scene are issues of origin in another sense: the anniversary repetitions of the story are also signs of repetition across generations; the father must have told this story – perhaps more than once – to his son.

For George Jr, what becomes the cake vignette, repeated almost verbatim from year to year, is also a way of integrating Jack Pattisson into the family system via the family story: almost every annual mention in the son's diary notes Jack's presence at Mrs Scharf's funeral. It is tempting to see the coincidence of the mother's funeral with the long-dead father's arrival in London as staging and resolving a family drama in which estranged parents resolve their differences after death, leaving Jack and George Jr to mourn as children of the Scharfs' strange marriage.

One of the appearances of the cake vignette in George Jr's diary occurs when he was fifty-seven years old, eighteen years after Mrs Scharf's death; at this point it has taken on a wider history and another temporality:

This day in 1869 my Mother was buried in Brompton cemetery. J.L.P. and I alone attended.

This day in 1816 my Father first arrived in London from Dover. Twelfth cakes then were all the rage. (D 6 January 1887)

By noting the distance between the moment of (re)telling the story and its origin ('Twelfth cakes then were all the rage'), this version of the cake story integrates it into history as it is measured by the passage of generations. Scharf's comment from the late 1880s looks back in a historicising idiom on London trends from before he was born, perhaps allowing the moment of seeing and desiring cake and all it represented for his father to recede into the distance. A developmental narrative – perhaps a therapeutic one – might frame this as a healthy step, consigning to the past something that George Jr had for many years apparently felt doomed to repeat.

The cake vignette in all its iterations suggests both distancing and identification. Frequently the only mention of George Sr in an entire year of diary entries after the father's death, it brings the father into the picture in a way that is controlled by the passage of time and all but obscured by the second, traumatic anniversary event of the death of the mother. But why this need for distance and for the elaborate mechanisms of recording and repetition, marking and unsaying? A traditional psychoanalytic account would, of course, suggest that these structures are universal and inevitable. Our own interest lies in the specifics of the story of this father and this son and how they accede to and refuse the master-narrative of differentiation.

Until George Jr was in his late teens, George Sr might have looked as if he were in a plot of professional development of his own. As a Bavarian national who joined the British army on the continent in time to fight at Waterloo, George Sr's move to London seemed promising. During his first decade or so in England, Scharf obviously saw himself as a portrait painter; he exhibited multiple portraits at the Royal Academy and had others engraved. To support himself at this time, he drew on his skills as a lithographer, which he had honed in Munich under Joseph Huber. In August of 1820 he married Elizabeth Hicks, who co-owned with her sister Mary a grocery and cheese shop in St Martin's Lane. George Jr was born a rather disreputable four months after the wedding. The birth of George Jr, and later of his brother, Henry, meant that George Sr had to turn from portrait painting to more immediately financially rewarding jobs. His hard work and talents as a watercolourist and lithographer, as well as his eye for interesting scenes, kept him in steady work for several decades. In the 1830s Scharf also produced scientific drawings for the Royal College of Surgeons and the Royal Zoological Society; he drew fossils for Darwin and Owen and worked for other established scientists. As the father of two young boys, George Sr seems to have done at least moderately well financially. While he did fail to sell a single one of his paintings, he exhibited more than forty of them at the Royal Academy and other prestigious venues. While Peter Jackson suggests (sympathetically) that George Sr was 'hopeless at business', not always selling his sketches and watercolours, he certainly produced an impressive number of them; at this point, at any rate, there could be no question about his work ethic (*London*, p. 7).

Throughout the 1820s and 1830s George Sr enjoyed some professional success as a watercolourist and as a scientific illustrator. George Sr's topical prints and watercolours found some buyers, although he was disappointed in the public reaction to his massive watercolour depicting the Houses of Parliament after the fire of 1834. His most popularly successful drawings – Jackson calls them 'Scharf's bestseller' (*London*, p. 12) – depicted the newly imported giraffes at the London Zoo in 1836 (Fig. 3.1). Queen Victoria bought three copies, and the Queen of Bavaria bought some as well, paying much more handsomely for them than did the British monarch. The fifteen-year-old George Jr came along on the drawing expeditions to the Houses of Parliament and to London Zoo, making his own watercolours of the scenes.

Despite the brief shining moment of the two queens' patronage, 1836 seems to have marked a downturn in the family finances, although, as we shall see, the decline in fortune might not have been as steep as Jackson believes. This was the year that George Sr pulled Henry out of the University College School he had chosen for both boys and arranged for him to study anatomical drawing at the College of Surgeons. This was also the year that the elder Scharf resigned from the New Water Colour Society because he was unable to pay his dues. In 1837 George Sr quarrelled with Darwin, who accused him (unfairly, according to Jackson) of overcharging for his drawings. Another employer accused him of spending too much time on his work. It is in answer to this rebuke that we get George Sr's most definitive statement about his identity as an artist: 'Artists ought not to be treated or spoken to like a common mechanic or servant,' he told his employer (*London*, p. 14). Although these conflicts must have been difficult, the diary/account books for 1840

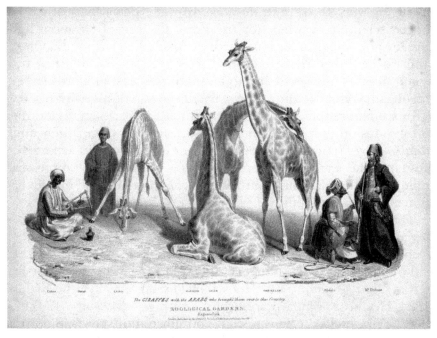

Fig. 3.1 Giraffes at the Regent's Park Zoo by
George Scharf Sr: his 'bestseller'.
©Trustees of the British Museum.

show George Sr to be still very busy (and still working for Darwin),
making more than £150 a year.[5]

Although we know very little about George Jr's childhood and early
youth, we do have a variety of sources for the relationship between
father and son for the long middle of George Jr's life, beginning
around 1852, when, at the age of thirty-two, he was clearly taking
up the role of main breadwinner. Before the major breakthrough
of his appointment as art secretary for the 1857 Manchester Art
Treasures Exhibition, George Jr held down a number of different
jobs based on his sketching skills, some of which required extensive travel. It made us tired to think of his comings and goings, his
consulting of train schedules and his writing to his parents with
stories of triumphs and penury and with requests for materials,
money or celebratory food for his many returns home. During the
1840s and the 1850s, George Jr patched together a living as best
he could from teaching, illustrating and lecturing. As we noted in
the introduction, the younger Scharf was intermittently employed,
for most of that period, as a drawing master. He gave lectures at

London clubs and societies as well as in cities and towns from Bath to Liverpool. He sketched and photographed English cathedrals in what appears to have been a long-term project with John Murray, who, much later, published a series of guides to cathedrals in the various regions of Great Britain, illustrated not by George Jr but by Orlando Jewitt. George Jr's illustrations did make their way into many published books during that period, including what would now be called a coffee-table book, *The Fine Arts: Their Nature and Relations*, by François Pierre Guillaume Guizot. In 1853 George Jr illustrated Chapman and Hall's edition of the *Divine Comedy*, translated by Frederick Pollack. In 1854 he arranged the Greek, Roman and Pompeian Courts at the Crystal Palace and wrote a guidebook to the exhibits. In the early 1850s he designed costumes and scenery for Charles Kean's revivals of Shakespeare's Greek and Roman plays at Covent Garden Theatre.

At least from 1852 on, when George Sr began keeping a new diary, the father was working as assistant to his more successful – or at least much busier – son. On 8 February 1853, for example, George Sr notes that he is working on illustrations for George Jr's lectures on Pompeii and Nineveh (GSS 8 February 1853). George Sr also, at least nominally, hosted dinners for some of George Jr's connections, including Murray. George Jr's table plan for a dinner he recorded in his diary on 23 May 1853 shows his father is at the head of the table, and himself at the foot. Despite the seating chart – always, as we have seen in Chapter 1, so central to George Jr's imagination of relationships – George Sr clearly saw his son as host of that party, noting the next day that 'George had a dinner party'.

By the 1850s George Sr was not in any sense the head of the household. George Sr's diaries make this very clear. On 31 December 1852, for example, he notes, 'George was so kind as to pay my yearly subscription to the Artists [sic] Amicable Fund [. . .] [H]e has also had another Great winter Coat made for me, as the one he gave me some months before was <u>stollen</u> [sic] from the Passage.' George Jr continues to supply clothes to his father. On 17 June 1854 George Sr writes in an identically grateful register, 'George was so kind as to have a new Frock Coat, a pair of Trowsers [sic] and Waist Coat made for me'. When he is not specifically noting that an item is a gift, it is unclear who pays for George Sr's clothing. George Sr will sometimes use the first-person singular when noting payment for an item, but it is unclear where he got the money in the first place.

More striking even than the economic dependence of father on son is an implied assumption in George Sr's diaries after the mid-1840s, as in those of Mrs Scharf and her sister, that George Jr is the most important person in the household. Readers of George Sr's diaries can follow the arc of his son's career, as he notes each new enterprise with fatherly pride. An entry in May 1856 celebrates his son's connections with Charles Kean:

> Mr Charles Kean reproduced now the Play of the Winter's Tale, at the Princess Theatre, Oxford Street, to which George gave much assistance as to Costume and scenery, and it was very successfull [sic] and pleasant for him to be on the free list, and to be able to take a friend; I, his Mother and Aunt went several times. The Play had more than a hundred nights [sic] run, and deserved it, being splendidly got up, such as I never saw, although I saw some of the finest Plays ever acted, in Munich, Paris and London. (no day)

This testament to George Jr's talents is also, of course, revealing about how the son's success opens up new worlds for his father. The entry ends, however, with a gesture towards the expansiveness of George Sr's worlds and to a cosmopolitanism clearly not part of his son's experience.

George Sr's pride in his son also comes through in rarely recorded moments of failure, as when George Jr did not get the position of secretary of the National Gallery for which he applied. In an entry in his 1854 diary, George Sr writes:

> The situation of <u>Secretary</u> [...] having now become vacant, <u>George applied</u> for it, for which purpose he wrote to several of his distinguished acquaintances such as Lord Overstone, Bishop of Lincoln [...] etc. who gave him most <u>excellent Testimonials</u> yet he could not get it; Mr Wornum obtained it [...] Mr Wornum having had to do for the Collections of Pictures, such as Prince Albert's, whose interest was of course in his favour. (GSS no day, November; underlining in original)

Ironically, in view of how important titled connections would become in George Jr's future career – and perhaps even in view of the testimonials his father mentions, now bound and available at the British Library – George Sr evidently believed that Mr Wornum got the National Gallery job by knowing the right people. When, three years later, George Jr applied for and obtained the equivalent position at the National Portrait Gallery, George Sr records the moment in triumphal orthography. In bold, black ink and large letters, he underlines every word in the following announcement: '<u>George was now appointed Secretary to the National Portrait Gallery</u>' (GSS

18 March 1857). The recording of such landmarks can easily be attributed to fatherly pride in what was obviously a developing career. Pride, however, does not completely explain other entries about George Jr in his father's diary, some of them oddly disjoined from their dates, like George Sr's note on 2 October 1853, that 'the 20th last month George changed his young man servant' (GSS 10 February 1853).

If George Sr had by the 1850s adopted a deferential tone – even, or perhaps especially, in his diary – about his son, what was the attitude of the younger George towards his father? The letters George Jr writes home from his many professional trips in the 1850s, although addressed to his mother, mention his father quite often. While he might also have written letters to George Sr that were not preserved, the internal evidence of the letters to Mrs Scharf shows that she was the conduit for messages to her husband, even those about the Georges' joint business concerns. In a 1 January 1855 letter from Rempstone Hall, the home of Lady Sitwell, George Jr writes to his mother alluding to a party there. While later letters from the same place will dwell on the connections George Jr is making at Rempstone, this one focuses on two issues relating to George Sr: George Jr's promise to draw the Rempstone Christmas tree for his father and the necessity for George Sr to represent him in negotiations to stave off a family financial crisis. Because this letter to his mother takes up so many issues pertinent to George Jr's relation to his family, to his work and to his networks, it is worth quoting at length:

> Many, many happy new years to you. I have only a moment to write but should be sorry to miss sending good wishes on the 1st of January 1855. I mean to start for Gloucester some time on Monday [. . .] I shall stay there a day & a night, after that letters may be sent to the <u>White Lion Hotel</u> [. . .] <u>Bath</u>.
> I have written to Lloyd asking him for a £10 note. Get Father to go to Snow Hill on Monday afternoon & bring what he can. Tell him also to write me a line on Monday to Gloucester so that I may be at rest or gain time for some other operation. He may be out of town & there must be no delay in meeting a bill [. . .] I hope to make a sketch of the tree for Father but find so much occupation & engagements in the house that it can only be a very hasty one. It was a brilliant affair & the tree itself, 8 feet high, a handsome specimen & too good almost to sacrifice. It all went off so well, after so many fears as poor Lady Sitwell was mightily anxious about it. She had really set her heart upon it [. . .]
> Tell aunty to use her discretion with regard to Miss Martin's gift. I thought Pork would do her good & 'buck her up'

I shall of course have a little money on hand when I return home but it will be very little. I hardly know what could have been done without aunt's contribution. I hope all goes on well. Don't forget the slices of pine-apple that I bought in Oxford St last Saturday. Have some on Monday for lunch. (George to Elizabeth Scharf, ESC no date, late 1854 or early 1855)

The picture of the Christmas tree, mentioned again in the letters and in the diary, suggests a connection between father and son through drawing and through a shared German heritage that included Christmas trees. It is also, however, a marker of George Jr's new life, as he merrily spends the holidays among the upper classes, 'contributing' 'with pleasure', as he says in his year-end summary for 1854, to a 'brilliant Christmas tree' (D 31 December 1854). Those contributions, whatever they may have been, link aristocratic hostess and humble guest with an exchange system in which he is, notwithstanding his obviously dependent position, eager to define himself as a giver.

At the same time, the tree – or at least the picture of it – is a link to his family and, particularly, to his father. Whether or not George Jr is responding to a direct request from his father, the offer to draw the tree – even if it will only be sketched between other engagements that clearly take priority – is a gift quite different in kind from the coat, 'Trowsers' and other necessities that George Jr so 'kindly' provides to his father. The tree belongs not just to the aristocratic gift economy operating at Rempstone Hall but also to a family gift economy that surfaces, for example, in George Jr's assumption that his aunt will be giving her friend Miss Martin a Christmas gift, even during the difficult financial times the letter also references. George Jr also has apparently taken on the power of choosing that gift of tantalisingly capitalised 'Pork', despite his assertion that his aunt should use her own 'discretion'. George's control in addition extends to the afterlife of gifts: he goes so far as to instruct his family on when they should eat the pineapple he bought.

Shadows of another economy of necessity, and of other places in the exchange network, are, of course, also present in this characteristic letter in which George Jr delivers the command that his father go to Snow Hill to pay a bill. The burden, at least as George Jr expresses it, is ultimately on himself; if his father cannot come up with part of the money, George Jr will have to 'gain time for another operation'. While we will discuss later in more detail the family economy that emerges from the Scharfs' many anxious accountings, this letter and others like it show something about how the father and son negotiate their joint economic situation, with George Jr consistently assuming the mantles both of obligation and of authority.

Throughout the mid-1850s, George Jr wrote to his mother with similar instructions for his father to perform for him in financial matters. An atypically unpunctuated (and undated) letter from the 1850s makes this request of his mother:

> Please ask father to take this accompanying – if fine weather to wait & see if it is alright to Longmans & if they pay the account to give £4 to Salandri who is to call this evening if not he must have it Monday – his case is urgent & my ready money prospects desperate. (ESC no date)

The word 'desperate' with which this letter ends is unique in the Scharf record. While at the beginning of this confusing sentence George Jr seems to be thinking of the 'urgent' case of his occasional employee in print making, Salandri, in the end his own 'case' – expressed in the singular – trumps Salandri's. George Jr is sending his father on a errand to the son's own publishers; the unnamed sum of money in George Jr's account seems clearly to be his alone. George Jr's request by proxy frames his father simultaneously as an errand boy and as a representative.

The conditional 'if fine weather' implies, however, a concern for his father's health frequently echoed in the letters and diaries. In July of 1857 he writes that he is glad that his father is working for a Mr Yates but advises that his father 'must take care not to catch cold in this showery & uncertain weather' (ESC 23 July). George Jr's sense of his father's vulnerability to illness is, however, complicated. In the year-end summary for 1854, written from Rempstone Hall during the Christmas-tree visit, George Jr turns to family matters just after the clock strikes midnight. His aunt, he says, is well, but 'My Father less so. He stoops & seems to give way to the shaking violence of his coughs. He is more susceptible to cold & gives way to outward affections' (D 31 December 1854). Twice in these two summary sentences, George Jr uses the phrase 'give[s] way', as if there is some connection between his father's illness and a lack of will. As we understand it, George Jr is calling his father inappropriately demonstrative, incapable of a proper reserve. His father's body traffics in violence and messiness, something his son might have associated with his inability to succeed in other registers.

George Jr's sense of his father's failure might have contributed to what remains for us a mysterious rupture in the Scharf household. Something happened on or about 1856 that caused George Jr to take the initiative in removing his mother, his aunt and himself out of Torrington Square in Bloomsbury and into Eastcott Place in Camden Town, forming a new ménage that did not include George Sr. We believe that the move from Bloomsbury to Camden was meant to address the chronic shortage of cash that was exacerbated by the high rent in Bloomsbury, but for George Jr it appears also to have been a way of forcing his father to shift for himself. Wishing as always to think the best of the son, we assumed when we first began piecing this part of the story together that the father must somehow have deserved to be cut off in this way.

We looked to George Jr's archive for an explanation, but we found that the strangest thing about the break-up of the family is George Jr's silence about it. Not once does George Jr's diary for 1856 allude to reasons or plans for separating George Sr from the family. Preparations for the move to Camden are duly recorded in the diary of his Aunt Mary, who begins mentioning the hunt for a suitable residence as early as May of that year, writing that 'Mrs S. and I went *again* to Camden Town to look about a house' but found 'nothing likely to suit' (MH 20 May 1856; italics added). That same day, 'Mrs S. and I' went further west 'to Notting Hill, saw several houses very cheap but I think too small for our convenience of accommodation'. In the first week of June they were back to looking in Camden. Miss Hicks notes that she and her sister '[w]ent with George to Haverstock Hill to look at several houses' (MH 2 June 1856) and they saw 'a house that I think likely to suit at Roxbury Terrace Camden Town' (MH 7 June 1856). By the first of July the two ladies had not yet settled on a house, but a week later, 'George saw a house that he approved of' in Camden Town (MH 7 July 1856), and the next day 'Mrs S. and I went to look over the house at George's request' (MH 8 July 1856). On 12 July George made arrangements to take the house at 1 Eastcott Place in Camden Town at Michaelmas, the traditional season for moving households in England. They took possession on 1 September, and by the end of October, George Jr, his mother and his aunt had settled into their new home. George Jr wrote to his mother from Chichester, 'You & aunt must now feel thoroughly set up for the winter. I hope the smell of paint is quite gone off as the weather has been so clear & favourable for drying' (ESC 29 October 1856). Altogether, the ladies went out on at least six days between May and

July to look at potential homes. It is striking that both Miss Hicks's diary and George's letters address the situation as if it only included three people. But while all this house-hunting and actual relocation was going on, where was George Sr?

Throughout the spring and summer of 1856, George Sr's diaries appear serenely oblivious of the activities of his family and the changes these might portend. In May 1856, as we have already seen, he reported on George Jr's theatrical collaboration with Kean in his typically enthusiastic, proud-paternal mode. George Sr's entries for June simply record business-as-usual, including a loan of his 'views of Old London' to Mr Franks at the British Museum, 'to show at an Evening Party of his Friends, particularly a Mr Penny, who collects such subjects, yet seldom buys any' (GSS 12 June 1856), and a notation that 'Mrs S. and her Sister' went to a violin concert (GSS 20 June 1856). On 15 July, three days after George Jr signed the lease on the Eastcott Place house for himself and the two ladies, George Sr notes that he has paid his subscription to the Artists Fund, bought two pairs of shoes and attended the 'Exhibition of the Royal Academy, where there were very good pictures and sculptures', but still does not mention the domestic transition in progress. Aunt Mary's diaries for July – full of details about carpet cleaning and rug sewing, dusting and packing – say nothing about how the move will affect George Sr.

Finding no indication that George Sr knew his family planned to relocate to Camden without him, and faced with his son's total silence on the matter, we have (of course) read between the lines of the aunt's and father's diaries. We thought we could trace signs of the son's increasing irritability around his father during the summer of 1856. Both the aunt's and the father's diaries report that George Jr was tired and ill (GSS 6 August 1856 and GSS 11 August 1856). According to both their accounts, George Jr was suffering from haemorrhoids, being – as Aunt Mary puts it – 'very uneasy in his seat from riding so far' and – to quote his father – 'having irruption coming out on the skin' (MH 2 August 1856 and GSS 11 August 1856). George Jr appears to have taken this malady very seriously. A little less than a week after the end of his long trip, Aunt Mary alludes to an unusual flare-up of family tempers: 'Very sorry to hear from George that he was much displeased with his Father's conduct towards him on his return' (MH 16 August 1856). After ten days of George Jr's being at home and having trouble with his 'complaint' (which Aunt Mary describes on 30

August as 'serious and most painful'), his father's diary tells of their quarrel:

> George still continues unwell and is rather ill humoured with me, reproaching me with not showing him enough attention in regard to his illness, as [sic] also not attending to give him assistance in doing Diagrams for his Lectures, which hurts my feelings much, as I always take great interest in anything which concerns him, but unfortunately, he will not believe me. (GSS 26 August 1856)

As we have seen, the evidence of his previous diary entries certainly corroborates George Sr's protestation that he 'always takes great interest in anything which concerns' his son. What sort of attention George Jr was seeking in acknowledgement of his haemorrhoids is hard to imagine. His refusal to believe that his father cared about his condition does seem 'ill humoured', as George Sr says, because it is so disproportional to his father's alleged offence. Like George Sr, we found George Jr's anger perplexing.

Surely, we concluded, there was a subtext to George Jr's ire – one which our evidence suggests the father did not fully understand until later on. Four weeks had passed since George Jr had signed the lease on Eastcott Place. When his father was pleading his deep interest in George Jr's condition, the son knew the father was on his way out of the family home. While it hardly seems possible that the father was still oblivious to the impending move, he evidently did not yet know the specifics of what his son was planning for him. In a note squeezed into the margin of the diary entry for 26 August, George Sr provides – apparently at a later date – an explanation of what was going on when his son was so annoyed with him:

> George had now decided on taking a House on the Hampstead Road, No. 1 at Eastcott Place, Camden Town, and I took lodging in a first Floor front Room, at 37 Preston Street Camden Town, near him, Mrs S. and Miss Hicks, I going to sleep & dine with them; it is a very pleasant situation with a Garden; and is only a 3 penny ride in an Omnibus from Town, by way of Tottenham Court Road, and Hungerford Market; much time is however lost in going backwards & forwards.

From our privileged perspective as reconstructors of his son's life story, we felt the poignancy of George Sr's expectations for what the arrangement would entail. George Sr was to 'dine with them' regularly, as his entry for Christmas Day of 1856 suggests ('I had the pleasure of dining, as usual, with Mrs S. and Miss Hicks in Eastcott

Place'). But he certainly was not to sleep at the family home, and we can hardly help wondering whether he ever knew exactly why. He must have suffered from his exile, as he certainly did after his health began to fail in 1859, when on 16 May he commented in his diary that he was still 'lodging in Preston Street, where I feel much annoyed, being left alone in the house'. He was to continue alone in that first-floor front room until a few weeks before he died, four years after the family break-up.

Over the years we have wondered about what happened in the Scharf ménage. Reading with the grain of the narrative of differentiation, it was easy for us to see George Jr's illness and his anger over it as inevitable. In this reading, almost anything would have done as an excuse to expel the father from the house: the haemorrhoids become, then, the occasion, rather than the reason, for George to form his own household. It is also possible, of course, to read the decision in the more local idiom of family accounting, to join the family in nervous calculations.

Would keeping the family together have meant finding a larger house for rent? Would the rent on a larger home have been more expensive than renting a smaller one plus a separate, one-room lodging for the fourth person? Not, we reasoned, as long as the rent for the room was coming out of the pocket of someone other than the renter of the house – and it seems from George Sr's weekly notations about paying the rent for his room that he might have been using his Artist's Fund pension. It is also possible that the Scharfs had a legal reason – perhaps impending bankruptcy – to separate their finances, although there is no mention of this possibility in any of the diaries. We realise, of course, that despite (or perhaps because) of the many figures the Scharfs have left in the archive, we cannot say for certain what the financial implications of the move might have been.

The answer to the mystery might have lain with the third member of the classic triangle, Mrs Scharf. We considered the possibility that Mrs Scharf must have played some role in kicking her husband out. We know that before the passage of the Matrimonial Causes Act in 1857 – and after, for most people too poor or respectable to go through its protocols – couples had to be inventive in shaping their lives around unsuccessful marriages. If a middle-class woman was simply fed up with her husband, we reasoned, and if she could get her gainfully employed son to agree to support her and her beloved sister, then maybe she could leave her marriage in this way.[6] But there is no sign of acrimony between Mr and Mrs Scharf in any of the diaries. Indeed, George Sr has only nice things to say about his spouse, as in his comment on 29 January 1859, that 'Mrs S. and her sister [were] behaving very kind during that time I almost lost my appetite and had great pain in my inside from that time after'. Perhaps his finding this behaviour notable enough to record in his diary implies that George Sr was not accustomed to receiving kindness at his wife's hands. Mrs Scharf's diary certainly does not speak warmly of the man she calls 'Mr Scharf' – but then again, her diaries say very little about anyone other than her son and are not records of feeling. We have no way of knowing whether her first use of the term 'husband' in the phrase 'My dear husband' on the day of his death is conventional or evidence of real affection (ES 11 November 60). Maybe Mrs Scharf was indifferent to her husband, but we have no evidence that she actively disliked him.

Sometimes, of course, a haemorrhoid is really a haemorrhoid, but the place of George Jr's illness in the affective economy of the Scharf family is of interest, especially given that George Jr seems to have attributed it to the kind of professional travel that defined him against his father and redefined him as head of the family. Also interesting (to us at least) is how George Jr, and perhaps his mother as well, used the home and the household to express their desires as, of course, George was to do later in the case of Jack.

George Sr was to return to the bosom of his family in his last illness four years after the family break-up, dying in 1860 in the top-floor apartment George Jr had just moved the ladies into at the National Portrait Gallery. This is chronologically the first of three major deaths recorded in the diary, and the first we visit in our story of *Bildung*. In September of 1860, two months before George Sr's death on 11 November, George Jr wrote to his mother from Lord Stanhope's house in Chevening; the letter contains the warmest expression of concern for his father we have been able to find, although it is tellingly sandwiched between items of news about the Stanhope family and comes only after a mention of the ill health of his hostess.

> Lord & Lady Stanhope press me to stay till Wednesday morning [. . .]
> Lady S still suffers much pain from her arm [. . .] I hope you feed father well with warm & nourishing things & above all keep up a good fire for him [. . .]
> We had a large party at dinner today. It was Lady Stanhope's birthday & her eldest son Lord Mahon came down from London quite unex-

pectedly. The harvest seems to be getting in very favourably. (ESC 10 September 1860)

In the letter, written on Chevening stationery, George Jr makes no apology for his absence from his father's sickbed; perhaps a feature of the Scharf family narrative – and the Scharf family economy – was an understanding that George Jr's visits to great houses were necessary sacrifices for the sake of the Scharf household. This letter from Chevening is written at a relatively early moment in the relationship with Lord Stanhope that we examine more closely in Chapter 4. The friendship with Stanhope – so crucial to George Jr in so many ways – might still have been quite fragile. Even so, George Jr's proprietary way of speaking about the state of affairs at the Stanhopes ('We had a large party at dinner today'; 'the harvest seems to be getting in very favourably') suggests that he feels himself to be in his proper place in the rarified air of Chevening.

George Jr is again absent, this time at Lord Overstone's, for the actual death of his father. The diary entry describing the death is very short: 'Father died quite calmly at 10 minutes past 9 a.m. during my absence at Overstone' (D 11 November 1860). Later in this book we will explore George Jr's very emotional descriptions of his mother's death and the death of Lord Stanhope, both of which are explicit about the importance of being present at a deathbed or a funeral. If George Jr himself couldn't be there, the death notice of George Sr in *The Times* – almost pathetically short compared to George Jr's obituary many years later – does the work of bringing father and son together at the end by noting that George Sr died 'at his son's residence' ('Deaths', 14 November 1860).

It has always been difficult for us not to read George Jr's absence at his father's deathbed symptomatically; why was he not, to put it crudely, in at the death? Was it simply a matter of timing? Did he not know soon enough that his father was actively dying? When we think of the journeys Victorian sons undertake in novels and in history to attend their father's deathbeds, we wonder why George Jr could not have caught the train from Overstone, just outside of Northampton, sixty miles from London. We are not judgemental about successful arrivals; we can make allowances for the idiosyncrasies of postal, railway and telegraph systems, for the whole creaky but actually quite efficient Victorian transportation and communication network that allowed George Jr to write letters to his mother on a given morning ordering ducks for dinner that night. But as far as we know, George Jr did not try to make it – there are no signs of railway fares or frustration, nothing in the financial or affective accounting that would explain his absence.

Our sense that George Jr should have been with his dying father is compounded by textual absences in the diary and (as far as we know) the correspondence. If we cannot have George Jr at the deathbed, we could, perhaps, have words about the death. No doubt this desire, and our faith in the substitution of text for body, has something to do with our allegiance to novels with their extended death scenes or, as Garrett Stewart would put it, 'death sentences'.[7] It is not only Victorian *novels*, however, that value the textual and visual representation of death. Patricia Jalland has documented the propensity among the Victorian middle and upper classes to document details of death and dying in letters, diaries and 'deathbed memorials' against which subsequent generations recoiled (pp. 10–11). Our experience with the Victorian culture of death suggests that there was something missing (besides George Jr) during the last days of the elder George Scharf. It is difficult not to read the absence of body and words as a sign of anger or resentment.

In (re)producing an Oedipal narrative that distinguishes father and son, George Scharf from George Scharf, we are no doubt guilty of a certain imaginative laziness, one compounded by what we might call a death-forward or thanatocentric reading of George Jr's family life. This is partly because, again, we happened to read the diaries first, and our search for narrative made us alert – especially in the absence of a marriage plot – to death as a vehicle for narrative movement and an occasion for textual eruptions of interiority. These two elements are present, as we shall see, in the description of the deaths of Mrs Scharf and of Stanhope; they are missing in the non-story of George Sr's death and dying.

The letters engage not with a single affect but with many, often in the same sentence. George Jr can, in one letter, note that he is making an emotionally meaningful drawing for his father and also that his holidays among the aristocracy leave him little time for family. He can order his father to take financial action and take final responsibility himself for the family finances. He can complain about having no money and prescribe a gift for a family friend. He can boast about the splendours of Christmas at great houses and remember a piece of 'pine-apple' at home that he wants his family to eat for lunch on a particular day. In this case the letters tell us much more than the diary; they can speak more complexly to the contradictions and recursiveness of *Bildung*.

Another problem with thanatic readings is that they tend to end – not surprisingly – with death. George Jr's diary entries about his father become more complex after the latter's death. Although George Sr's death, in contrast to that of Mrs Scharf, does not always appear in the annual entries that are part of the diaries' anniversary structure, entries after George Sr's death begin to include, for the first time, a mention of the father as artist. In the year-end summary for 1862, two years after his father's demise, George Jr introduces his father's drawings into his annual accounting:

> The sale of my Father's drawings to the British Museum has been an important source of revenue to us, & the distribution of his lithographs among friends and public Institutions may become an important means of perpetuating and disseminating his name.

Although George Jr begins with the ever-important financial considerations, he ends by moving out beyond the economic and, crucially, to the issue of his father's name and reputation. Until this moment the father's artistic efforts are represented in the son's diary merely as an aid to George Jr's art, George Jr's career: reading through them one would have thought of George Sr as a somewhat unreliable assistant to his son. By shedding the infantilising suffix, the man formerly known as George Jr allows his name to take on a life of its own, but the name of the father seems slowly to become something worth passing on.

Incorporating the elderlies: mother and aunt

We have mentioned in Chapter 2 that George Jr loved his mother. This is simultaneously a diagnostic cliché and an understatement. As a diagnosis it fits perfectly with homophobic and some homophilic narratives of sexual development. In George Jr's diaries this feeling of love for his mother is a daily reality that makes its way into all of the temporalities and technologies of representation we have discussed so far: his accounting, his recording of anniversaries and his rare textual moments of emotional display.

Many entries in Scharf's diaries from the late 1850s to 1869, the year his mother died, include in their accounting section some mention of gifts for his aunt and mother. These often took the form of luxuries: cream or collars, wine or cakes. For the most part, the gifts stay, as it were, in the accounts and do not stray to the narrative entries. Mrs Scharf's diaries add some narrative detail. On 1 January 1859, 'George came and took tea with us he brought us both a pair of warm house shoes for our comfort; likewise some cakes. He gave me a sovereign for the coals and his aunt one for the papers'. Later that week she records that he sent '3 bottles of Elder Wine and Some Brandy' (ESD 4 January) as well as 'a truffle cake a jelly and a cream' (ESD 6 January). When George joined his mother and aunt for tea, he would bring some food items along. On 11 January 1859 it was 'biscuits sardines & lemons'.

George Jr's mother – and his aunt while she was still alive – form part of the backbone of his year-end summaries and birthday entries; comments about the health of the 'Elderlies', as he began to call them – irresistibly reminding us of Dickens's Mr Wemmick and his 'Aged P' in *Great Expectations* – are often incorporated into entries or even sentences about professional landmarks. The year-end summary from 1854, written from Rempstone Hall and quoted above, proceeds from a listing of his 'successes, hopes [. . .] friends made' to a discussion of Lady Sitwell's friendship. He continues in a less exalted vein about a more homely social occasion:

> I must also record thankfully my Mother's improvement in health. On Christmas day when Dr Sattler dined with us she was [unreadable] well and had the day before enjoyed in company with Miss Martin a Roast Pig and champagne. [The very pork, no doubt, that George Jr told Aunt Mary to give Miss Martin for Christmas!] The year before she dined alone in her room being kept upstairs in her room by an attack of bronchitis.

As will be typical in the later summaries, George Jr uses New Year's Eve to look back not only on the preceding year but to the last holiday season. When his mother is mentioned in the summary, it is most often with attention to her health and to what is to George Jr its most legible sign – her appetite for holiday foods.[8]

The oscillation in his field of attention between professional 'successes' and 'hopes' and the physical well-being of his family continues. The summary for 1856 moves from the Manchester Exhibition, a crucial professional coup that we will discuss in more detail below and in Chapter 4, to an unpunctuated expression of thankfulness about his 'Mother and Aunt', who are 'as well as ever'. Annual references to the Elderlies' health continue until the death of his mother in 1869: they are 'wonderfully recovered' in his entry for the final day of 1858, 'well and happy' in his year-end summary for

1859 (D 1 January 1860). In 1864 George Jr's 'first thought' in summarising the year is the 'loss of my dearest Old Aunty'.

From the beginning of the diaries in 1858 to the death of Mrs Scharf in 1869, the well-being of the mother and aunt is integrated almost seamlessly into George Jr's narrative of professional progress. In a passage we have previously quoted from December 1863 he moves easily and within the same sentence from the personal and familial to the professional: 'I have great reason to be thankful for the continued good health of my Mother & Aunt & for the favour and friendly interest of Lord & Lady Stanhope & the Duke & Duchess of Marlborough.' In this entry, his closest relatives' 'good health' is grammatically and emotionally parallel to 'the favour and friendly interest' of his titled friends. Both are things for which to be thankful; both occupy a temporality that is at once about continuity and progress (D 30 December 1863). Except, of course, for their deaths, mother and aunt only rarely appear in the diaries' idiom of the milestone or landmark. Two deviations from this pattern occur in the year-end summary for 1860, which is, unusually, formatted as a list, with each item on a separate line. Under the heading of 'Leading events of 1860', Scharf lists, first, 'My Father's Illness and death' and, then, two items later, 'Removal of the Elderlies from Eastcott Place to Gt George Street through the kindness of Lord Stanhope' (no date; added to diary for 1860). While, as we will discuss later in this section, the move of Mrs Scharf and her sister to lodgings at the National Portrait Gallery – which actually happened before George Sr's death in November of the year – was an important moment in the story of George Jr's professional development, the structure of the list is unusual in producing familial life as recordable event. Even less predictable is George Jr's inclusion, lower down on the list of 'leading events', of 'Photographic Portraits of My Mother & Aunt'.

A year before Mrs Scharf and Miss Hicks moved into the attic at Great George Street, the National Portrait Gallery first opened its doors to visitors without special invitations. By the time the Elderlies had settled in, the NPG had fully taken on the partly public, partly private status it would maintain until 1869, when the gallery moved to less expensive, more capacious quarters among the other Victorian museums on Exhibition Road in South Kensington and when George Jr had to find somewhere else to live. For the decade of the 1860s, 29 Great George Street was both home and workplace for George Jr. In contrast to the grand edifice that houses

Fig. 3.2 GS sketch of paintings crowded onto the walls at
the NPG in Great George Street, September 1869.
©Trustees of the British Museum.

the National Portrait Gallery in Trafalgar Square today, this was a modest building – a large but by no means imposing Georgian house in a simple, neoclassical style with a pediment and very regularly spaced windows, two of them on the ground floor and three on each of the floors above. The attic space where the Elderlies lived was located behind the pediment. The paintings were crowded into the ground level and next floor, taking up all available space on the walls and along the staircase (Fig. 3.2). Because it had been built as a home and not a museum, the gallery space at Great George Street was poorly lit for the viewing of paintings, and it turned out in the end not to be an ideal space for its public purpose. It wasn't, at least on the surface, ideal for the Scharfs' private purposes either, as it contained no bathing facilities. George Jr complained to the gallery's trustees that he 'had to go to the public baths every six weeks until he bought a hip bath from a servant' (Hulme et al., p. 27).

Great George Street, then, did not have all the comforts a home back in Bloomsbury, for example, would have had in the 1860s, but it made George Jr comfortable in many ways. Living above the gallery meant he had no commute to work, giving him plenty of time to walk up to Camden and back for visits to his mother and aunt before they came to live with him. It must also have felt similar to living above a storefront, the way George Jr's mother, née Elizabeth Hicks, must have done as a girl growing up in a grocer's family in St Martin's Lane. It was economical to have the ladies move in there. The space above the gallery, including the attic, appears to have been given to George rent-free. George Jr's mother and aunt maintained their own separate housekeeping upstairs, though George Jr continued bringing them presents of little luxuries such as lemons and lace. The vertical arrangement of space allowed for the proximity of the women in his life and for a certain amount of privacy. It seems from the seating charts of dinners George Jr gave at the NPG that women were never present. It seems that this home could function as a bachelor lodging, despite the presence of the two old women upstairs.

While histories of the period suggest an increasing division in middle- and upper-middle-class households between home and work, the Scharf family offers a striking counter-example. Once the mother and aunt moved in, the building in Great George Street – with the public rooms on the ground floor and first floor, George Jr on the middle floor and the Elderlies in the attic – could serve as a model for the integration of the public and the private, the

145

professional and the personal. That middle floor was where George Jr slept, wrote and held his dinner parties. This was a bachelor's flat, with nothing of the makeshift arrangements that category might invoke, as we see from George Jr's beautiful set of sketches showing all the contents of his bedroom, library and study on the floor he occupied alone as well as two views from opposite ends of the upstairs parlour he shared with the Elderlies (see Figs 2.6, 3.2 and 3.3). Peter Jackson, who edited a collection of Scharf's sketches, remarks that George Jr made them after learning he would soon have to leave this home. 'It must have been a considerable wrench,' Jackson observes. 'The meticulous care he took in depicting every detail shows how devoted he was to these comfortable, cluttered apartments' (see Jackson, *Drawings of Westminster*, p. 38). Looking at the way George Jr reproduced every curlicue on each piece of furniture, drew in all the bindings on all the books, and even noted 'the reflection of books in [the] mahogany' of a desk in the library (Jackson, *Drawings of Westminster*, p. 41), we heartily agree with Jackson's impression. The drawings are a testament to the space and to the nine happy years George lived there. Even more, though, we see the drawings as a memorial of the relationships that made those years so happy. Two drawings of the library show Jack Pattisson studiously making notes on two separate sets of books and papers, doing the public work of the NPG here and looking very much at home (see Fig. 2.6). There are two drawings of the upstairs sitting-room, as well, one of them dated 27 August 1869, within the two-month period when all but one of the other sketches were made. The second picture of the sitting-room shows a lady seated at a table reading papers, her face turned away from the artist (Fig. 3.3). Along with the many other labels George Jr has inserted into this – as into the other sketches ('plain pale stone colour', 'floor cloth', 'carpet', 'hearth rug', 'crumb cloth', 'brown mahogany' etc.) – he has written beneath this lady, 'my Mother'. This sketch is dated September 1868, a year before the other drawings of the apartment were made and six months before Mrs Scharf's death.

Before moving George Jr out of Great George Street and removing his mother from the scene, though, we want to dwell for a few more moments on the pleasures of George Jr's life above the NPG. The loss of Aunt Mary, ten years older than her sister, was a painful blow in 1864, but the diaries for the five years between her death and that of George Jr's mother represent a kind of domestic bliss that suggests a complicated relationship with the plot of differen-

Fig. 3.3 GS sketch of his mother's sitting-room at
the NPG in Great George Street, September 1868.
©Trustees of the British Museum.

tiation. At this point in his life, George's household was free – and
we have to put it this way – of his father and his brother, although
it included or at least was open to a specially chosen quasi-brother,
Jack, who, according to the idiom of family systems, was comfortably triangulated with George Jr and his mother. Typically Jack
was there in the evenings, whether George Jr was present or away
on one of his portrait-sketching or lecturing trips. 'Faithful Jack'
(as George Jr calls him in the diary's narrative of his mother's
funeral) became very attached to Mrs Scharf, who seems to have
been a pleasant, jolly and intelligent woman. As far as we can tell
from the evidence of the archive, George Jr was always completely
in harmony with his mother. Whether Jack was there of an evening
or not, Mrs Scharf would sing her 'old songs', including one she
called 'the Jack song', 'Gaffer Grist' (D 13 December 1868). She
liked to play card games and cribbage, and she delighted in doing
word scrambles, either deciphering words George Jr or Jack set
out for her or, more rarely, giving them scrambles to work out for
themselves. During her last illness, just a few days before she would

become too weak to leave her bed again, George Jr noted that, on a rare appearance at a meal, 'when Mother was sitting at dinner with me she took out her spectacles, put them on, and wrote chump as a word that reads the same backwards or upside down' (D 26 December 1868).[9] We do not know what words she used to describe to herself or others her son's relationship with Jack, but he was present and part of home life – if not (yet) the household – during the last years of her (domestic) life.

Turning back to George Jr's diaries, we can see that Mrs Scharf's death represents not only a sharp discontinuity in her son's living arrangements but also a move into an entirely different register of writing. The first sign of writerly disturbance is the break, in George Jr's recording of her final illness, with anniversary convention. On 16 December 1868, George Jr goes against his tradition of birthday review and retrospection to produce a long narrative entry about his mother's current state:

> My 48th Birthday, a far less cheerful one than last year. As the clock struck 12 I was in great anxiety about Mother's health. She had gone to bed so utterly exhausted. I was reading the lives of the Princes of Orange. After that I collated the text of Rossini's History of Painting, Gibson's copy, which I had just bought from Rinnell. Went to bed at 2.30. Very restless night. In the morning found Mother better. She had turtle soup for lunch with me and I showed her various miniatures by Father & two of herself. Touched upon my enlarged copy of the photograph of Miss Bayley with her dog Cally. Reginald Worsley called from his brother Dick (kept at home by a bad knee) to enquire after Mother. Jack Pattisson came to an early dinner with us. Mother was very cheerful. I began a sketch of her before dinner. She was very chatty. After dinner she lost spirit & was much inclined to sleep. Jack & I smoked a quiet cigar in the library. We had music after tea, & she attempted to sing two songs 'Gaffer Grist' & 'Go George I can't endure you' but desisted for want of breath. She spelt two words with letters which Jack set for her. She however sat down at the piano & was amused at my singing 'The Old Bean', 'The Cork Leg', 'Taking Tea in the Arbour', 'Nothings', and 'The One Horse Shay'. She went to bed very tired. Attending to her prevented me from writing letters to friends as usual. I could scarcely do more than open my papers for the Knowsley catalogue.

Framed, as is the year-end summary from 1862 referencing Jack, by the striking of a clock at midnight, the entry betrays temporal anxiety and confusion. His mother's illness interrupts his work and the usual arrangements of the day, as it interrupts the strategies by which he represents that illness. The entry seems to describe two days in which his mother goes to bed 'exhausted' or 'tired'; they run into each other in a way that mimics, with moving intensity, the disturbances in time that characterise periods of illness and caretaking. It is unclear when George Jr wrote various parts of the entry: on his birthday, on the following day, or both. Three lines on that same page seem to be inserted later. 'Very restless night' and 'Jack and I smoked a quiet cigar' are, from the look of the ink and the handwriting, clearly added later than the body of the entry but, perhaps, not at the same time as each other. 'She sang only once more after that on the 20th' must be a post-mortem entry, in some ways an anniversary marker and in some ways an anti-anniversary one recording the fact of something that will never happen again.

Running throughout the entry is a feeling of running out of time: on the most literal level, this would be the time to do the many different kinds of work George Jr undertook in a given day. 'Attending to' Mrs Scharf prevents him from his 'usual' activities – professional, personal and in between. Of course, we as archival readers knew that Mrs Scharf was herself running out of time; George Jr must have sensed or at least feared this as well, despite his clinging to the comforting signs of (daily) life apparent in his mother's singing and playing her favourite word game. The temporal dislocation of the entry, however, strikes at the heart of dailiness, contributing to the dominant tone of 'anxiety' – and this time, that's George Jr's word, not ours – of the entry.

Not many of George Jr's diary entries can be said to have a dominant tone – or a dominant feeling. The entries around his mother's death, however, take us into a mood of deep and sustained sadness that works its way into the structure of the diaries for the rest of George Jr's life. The actual descriptions of Mrs Scharf's final illness read very much like the examples from Jalland with their insistence on the detail of the process of dying. On 1 January 1869 he opens with an entry that is both summary and narrative: 'This year begins most sadly with my dearest Mother's extreme illness, a steadily increasing decay of nature.' The entry for 2 January contains the kind of domestic realist detail we associate with the Victorian novel:

> Took lunch, a plain mutton chop, with Mother in her bedroom, she sitting before me at the little round table. I helped to feed her & held the glass of brandy & water to her lips & guided her trembling hands, like feeding a child. Very painful. It was the <u>last time</u>. Afterwards when Jack & I came up before 5 o'clock, Mrs. Parlett said she was much changed & we had best not go into the room.

The mutton chop, the little round table, the glass of brandy and water all bring a bodily materiality to the scene, sharpening the effect of the rare affective adjective 'painful'. The underlined 'It was the <u>last time</u>' tells us that this entry was written later, the scene called up, with all its resonant details, from memory. The last few lines of the paragraph suggest that George Jr (and the faithful Jack) were to be excluded from the final scene of death, from the 'change' that Mrs Partlett assumed George could not bear to witness.

For whatever reason, George Jr does witness – and bear witness in the diary to – that change the next day. In an entry bearing a black cross at the top, George details the transformation of his mother's body:

> Found Mother very low indeed & breathing with labour & much moaning, after a sleepless night. Mr. Lidiard [a doctor] called [. . .] & said that she was much worse than when Mr. Collambull [the family doctor] had seen her. I went in & sat with her. The right hand, as she laid on that arm, was much swollen & quite cold. She would not have her head raised from the pillow. Her last looks with straining eyes [. . .] I never can forget.

The mother, who had turned into a child in the feeding scene of the earlier entry, is now turning into a body, her arm turning cold before she does. The passage embodies the final anxious inventory of the son: breath, arm, head and, finally, the eyes that still strain, as we assume, to see him. George Jr leaves the room, but only to go to his library downstairs:

> I went down into my library where Jack was sitting & looked at my old Journals of 1860, for facts & dates of my Father & Aunt's death & then, preparatory to dinner being announced, began to touch upon my last sketch of my Mother. At that time, 2 o'clock, she died, & Mrs Parlett came into the room & said 'She's Mrs Scharf is gone, Sir!' We were much shocked & at once went up into the room and found her very blue in the position as I had left her. She went off sleeping.

George Jr leaves to join Jack and to do two kinds of very George-like work: the insertion of his mother's death into a chronology of family deaths and the touching 'touching up' of a last sketch. Two more typical attempts to manage the pain of the moment cannot be imagined: George Jr's sense of order, his anniversary impulse, comes to the fore along with his almost reflexive need to draw. We avoid saying sketching here, because George Jr is emphasising the act of touching-up, of making the portrait both correct and final.

Mrs Scharf's dying is simultaneous with George Jr's rituals of recording; Jack and George Jr are nonetheless 'shocked', a word that will resonate later in George Jr's life, as we have discussed in Chapter 2, in his other central emotional relationship. George Jr's diary, which does not often traffic in the simultaneous, captures in moving prose the sense of an inevitable process unfolding upstairs as George Jr goes about the pre-emptive work of mourning downstairs. As with the final sketch, this entry is itself subject to revision: at some point George Jr goes back to replace the 'She's' with the more formal and more final 'Mrs Scharf'.

George Jr's restless movements within the family space place the son with respect to his mother's death very differently from his father's. Excluded from his mother's room by her attendant, he returns as a witness and, perhaps, as a comforter. Even in his absence, he does not, of course, stray very far. One cannot imagine George Jr being called away here – not to Overstone, not to Blenheim, not even to Chevening. His place is with his mother and within the complicated spatial configuration that is his domain in Great George Street.

The keynote of what we have been calling *Bildung* is, of course, the breaking away or, more benignly, the moving away from the family. We have seen the distance George Jr travelled from his father and the orthographic changes that follow as he begins – albeit inconsistently – to exclude the 'Jr' from his signature. Ironically perhaps, in this patriarchal and patrimonial story, the greater change to his signature follows his mother's death. On 4 January, the day after his mother's death, George Jr follows his note that he has given away all his coloured clothing and had ordered a set of 'new things as mourning' with the following statement: 'Today I make a change in my mode of signature, three marks instead of two.' Below this statement he writes his name twice, once with his old signature and the second time with his new one, identical except for a curved line under it, crossed and dotted in the middle. The line looks like the mark that often accompanied 'finis' at a book's ending. The 'three marks' are evidently the two names, 'George' and 'Scharf', plus the new flourish underlining them. Three marks: the son and his two now-absent parents? The flourish: an arrogation of the new self-importance that comes to the oldest living member of a family? Or is the line really 'finis', a reminder of the end of his mother's life to be revisited with every subsequent writing of his signature? The gesture seems so poignant, but it represents another of those diary moments that baffle the insight they appear to invite.

If his mother's death inspired a new way of writing his name, it also incited a new mode of writing in his diary, if only for a day. The rhetoric of George Jr's entry for the day of his mother's funeral, 6 January 1869, rings out in a resonant anaphora, a repetition of parallel clauses that suggest the tolling of the bell in Brompton Cemetery where she was laid:

> This night last year I was dancing at the servant's Ball at Blenheim. I opened the Ball with Lady Cornelia.
> This day in 1816 my Father arrived in London at Whitehorse Piccadilly & was surprised at the crowds of people looking at white cakes in the shop windows.
> This present day I have seen the last of my dearest mother.

This entry he signed with his painterly 'GS', the stylised initials he always used to identify his drawings and sketches, his art. The layering of the three events does go further than Scharf's prose usually does towards something like an artful representation of consciousness.

And it is a consciousness – and perhaps a subjectivity – that is profoundly shaped by the fact of the mother's death. We can see the new signature as a final attempt to incorporate the mother: if the living woman could be incorporated through the careful arrangement of living spaces, the dead mother could only remain present on the page and on the canvas in the contour of her son's name. We have mentioned the often homophobically inflected narrative (or rather, anti-narrative) that makes the gay man the perpetual son of a usually domineering mother. If we abandon the need for canonical stories of development, however, we can perhaps appreciate and find words for the relationship and the household in which George Jr seems to have felt most at peace. Jack's presence at the edges of that household is, of course, crucial, but the mother remains central. It was only when we were able – for a moment – to put the urgency of Jack aside that we realised that the entries leading up to Mrs Scharf's death contain one of the very few pieces of evidence we have found that George Jr touched or was touched by another person.

Horizontal narratives 1: family (accounting) systems

In a psychoanalytic narrative the death of Mrs Scharf provides both an end and a beginning. In a narrative of *Bildung* the death of the last generation cements the triumph (however painful) of the next. The family narrative can, of course, be told another way, less nuclear but in some ways more intimate, less intensely vertical in its emphasis and affect. To tell this other story we must go back, if not to the beginning, to the time before the deaths of the elder Scharfs and to relationships that unfold – generationally speaking – horizontally as well as vertically. That sense of the horizontal has a temporal dimension as well: this attempt to tell the story will feature not so much a diachronic narrative that unfolds over time, moving towards the death of the parents and the professional success of the son, but a synchronic narrative in which multiple family members are doing things and writing about them at the same time. This new narrative also moves from the highly emotional language of George Jr's 1869 diary to the less superficially affective language of accounting – a distinction that dissolves quickly under the weight of debt and anxiety.

No narrative of George Jr's professional advancement would be complete without attention to the financial accounts that appear across the archive, not only in George Jr's diaries but also in those of his mother, his father and aunt as well as in his letters to his mother and from other correspondents. Without looking, as it were, at the bottom line, we can read the story of George Jr's professional advancement as a shapely arc from self-employment and piece-work to a salaried and stable professional position at the NPG. As George Jr's year-end summaries (with one partial exception) continually remind us (and him), each new year, with its widening circles of friends and patrons, jobs and possibilities, marked a further step along the path to professional success. If we follow the money, however, and linger once again in the idiom of accounting, what becomes visible is the precariousness of the family situation: the moments of anxiety and financial desperation and the many separate acts of compounding and putting off payment of debt and of making complex logistical arrangements for the payment or non-payment of small sums that make the larger, progressivist narrative possible.

The richest sources for this kind of focused reading come from a specific period in George Jr's life (and in the life of his family) that we have already identified as crucial to the master-narrative of development; the family's economic anxiety (if not their actual financial situation) seems to have reached its nadir in 1856, the year of George Sr's ejection from the household.[10] In focusing on a particular year, we risk falling into the method that Helena calls 'annualising', the problematic emphasis on a given period defined arbitrarily in terms of dates. We do, however, want to register the shock – in its way as profound although not as emotionally fraught as the one we experienced reading, with George, of Jack's marriage – that we felt when we realised that almost all of our disparate sources about financial anxiety were written in (and around) the same year. Initially we read individual items in the Scharf archives – family letters, diaries of individuals – from beginning to end in what we hoped (in the case of the letters) and knew (in the case of the diaries) was chronological order. Each individual diary, helpfully marked by dates, was a mini-narrative; while there were gaps and blanks in the diaries, the stories they told were ordered. We were encouraged, of course, in this procedure both by the convention of dating itself – a convention very much at work (although not always followed) in letters and diaries – and by the procedures of the archive which ensured that we were each given only one item at a time. We understood that we were reading along the diachronic or sequential axis of history, looking for change over time. When we read the diaries of different family members together, deciding to 'linger', as Helena put it in a different context, 'on the synchronic axis', we were able to see events unfold at approximately the same time (Michie, 'Victorian(ist) "Whiles"', p. 278). Synchrony, of course, produces its own master-narratives, its own limitations: in this section we want to register both that members of the Scharf family were making decisions, feeling anxious and writing in their diaries at the same time and that they were living in their own day-to-day temporalities. This disjunction is most evident, of course, in the case of George Sr, who wrote in his diary almost every day, describing incidents that are also described by his son and sister-in-law, but whose knowledge of crucial family decisions was belated.

Before we turn to the minutiae of 1856, it will be useful to look more closely at how the various members of the family used – or rather attempted to use – their diaries as tools or technologies for money management. We have seen that George Jr's daily diary entries usually end with a list of expenditures. This is also true of those of his aunt and father. Miss Hicks, George Jr's Aunt Mary

– for whom we have a diary only for the crucial year 1856 when the family moved, as we have assumed for financial reasons, from Torrington Square to Camden Town – used the lower-case abbreviation 'mem' in her diary entries to signal the transition to accounting or, sometimes – tellingly – for expressions of financial worry. George Sr, as we have seen, also used his diaries as account books; his early diaries keep a running total of hours worked and money earned, while the later ones follow narrative entries with lists of expenditures and notes about whether it was he or his son who paid for them. George Jr's diaries are particularly rich in financial technologies: he used the preprinted 'Almanac' section of the Lett's diaries to mark quarter-days when his rents were due; in the years when he gave private art lessons, he used numbered diamonds on the day of each lesson to keep track of how many he had given; his early diaries also act as receipt books, where he had a landlord or an employee sign a page in the diary as evidence of payment; in the early diaries he calculated the total cost of a day in pencil and wrote the total in pen; and he used the first or last pages of several of his diaries to attempt a total of expenditures for the year. All these efforts at adding up added up, to these archival readers at least, to a sense of over-complication. Financial issues could also cause a cross-contamination of categories: we found, stuck in the back of his 1853 diary, a letter from a creditor, as if a missive from outside had entered the individual and ordered world of the diary.

A case study of the diaries for Miss Hicks and of the two Georges reveals, for that anxious year, a series of interlocking strategies for managing both money and anxiety about money. Miss Hicks's diary for 1856 tracks intrafamilial debt:

> Received from George 6 lots of money totaling [sic] 8 pounds 15, mostly 1 pound at a time
> Lent Mrs Scharf 5 pounds 30 s (6.10) 6 occasions, 1 pound (x3); 2 pounds in Oct, 3 lots of 10s (MH end of year accounting, after entries for December 1856)

While these notations might have been clearer to Miss Hicks than they were to Helena – who became for a time, with no particular skills for this position, the Scharf family accountant – like many of the Scharf entries involving money these do not, finally, make numerical sense. The entry 'received from George' is fairly clear, although a reader might wonder whether the inclusion of the 'mostly 1 pound at a time' is strictly necessary. The record of loans to her sister, however, is really quite confusing; we assume that the entry '6 occasions' refers to the total of '5 pounds 30 s', but we are not sure why the other debts are listed separately and why only one sum is dated. In any case, the precision of the whole, signified if not fully realised by the arithmetical markers, collapses with the 'lots of 10s'. These are not usable figures: if the debts to George Jr are meant to be balanced against the total of the loans to his mother, it is hard to say how much the rest of the family 'owes' Miss Hicks. In other words, the insistence on numbers is more about recording than about calculation; nothing follows from their existence except the (salient) fact of the recording itself.

George Sr's diary for the same year includes financial notations that are similarly confusing. In that same stressful year of 1856, he writes:

> Paid my subscription to Artists Fund 3. 2 .5
> Two pairs of shoes for myself 0. 14 . 6
> For me to see the Exhibition of the Royal Academy, where there were very good pictures and sculptures – – – – – – – – – 0..1..0
> Beginning of August, I made a present to Mrs Scharf from the £20 [. . .] (which I had received from the Prince of Thurn and Taxis, as a very liberal reward for a View of Belvoir Castle, the Seat of the Duke of Rutland, to Miss Hicks from me of the same £1). (GSS 15 July 1856)

This is, to coin a phrase, mixed-genre accounting. The two opening entries are traditional in their use of brief categories and their aligned figures. The third entry includes a mini-review of the Exhibition on which he spent a shilling. George Sr's (rare) recording of a gift from himself to other family members is very tangled; like his sister-in-law's entry above, this one starts out bravely looking money in the face and ends up enmeshed in dominant family narratives and unspoken family histories.

Part of their problem with adding up comes from the equivocal relation of the family economy to the very different economies of gift and debt. In a family like the Scharfs' is the family one unit or is it made up of competing interests?[11] How can a family whose members are in debt to each other make gifts to one another? One example of this incoherence occurs in the summer of 1856. On 30 July, Miss Hicks notes that George Jr has written to her from out of town asking for a 'remittance'; she sends him five shillings. Only ten days later, George Jr returns home with expensive gifts: 'George brought Mrs S & me a nice plaid dress Ribbons [sic] broach [sic] &

scarf from Edinburgh' (MH 9 August 1856). The amount George Jr spent on these gifts is unrecorded, although they must have cost more than the emergency five shillings. In reading these accounts it is hard to say what items are meant as gifts and what fall into some other accounting category – say, 'clothing' or 'necessities'. George Jr seems to have paid for many items of clothing for the members of the older generation – bonnets for his aunt and mother in June and shoes for his father, for example – but this sudden influx of goods from Edinburgh suggests a different economic register.

What figures do not explicitly record is the anxiety they generate; we can, of course, choose to see their very incoherence as a self-fulfilling prophecy, pointing to a fundamental fear that the numbers will never quite come right. But other entries in the aunt's diaries are explicit about the affective cost of the Scharfs' financial situation. The period from May to July 1856, when George Jr, his mother and aunt were looking for a cheaper place to live seems to have been particularly difficult. On 17 May Miss Hicks notes in the 'mem' section of her entry that she is 'still very uneasy about the state of affairs'. On 23 May she is 'very anxious & nervous concerning our removal', and on 19 July 'very anxious about moving'. The anxiety moves back and forth between the 'mem' section and the narrative portions of the entry, betraying perhaps its power to insinuate itself into all aspects of daily life.

It seems that the ever-generous Miss Bayley may have helped in a concrete way. On 19 May Miss Hicks notes that George Jr was not home to receive a visit from Miss Bayley and a Mrs Baron, but that they were 'very kind [. . .] concerning his affairs'. In June the situation seemed to improve a little: Miss Hicks records that 'Mrs S went to Holburn & paid the remainder of the bill [. . .] [M]y mind much relieved by George's being enabled to pay our Tradesmen's Bills for which I am very thankfull [sic]' (MH 21 June 1856).

George Jr's uncharacteristically pessimistic year-end summary for 1856, quoted at length in Chapter 2, is worth quoting again in this context. In it, we get in summary form what we see in a more fine-grained way in his father's and aunt's diaries:

Few years have contained so many varieties for me as 1856, anxieties support & losses characterise it [. . .] Oxford lectures & at Leeds also in Passion week. Charles Kean's seeking my aid for the Winter's Tale. Roger's sale, sketching his house. My financial embarrassments, kind help from Franks and Enfield. Loans & presents from friends. Leaving Torrington Square. Expenses of moving & repairs. Honourable expedition to Edinburgh at

expense of the Archbishop [. . .] My illness. Great incidental expenses.
Manchester exhibition. Kind friends. New life, numerous introductions
& good prospects for future. Mother and aunt well as ever, especially the
latter thank God

[. . .] Mr Kenyon's legacy of 500£ and other helps from him, from Miss
Bayley, Crabb Robinson, Enfield & Lord Overstone have combined to
maintain my position & feel on a surer basis.

This is the last year-end summary that explicitly mentions money.
In it we see the beginnings of a rhetorical transformation from
help with money to help with position, from cash to connections.
'[N]umerous introductions & good prospects for future' suggests a
form of long-term investment in networking that partakes of a temporality different from that of Miss Hicks's diaries, where a specific
sum is required to meet immediate expenses.

George Jr's letters home for 1855 and 1856 oscillate between the
two modes of investment and emergency. In 1855 he is developing
the acquaintance of Lord Overstone, who would, as the chairman of
the General Committee for the Manchester Art Treasures Exhibit,
later employ George Jr as the organisation's secretary. George Jr
writes to his mother, as he often does, to tell her he will be staying
away from home longer than expected:

As Lady Sitwell insists on my staying over Monday for dinner, some people
having been invited especially to meet me, I seize this opportunity of letting you know that there is no need of waiting for me at night. My visit
has been a very successful one; it has just afforded me the opportunity I
hoped for with Lord Overstone. He has been consulting me upon a new
Institution & one that when I told him of my wishes upon the subject he
told me had already occurred to him. These sorts of coincidences are
always fortunate when they do happen and I trust will. He desires me to
leave my card on [sic] him when I return to town. My music was very successful with Lady Constance. The daughter (an only child about 13 and
who will have 3 millions for her fortune) was expressly sent for to hear
me sing [. . .] I have no time for more but was sure however you wd [sic]
be pleased to know this & to hear I am now with the Nightingales who are
very delightful. (ESC 'Sunday', no day and month, 1855)

Travelling between Rempstone and Embley, the home of the
Nightingales (where he was to make a now-famous sketch of
Florence Nightingale), George Jr moved in rarified circles. Lord
Overstone is, of course, the key figure here, since he can 'help' in
concrete, if not immediately negotiable ways: as usual, George Jr
keeps his mostly middle-class friends who loan him money sepa-

rate from aristocratic friends who will help him professionally in the long term. Here, George Jr seems content to let the relationship unfold: 'These sorts of coincidences are always fortunate when they do happen and I trust will.' The temporality of this sentence is a little awkward; presumably the 'coincidence' of interests has already happened, and what he 'trusts' will happen is the joint project between himself and Lord Overstone; perhaps George Jr was less comfortable with futurity than his breezy 'always' might suggest. A long-term approach to money and to progress is associated with the aristocracy, as his somewhat odd comment about the young heiress implies. Demands for immediate cash are, predictably, associated with his family and with the (precariously) middle class.

In his letters from this year and next, George Jr continues to oscillate between these two temporalities and two economic modes as he tries to develop connections while keeping the family afloat. A letter from 29 October 1856 celebrates his new connections with uncharacteristic bluntness and then descends abruptly into financial minutiae:

> The great kindness of Lady Charlotte Guest at Canford, where I have been staying, detained me over yesterday. My visit has been charming and I have gained a host more friends & aristocrat ones too. The lecture went off admirably and Layard's presence only gave a brilliancy to the scene. I must stay here at the Cathedral tomorrow forenoon & then I shall travel on to Canterbury where I intend to stay for a couple of days & make arrangements for your departure [. . .] I feel so anxious to get home again. I hope father sent you the £3 in good time and that they did the necessary service.

George Jr is at his most candid here: the proud mention of 'a host more friends & aristocrat ones too' suggests an almost childish glee in telling his mother about his growing list of titled connections. Halfway through the letter, however, the word 'anxious' appears like a ghost from the Scharfian financial and emotional lexicon. He is not, it seems, using the word casually as he might to indicate an eagerness to return to the family. The word is followed quickly by a mention of a typically small sum of money assumed (hoped) to have travelled along the family network to do a 'necessary service'. The 'charming' visit and the professional successes that follow its mention in the letter collapse as the letter unfolds into discussions of the small but crucial sums of money that make George Jr's travels possible.

The conflict between George Jr's professional and social life, on the one hand, and his family life, on the other, is shown more clearly – and in barer economic terms – in another letter that inverts the class order of the last:

> I am glad to hear a good report through aunty & hope father will go to the New Philharmonic. I owe the Queen for taxes £15 7 get Father to pay Mr [illegible] Give Salandri £1.10 on Saturday evening [...] Keep the rest. I cannot come away from here without more money. Perhaps Mr Dundas will help again. A post office order on Monday for £5 will be sufficient perhaps [sic] he will give father £10 in case I write for further supply. I shall dismiss Warren probably tomorrow but I must visit Longford Castle & make some drawings. Lady Henrietta Lewis has sent me an introduction to Lord & Lady Folkestone to whom the Castle belongs. (ESC 24 July 1857)

This letter begins with the slightly incoherent prose we now recognise as typical of George's representation (verbal and numeric) of financial affairs. Halfway through the letter comes an arresting moment: George Jr 'cannot come away from here without more money'. George Jr's very mobility, in the sense of both class and geography, is threatened by the want of five (make that ten!) pounds. His professional life, his very career, demand that he be on the move, in this case to Longford Castle and to new potential 'aristocrat' friends, Lord and Lady Folkestone. But for the first time in our reading of the letters and diaries, the financial basis of that very movement is revealed in all its vulnerability and messiness.

We think of the time before George Jr's appointment to a salaried position at the NPG as his 'middle period', with an eye both to chronology and his especially fraught position between worlds and between classes. As we note later, the tensions persisted after he was, in all senses, more comfortable, but they would never again be so starkly rendered as they were in the kinds of economies and temporalities that characterised the period before 1857. The story we have told so far depends, of course, on a turning point that is part of a narrative of professional development: we have indexed George Jr's salary along with the permanence of his position at the NPG, as a marker not only for George Scharf Jr but also, perhaps, for Victorian culture more widely. George Jr can easily be interpolated into a narrative of the rise of the professional class, his sometimes unpredictable movements all over the country, documented in often-undated letters, collected into the sleekness of a professional narrative.

This narrative, too, can, of course, be written just a little differently. We could have used another moment in George Jr's career as a turning point, although it does not fit quite as neatly into the cultural and individual narrative of professionalisation. George Jr's appointment as secretary to the Manchester Arts Treasures Exhibition, which pre-dated his NPG appointment by a year, was, although only a temporary position, a crucial change in his fortunes. It was as the art secretary of the Manchester Exhibition that his movements began to be traced by people other than his family. It was his journeys as art secretary that earned him a mention in the *Times* beyond the classified section: 'Mr. George Scharf [. . .] will on Monday visit Knowsley, to select from the Earl of Derby's collection, and will afterwards proceed to several important depositories of art in the midland counties' ('Art Treasures Exhibition'). From that point on, George Scharf Jr was more or less in the public eye. In other words, the story of professionalisation that depends on the economic stability of a salary lags a little (one year) behind a story of public visibility.

Running throughout the story of George Jr's professional success in this middle period is the issue of his relationship with his titled friends. Our questions about this will take a slightly different shape in the two case studies that form Chapter 4: we will then be investigating in detail the extent of his personal intimacy with two titled men and their houses. At this period of George Jr's career, the category of intimacy seems less relevant – if only because George Jr, for whatever reason, did not have recourse to an affective vocabulary when he talked about his titled connections – even 'my excellent friend' Lady Sitwell (D 31 December 1854). After we had read the diaries and in particular the letters from his early and middle periods, we asked not about degrees of intimacy but a perhaps shallower and more instrumental question: what was it about George Jr in his role as guest that resulted in so many titled hosts asking him to spend another night at their homes? For this, as we have noted, is the characteristic occasion of his letters home – or the way he chose to open them. He was often at this period writing, at least on the face of it, to tell his mother not to expect him home because some 'aristocrat', as he likes to say, had insisted on his remaining with them a little longer. Whatever work the letters perform besides (and usually after) their statement that he will not be home when expected, they act almost as telegrams might: changing – that is to say postponing at very short notice – plans for getting together with his family. While we think we know something about how such announcements worked to express George Jr's divided identifications, we have no idea what made him so desirable a guest. We do not know what 'contributing' – to use his description of his activities at Lady Sitwell's party – might have meant. How did he contribute to that Christmas tree? Did he fashion some cunning ornaments? hang some up in the company of the family and other guests? draw a plan for the tree's decoration? Or perhaps – and we have tended to forget about this – he was as valued for his singing as his drawing.

Horizontal narratives 2: brother Henry disappears

One account we don't have is that of George Jr's only sibling, his younger brother Henry. An 'H' standing for Henry appears in the father's diaries, as do brief mentions in his older brother's. But what we do know is that at crucial moments Henry was *not* there, no longer officially part of the Scharf household. We would like to end with the story of his expulsion from the household, which eerily parallels his father's. Here we find ourselves trying on the paradigms of family-systems theory, with its moves beyond the Oedipal triangle, to trace out broader patterns of differentiation and identification. Family-systems theory resists pathologising the symptomatic individual, finding the source of dysfunction in patterns of alliance and othering that include all the members of a given family and that play out across generations. The paradigms we find most useful in the Scharfs' case are two different patterns through which individuals in a family become outsiders, two patterns that pertain both to George Sr and to Henry. The first is the triangle, not (or at least, not exclusively) the Freudian triad of mother–father–son, but rather a way of configuring all relationships between any two family members as mediated by their dual relation to a third. Every pair of individuals in a family is in a series of triangles with all the other family members, a pattern that turns out to be especially illuminating in the case of the Scharfs. The second family-systems paradigm we find useful is 'emotional cut-off', or what happens when an individual, whether on purpose or by circumstance, loses touch with the rest of the family. Patterns like cut-off and triangles repeat themselves within and across generations of a family, serving as conduits for the circulation of anxiety. In family-systems theory, the most anxious families are those in which the boundaries between individuals are blurriest, and the highest functioning people are those who can best manage their anxiety by achieving a higher level of differentiation.[12] As we have seen, the Scharfs' household accounting reveals a family baffled about who owes what to whom, perhaps in part because they are not at all clear about where one family member ends and the other begins. In this reading, George Jr's failure to differentiate – to play out the plot of *Bildung* – is over-determined by 'family process'.

While the Elderlies are vividly present in George Jr's diaries, Henry is not easy to locate there. We noticed him first in George Jr's entries around the time of their father's final illness, which prompted us to wonder why he was not present more often. It is clear from George Jr's diary that his brother could not offer much in the way of material help at his father's deathbed. George Jr's accounts tell us he had to give Henry cab fare for moving their father's 'things' from Camden to Great George Street (D 15 September 1860). The more we learned about Henry, the more we could see that this was typical: he was always 'one down', in the parlance of family-systems theory, and like his father, always on the outside of the family's triangles. In the triangle of Mrs Scharf, Aunt Mary and George Sr, the sisters are allied and the husband/ brother-in-law is on the outside; in the triangle of Mrs Scharf, George Jr and George Sr, the father is again the outsider. In the triangles of Mrs Scharf, George Jr and Henry and of George Sr, George Jr and Henry, however, it is the younger brother who falls outside, as the older son was the mother's favourite and the father devoted his skills to supporting the older son's professional ascent. The younger, less favoured son, standing on the outside of those triangles, as the family-systems story would have it, tried to differentiate himself from father and older brother by pursuing a different art form and becoming an actor.

Henry Scharf began and ended his adult life on the stage. He did not become a celebrity, though the London *Times* mentions his appearances in a few plays. A cataloguer of Shakespearian prompt-books found his name in a marked-up copy of *King John* at the Newberry Library, dated November 1844 and traceable to a pro-duction of the play at Sadler's Wells in that year (see Shattuck, pp. 195–6). A handbill for a June 1848 production in Birmingham by Charles Dickens's troupe of friends and family, the Amateurs, names Henry Scharf as the understudy for a member who was unable to make the trip from London.[13] Although we found no discussion of his decision to emigrate in any of the Scharfs' diaries, by 1852 Henry had gone to seek his fortune on the American stage, appearing that year as Moses in a New York production of *The School for Scandal* (see T. A. Brown, pp. 181–2). Leaving his country of origin to practise his art elsewhere, Henry was repeating George Sr's emigration from Germany to England. Like George Sr, Henry was not a success in the new land, and like George Sr, he gradually became cut off from his family of origin when his parents – who maintained a correspondence with their second son during their lifetimes – died and his older brother let the connection drop.[14] This is 'emotional cut-off', brought about partly by the prodigal son's departure and partly by the family's failure to keep the connection alive. Cut-off spells trouble not just for the outsider but for everyone in the system, as no one in the system functions well when one family member has become disconnected.

Henry found himself repeating his father's life story in more ways than one. Just a year after emigrating, George Sr's diary mentions receiving a letter from Henry, who was following in his father's footsteps by doing anatomical drawings for 'Professors', having almost given up on performing because he was 'little encouraged by the Managers of the Theatres' (GSS 15 March 1853). If Henry was not a particularly gifted actor, he did have the gift of the family genius – or at least the gene – for drawing. The work was generally not very lucrative. As Henry's concerned father notes in August of that year, Henry had become 'tired of working for the Doctors, as he was so indifferently payd [sic]'. Discouraged, Henry joined a company of strolling players in Pennsylvania (GSS 18 August 1853). Not long after that, he found employment at the University of Virginia, teaching elocution and anatomical drawing.[15] Charlottesville then was not what it is today, nor was teaching at UVA necessarily a path to self-supporting respectability. Repeating his father's fate, Henry would always be scrabbling to make a living.[16] For instance, he was paid $500 per year for six years' work on a set of anatomical drawings commissioned by the university. Sadly, what remains of Henry's labours is preserved only in a mention in a 1904 history of the University of Virginia:

> These colored drawings for the Medical Department were executed by an accomplished artist, Mr. Henry Scharf, who labored for six years, and 'accumulated an unequalled collection of plates, executed with an exquisite truth to nature, making them invaluable'. These rare plates, on which at least $3000 had been expended, were unfortunately destroyed in the fire that consumed the interior of the Medical Hall about 1886. (Barringer and Garnett, pp. 159–60)

The fire that wiped out Henry's life's work occurred thirty years after he began making the set of anatomical plates and just one year before his death. The disappearance of that work prefigures the disappearance of Henry himself under mysterious circumstances.

Henry Scharf was still a teacher in 1872, instructing young ladies in elocution at the Virginia Female Academy. By 1884, though, he had returned to the stage in Washington, DC, and eventually he was back where he had started more than three decades before, working as an actor in New York City. The *New York Times* item reporting his disappearance bears repeating in full:

AN OLD ACTOR DISAPPEARS

Henry Scharf, a genial old actor, who since the theatrical season closed has been boarding at 65 Irving-place, left that house on June 18, and has not been heard of since. The day before he left Mr. Scharf obtained the sum of $30 with which to buy himself a suit of clothes. He had no other money. He was an Englishman, 65 years of age, stoutly built, and almost bald, and had for the last three years played 'leading old man' parts in Miss Lizzie Evans' company [. . .] Mr. Scharf was much liked among his fellow-boarders, who are at a loss to imagine what has become of him.

One of his friends said yesterday that Mr. Scharf was convivially inclined, and he feared that he had, while intoxicated, been robbed, taken to court, sent to the Tombs, died there, and been buried in Potter's Field. Mr. Scharf suffered from heart disease and was nervous about himself. (8 July 1887)

We can't resist viewing the protagonist of this strange account as a specular portrait of Henry's older brother. Stout, almost bald, old, genial, convivially inclined and much liked among his fellow-boarders, Henry at age sixty-five must have closely resembled George Jr. Living from hand to mouth, borrowing money for a suit of clothes, having no accumulated assets to show for a life-time of work, Henry is only a slightly more extreme version of the overextended debtor George Jr never quite grew out of being. Not particularly healthy and chronically 'nervous about himself', Henry in his less prosperous way was living much as his brother lived, in a constant state of uneasiness about his body. His friend's thinking it likely the disappearance was a consequence of intoxication suggests that Henry, like George Jr, habitually drank more than was good for him. There, but for his position in the family system, might George Jr have gone.

Meanwhile, back in London, Henry's brother's diaries expressed no curiosity about what might have become of him. In the middle of August 1856, while packing up household goods for the move to Camden, George Jr had sent 'a large parcel of books and drawings to Henry in America' (D 23 August 1856). This parcel George Jr describes in retrospect as a 'present' to his brother in the year-end summary for 1856 we have quoted in its entirety in Chapter 2, adding that he had received from Henry a '[n]ote [. . .] of apology, reconciliation, etc.'. The 'etc.' sounds to us like the impatient dismissal of an apology the elder brother might have heard from the younger many times before, for we-know-not-what infraction. As far as we can tell, the two brothers saw each other only once in London after Henry's move to America, during those weeks before their father's death. From that time forward, George Jr was not just the alpha male in his family of origin, he was the only male.

As his years in America went by, Henry's existence seems to have commanded less and less of his older brother's attention. Though he had sent Henry a birthday greeting to Staunton, Virginia, the year their mother died (D 8 December 1869), on his own birthday a year later George told his diary, 'I intended to have written to Henry in America but could not make time' (D 16 December 1870). We are sceptical about this excuse. How likely is it that this man, who wrote down the minutiae of the weather on his very dullest days, could not find time to dash off a birthday note? The explanation he offers his diary for this negligence rings hollow, especially in the context of what happened in the next few years. In 1871 on Henry's birthday, George Jr wrote only to himself, 'I remember this day as my brother Henry's birthday. Still away in America. I hope he is well & that no news of him may be accepted as good news' (D 8 December 1871). Henry has become part of the anniversary technology of the diaries, as absent, in his way, as the deceased elder Scharfs. George Jr's diary for 1877 once again notes the date of Henry's birthday with the reminder that his brother was 'born 1822' (D 8 December 1877). That is the last mention of Henry we found in George's diary. Then, ten years later, George Jr's brother disappeared. If George Jr knew anything about it, we have not found evidence in his personal papers. The cut-off was complete.

The year Henry vanished George Jr was in poor health himself, suffering at various times from stiffness in his neck, intermittent deafness, chronic cough, and shortness of breath, but enjoying, as he recorded on Christmas Day of that year, 'a full sense of comfort, happiness, love of friends & I hope also proper contentment'. George Jr had, after all, replaced his blood brother with two more satisfactory substitutes, first Jack – whom George Jr described in his year-end summary for 1865 as acting like a brother and two years later as 'more brotherly than ever' (D 11 August 1869) – then Donny, whom, as we recounted in Chapter 2, George told his cook to regard 'in the light of a brother to me' (D 9 March 1888). Reverting from our family-systems analysis to our more typical psychoanalytic mode, however, we can see that George was uneasy about his estrangement from Henry: 'Had a remarkable dream of preparing for execution, to be beheaded in a state of dreadful calumnies. Reasoning upon it as something absolutely inevitable. Woke on remembering that I ought to write to my Brother' (D 28 October 1871). That was the year George Jr could not make time to send his brother a birthday greeting. Family-systems theory does not read dreams, but we cannot help noting this as another iteration of George Jr's characteristic nightmare. The uneasiness we read there expresses the damage done to the brother who stays in place when the brother who leaves home gets cut off.

If family-systems theory opens up the possibilities for thinking broadly and horizontally about the Scharf family, it still, of course, depends on a certain psychic geography charted by the triangle and the arc. The addition of multiple triangles takes the pressure off the parent/child dyad, only to reproduce its affective shape across the family and from one generation to the next. Family-systems analysis leaves in place even as it modifies the idea of development so crucial to the narrative of *Bildung*. Our struggles to comprehend the Scharf family dynamics have reminded us of our own investments in *Bildung*, initially less visible to us than our similar (and linked) investments in the romance plot. We have had to admit to ourselves that we wanted George Jr to grow up – and that growing up meant for us, as for Anglo-American culture for the last two hundred years, establishing a home of his own. At the same time, we have been appalled by the cost of that 'maturation' and at the psychic cost – to George Jr, to George Sr, to Henry and, perhaps, even to Mrs Scharf – of ejecting father and brother from the family. Finally, we have admired the flexibility and creativity of George Jr's creation of households and his negotiation of domestic topography to bring together – for a few years – mother, romance and work. For a while everything he loved – from his mother, to Jack, to books and to what we assume were spare artworks from the NPG – was brought together in one domestic space, albeit it a space carefully and creatively layered.

If we were invested in *Bildung* as we read family diaries and added up numbers, so, of course, was George Jr. *Bildung* is the master-narrative of the diaries with their progressivist year-end summaries. Like the curriculum vitae, which attends only to the landmarks of a life, the diary as a genre allows for a sense of progress, as year follows year. But, of course, the diaries, like George himself, inhabit smaller units and recursive temporalities that resist or simply cannot live up to the exigencies of *Bildung*. As we have seen in Scharf's early career, George Jr had to live simultaneously in the day and for the year, in the messy present, for the future, and with an eye towards the legacy of the past. If having to negotiate these different temporalities makes him typical, his resolutions of temporal conflicts suggest a particular creativity, even an artistry well worth tracing through the archive.

4

Reading for success: the professional plot

IN THE LAST TWO chapters we have read some key moments in Scharf's life with and against two dominant cultural narratives: the romance plot and the differentiation plot. These plots are intimately but complexly related to literary genres – the marriage-plot novel and the *Bildungsroman*. This chapter focuses not so much on a single plot as on a culturally privileged place that has generated a variety of literary plots. By telling the story of Scharf's relationship with two great country houses only seven miles apart, we cannot help invoking the frisson-inducing spectre of the Gothic and sensation novel and the linked cultural and literary plot of inheritance. Scharf's relationships with Knole, the home of the Sackville family, and Chevening, the seat of the earls of Stanhope (both located in Sevenoaks, Kent), brought up for us some of the central questions of Gothic and sensation novels: who belongs to the house, and who does not? Who is absorbable into the household, and who, finally, is foreign to it and must be thrust out into a different space, whether that be a prison, an asylum or another country?[1] Who represents the future of the house and who inherits it? If we see Scharf not as that urban extra man, Mr Twemlow of *Our Mutual Friend*, but as something more like Walter Hartwright, the drawing master who visits Limmeridge House in Wilkie Collins's *The Woman in White*, what would that shift tell us and how might it help us pose the question that bothered us so long: where in the class system of the last quarter of the nineteenth century did George Scharf belong?

Our answers, even if they unfold within a sensational structure, are realist in mode and method. As far as we know there are no bigamous marriages in the story of Scharf's visits to Knole and Chevening, no hidden offspring, no murdered heirs, in short, no paradigm-shifting secrets to which he was a party. We did eventually find a possible candidate for villain in the person of Mortimer, Lord Sackville, who – as we explain below – shifted in our imaginations from a dull and harmless snob to something more sinister. Knole was at the time of Scharf's visits the centre of a novel-worthy inheritance plot, and Lord Sackville was one of that plot's prime movers, but Scharf played only a supporting role. Our approach to the question of belonging includes mysteries, but they are small ones: what did Lord Sackville and George Scharf find to say to each other during their walks in the hops garden? Was Scharf housed in the family or guest wing at Knole? What happened between Lord Stanhope and Scharf during the trip to Canterbury that made the latter such a household intimate? All these questions, of course, bear on the central – and for us sensationally inflected – mystery of whether Scharf stayed in these houses as an employee, as a friend, as a quasi-family member or as a protégé. (How) did this immigrant's son, this man without a university degree, belong to Knole and to Chevening?

What follow are two case studies linked to the different houses. Our first focuses on Knole and on what we see as the strangeness of Scharf's relation to the house and to the eccentric Sackville family members who occupied it during the period of his extended visits there. The Knole case study takes us into questions of Scharf's expertise about portraits and portrait collections and back to his complicated role as guest, companion and diner-out. He is on many occasions at Knole the extra man at dinner and in the household, as those more firmly designated 'guests' leave after the end of a house party. In the role of extra man he acts as mediator, sounding board and supporter to titled friends engrossed in conflicts in which he can play no direct part.

The section on Chevening is a slightly different kind of case study. Here we look closely at the development of Scharf's professional relationship with Philip, the 5th Earl Stanhope, focusing on letters from Stanhope, chairman of the Board of Trustees of the newly founded National Portrait Gallery, to Scharf in his role as secretary. We try to pinpoint where and how that relationship became more personal, and to think through possible ways of naming that relationship. The more intimate relationship takes us – as it did Scharf himself – to Lord Stanhope's country house and to what we could find out about what Scharf did there on his frequent visits.

Desiring Knole

What would it mean to desire a house like Knole? It would certainly mean something different from, say, desiring the house next door: the one with the pool, the bigger third bedroom or the built-in bookcases in the living room. Desiring Knole would not, for most people, mean wanting to buy it or to live in it or even (more on this later) wanting to inherit it. Imagined by some to have been built as a calendar house, with 365 rooms, fifty-two staircases, twelve entrances and seven courtyards, Knole belongs to a different order of living from the apartment, the cottage or even the mansion – an order that is at once temporal and spatial, historical and contemporary, public and private. Its transformation in 1947 from the private home of the Sackville-West family to a public museum[2] (with visiting hours, cordoned off wings and a tearoom) further detaches desire from fantasies of ownership, if not of visual metonymy (look, but don't touch) or incorporation (the tearoom offers lunches featuring local foods).

Any discussion of our own desire for Knole must return once again to the album of menus with which this book – and this project – began. It is no accident that the first menu cards we touched and the first menus we copied out were from Knole. These touchings and transcribings were overdetermined gestures: the menus from Knole, so obviously meant to be folded into boxes, were more interactive, more numerous and just plain cuter than their fellows on the pages of the album. Those menus caught our imagination with their cavalcade of elegant French dishes organised into multi-course meals. But Knole was also a name we recognised, a name that was part not only of our sense of British history but of the history of second-wave feminism and of our own histories as feminist readers of modernist women's literature. Although Helena had visited the house as a tourist many years before we ever heard of George Scharf, and although she had at that time looked dutifully at its portraits of bewigged seventeenth-century aristocrats and smiling Restoration poets, Knole was to us chiefly the house that Vita Sackville-West adored but was barred from inheriting due to the fact that she was a woman. It was the house that Virginia Woolf offered up as a gift to Vita in imaginary form in *Orlando*, the novel that traces a fantastic (counter-)historical journey in which Vita's avatar – represented sometimes as a man and sometimes as a woman – gets to live out centuries of a blissfully literary existence at

171

Knole. Knole was for us part of the canon of female erotic friendship; it represented the triumph of Woolf's loving imagination and Vita's resistance to gender norms.

As with our discussion of Scharf's erotic life, these compelling elements of Knole can also be thought of as unfolding within a highly literary plot – in this case the ample Victorian plot of inheritance. Vita was, of course, enmeshed in the plot, but so were her nineteenth-century forebears, the inhabitants of Knole whom Scharf visited over a period of more than thirty years of contested ownership. Knole was an object of (often-thwarted) desire for a parade of Sackvilles, who gained and lost their rights to the great house and to family titles, who took each other to court, formed and unformed alliances; sold, stole or reclaimed precious artifacts belonging to the house; and barred and unbarred public access to its rooms and grounds.

As someone who found himself in the mid-Victorian middle – if by no means at the centre – of this inheritance plot and its events, George Scharf also desired Knole. His was a desire from outside, not the frustrated dream of inheritance of a daughter of the house, but a fantasy of belonging indulged by an immigrant's son whose mother had been a grocer in St Martin's Lane. Between 1858 and 1878 Scharf visited Knole at least seventeen times, sometimes spending two weeks or more in what he came to refer to as 'his' room next to the chapel. He paid visits to Knole during the tenure of at least three of its owners: his most frequent and intimate visits came after 1875 to Mortimer, the 1st Baron Sackville, and his wife, Elizabeth. Before 1875 Scharf visited Knole to do research on its portrait collection; he appears in the beginning not to have had much contact with the family or to have spent the night.

Eventually, Scharf assumed a more complex role in relation to the house and family at Knole: still focused on the portrait collection, he seems to have come – at Lord Sackville's request – to help rearrange the collection on the great house's walls, although he evidently did not produce, as he was hired to do at other houses like Knowlsey, a formal catalogue. At Knole he was simultaneously a guest and not a guest. Like other guests of the Sackvilles, he participated in musical evenings and took long walks with his hosts, sharing their elaborate meals and apparently sympathising with their legal and financial troubles. But he also did things guests would not typically do, like giving advice to the family servants, staying behind after house parties and even showing visitors around all three floors of the house. Scharf moved, it seemed, quite fluidly through Knole's many spaces, from the dining-room where he ate with family and guests, to the muniments room, where he studied the patents that embodied the history of the Sackville family, to the 'beer cellar and the laundry' (D 17 October 1878). His favourite word to describe his movements within Knole was 'wandering'; sometimes he did this alone, sometimes with people to whom he refers, with a slight sense of distance, as 'guests'. In a diary entry from 1877, he combines the authority of his 'wandering' with markers of differentiation from other visitors to Knole: 'wandering about the house with the guests, especially in the top rooms' (D 24 August). On 18 July 1878, he again draws a distinction between himself and 'guests': 'the guests departed leaving Sir F. Hamilton alone with me all day'. We believe he was never paid for these working trips to Knole. Indeed, the careful accounts in his diaries indicate no income to offset the considerable sums of money he spent on travel to Sevenoaks and on supplies for the work Lord Sackville evidently asked him to do. The question of Scharf's position in the Sackville family is, of course, in part a question of his desire to be associated with the family and the house. In this first half of our final chapter we ask, what did Scharf do for Knole and what, finally, did Knole do for Scharf?

To some extent we have let our own desires for Knole shape a story that Scharf might tell differently. If for us Knole came first, for Scharf Knole House was really only one of several country houses that offered him enhanced position and status. Despite the prominent place Knole's menus occupy in Scharf's album, Knole does not appear in his diaries' year-end summaries, nor is Lord Sackville mentioned as one of the many 'friends' for whom Scharf would remind himself at the turn of each New Year to be especially grateful. At first we found it strange that Knole did not figure as a landmark in Scharf's annual narrative of his own social and professional rise, although 'at Knole' and 'Knole' appear at the top of many pages in his diary throughout the 1870s. We now know Scharf's story of country-house desire would probably begin at the other end of the village of Sevenoaks, at Chevening, the country house belonging to Lord Stanhope, who – as we have mentioned – was Scharf's patron, friend and supervisor. It is Chevening that figures most prominently in Scharf's diaries as a marker of his social and professional advances, Chevening that continually serves as a landmark in those year-end summaries where Scharf charted his ascent.

The second half of this chapter traces Scharf's growing intimacy at Chevening, without which he never would have found his way into a bedchamber at neighbouring Knole, a seven-mile drive through the village from Lord Stanhope's country seat.

Certainly Knole and Chevening are intimately linked in the story of Scharf's professional life as we were able to reconstruct it from his diaries, his sketchbooks, his menus and his correspondence. In the early years of his on-site work in great country houses – from 1858 when he was named director of the NPG to 1875 – Chevening served as a home base in Kent from which Scharf could take day-trips to Knole. After Lord Stanhope's death in 1875, Scharf began to spend longer periods of time at Knole and sometimes to visit the surviving Stanhopes from there. This shift would, in part, be due to the death of his friend and patron at Chevening, although Scharf was to maintain lifelong friendships with Lord Stanhope's son and heir – the 6th Earl – and his wife, the younger Lady Stanhope. Our entry to the story, however, was our attempt to unravel the significance of Scharf's increasing intimacy with Mortimer Sackville and his wife, Lady Sackville, whom Scharf's diary calls in the early days, before Mortimer's inheritance was secure, 'Mrs West' (D 22 August 1875). In the course of our research we were ultimately to visit Knole, not as tourists, but as the professional guests of the present Lord Sackville, Robert Sackville-West, and to look around the house in the company of his mother, the Dowager Lady Sackville, who asked us to address her, too, as 'Mrs West'. Like Scharf himself, as we explored the private recesses of the grand old house, we could not help feeling we had somehow really arrived. This section of Chapter 4 ends with an account of what we discovered there.

To begin with Knole as the nexus of questions about class and profession is, then, to read against Scharf's desires and with the grain of our own; in choosing to place Knole at the centre of the story before looking at Chevening, we are, in fact, using Knole as a metonymy for our own preoccupations: food and inheritance. Our story of Knole circuits through a series of desires and ambitions, including Scharf's desire for status and for rich meals, the various Sackvilles' desire to claim their inheritance, our own desire for knowledge of Scharf and what we will be calling national desire – Knole's importance to Britain's idea of itself and its history.

Knole in the national imaginary

Virginia Woolf's identification with Knole, through her (usually) beloved Vita, has its own personal dynamic, but desire for Knole was common in the complex story of inheritance that marked Knole for four generations before Vita's birth into the Sackville-West family. Commenting on the mid-nineteenth-century legal battles over the possession of Knole, a writer for *The Times* stepped back from official accounts of the court proceedings to remark that the Baron of Buckhurst, Lord de la Warr – the brother of Mortimer and aspirant to the title Lord Sackville – could not be blamed for wanting 'to get back Knole for himself'. Though there are other, more magnificent houses, the author concedes that Knole has a special place in the national imaginary:

> It is too much to say there is no other place like [Knole] in England. The house may compare ill with many of the halls and palaces yet remaining among us which were built by the men who climbed into eminence upon the ruins of an older nobility in the reigns of Elizabeth and James [. . .] When every defect is noted, and all that can be said in depreciation of Knole has been exhausted, the associations of the house are irresistible. It is too full of the lives of statesmen and poets, of soldiers and of beauties, for criticism to maintain itself against the rush of memory; and if we escape from the traditions of 300 years to pass into the Park, we own that these woodlands and glades, these chestnuts and beeches, are nowhere outdone, if they can be anywhere matched, in beauty. ('Lord de la Warr', 14 November 1877, p. 9)

Unanchored here from a specific family member or indeed the family line, the 'rush of memory' suggests a fantasy past belonging to – even inherited by – the entire nation. Knole is portrayed, not as a 'monument' to Renaissance architecture, but as a sort of living museum, a container 'full of the lives of statesmen and poets, of soldiers and of beauties' (Fig. 4.1). The Park, explicitly exempt from the 'traditions of 300 years', offers an alternative temporality marked by a continuous present where the beauty of the trees is second to none.

Vita's 1922 description of the gardens at Knole participates in the same fantasy of the power that growing things have to connect the present to the house's deep past:

> The white rose which was planted under James I's room has climbed until it now reaches beyond his windows on the first floor [. . .] the magnolia

Fig. 4.1 GS sketch of Knole House in Kent, 1874.
©National Portrait Gallery, London.

outside the Poets' Parlour has grown nearly to the roof, and bears its mass of flame-shaped blossoms like a giant candelabrum; the beech hedge is twenty feet high; four centuries have winnowed the faultless turf. In spring the wisteria drips its fountains over the top of the wall into the park. The soil is rich and deep and old. The garden has been a garden for four hundred years. (V. Sackville-West, p. 209)

Here again, as in *The Times*' article, the lives of 'statesmen and poets' haunt the home through the traditional names for rooms they frequented, like King James's bedroom, containing a bed where he is supposed to have slept, and the Poets' Parlour, where the wood-panelled walls are lined with portraits of Johnson, Pope, Dryden and their cohorts. Connected by windows to these spaces that have been inhabited by mortals, the eternally living rose bushes, lime trees, magnolias and wisterias are still there centuries after the people have died. Through the vagaries of entailment and primogeniture, the real continuity of Knole is in the soil that supports the 'faultless turf'.

Not just for Vita, who had such a personal investment in the house, but for other historians of the place, part of the fascination of Knole has always been another form of continuity: perhaps ironically, in view of what was going to happen in the nineteenth and twentieth centuries, a continuity of inheritance itself. As the author of an 1817 guide to Knole writes,

It is not less singular than extraordinary, that during so many centuries as have elapsed since the [Norman] Conquest, filled with wars, rebellions and insurrections, in which the Nobility and Barons, chief instigators of those events have been engaged, while so many have become extinct and are forgotten; that [Knole] should have descended regularly from father to son during so long a period [. . .] There are many more ancient creations, but no other instance can be produced of a family inheriting in so direct a line. (John Bridgman, qtd in R. Sackville-West, p. 151)

Knole, then, is a triumph of the indicatively British narrative of primogeniture. For visitors and writers in the nineteenth century it embodied not only history – derived from the stories of those who lived there and from the portraits of those who did not – but also the principle on which that history was based.

The present holder of the title of Baron Sackville, Robert Sackville-West, suggests in his aptly titled *Inheritance,* a recent book about the house and family, that for Victorians Knole harked back to a definitional – if not always defined – moment in British history.

[I]n the nineteenth century [. . .] [t]he house caught the Victorian imagination as a perfectly preserved relic of 'the Olden Times', a period somewhere between the Tudors and the Stuarts, between the Middle Ages and modern times. It was an era popularised in the novels of Sir Walter Scott, whose portrait was – appropriately enough – acquired in 1822 and hung in the Poets' Parlour at Knole, complementing the collection of Restoration poets and playwrights. (R. Sackville-West, p. 152)

The capacious 'Olden Times', in their lack of specificity, embody a complex temporality, a nostalgia for Scott and also for the period about which Scott wrote.

If, for many Victorians, Knole represented what was best and most British about British history, the Victorian period and the nineteenth century, more generally, have not figured prominently in histories of Knole. Vita Sackville-West's *Knole and the Sackvilles,* replete with anecdotes about the first three centuries of the house's existence, ends with a short chapter on Knole in the nineteenth century that skips from 1825 to Vita's 'present day'. Of her grandfather William, the youngest brother of Mortimer, she writes:

And here, save for a few very brief notes to bring the history of the house down to the present day, these sketches must cease. The duchess Arabella Diana dying in 1825, her estate devolved upon her two daughters, Mary and Elizabeth. Elizabeth, my great-grandmother, who married John West, Lord de la Warr, and who died in 1870, left Buckhurst to her elder

> sons and Knole to her younger sons, one of whom was my grandfather. He was, as I remember him, a queer and silent old man. He knew nothing whatever about the works of art in the house; he spent hours gazing at the flowers, followed about the garden by two grave demoiselle cranes; he turned his back on all visitors, but sized them up after they had gone in one shrewd and sarcastic phrase [. . .] [H]e seemed to me, with his taciturnity and the never-mentioned background of his own not unromantic past, to stand conformably at the end of the long line of his ancestors. (V. Sackville-West, p. 210)

In portraying her grandfather William as the 'end' of a long line, Vita is minimising the future generations of Knole of which she is a part or, perhaps, merely sniffing at the claims of her male cousin to be the successor to a legacy she thought should have been her own. Her narrative suggests, however, that by the end of the nineteenth century the history of Knole is already over. The complex inheritance plot that pitted brother against brother in the 1870s and 1880s, is subsumed here under the oddly general observation that Elizabeth left 'Buckhurst to her elder sons, and Knole to her younger sons, one of whom was my grandfather'. While there are good reasons to resist representing or even attempting to untangle the snarl of Mary's and Elizabeth's bequests, and while it was possible that Vita knew only selected details of the case, the idea that Knole was left by a female owner to the 'younger sons' suggests a collapse of temporality and financial interest that contradicts the long-term story of Knole as the classic emblem of primogeniture.[3]

Vita's history of her ancestral home says very little about her own problematic relation to that history. In the revised 1958 edition she includes an appendix referring to a second 'giv[ing] over' of Knole:

> I have to record with sorrow that Knole was given over to the National Trust in 1947. It was the only thing to do, and as a potential inheritor of Knole I had to sign documents giving Knole away. It nearly broke my heart, putting my signature to what I couldn't help regarding as a betrayal of all the tradition of my ancestors and the house I loved. (V. Sackville-West, p. 215)

Ironically surfacing as a 'potential inheritor' of the property only at the moment when it was to be 'given over', Vita relegates to this second appendix a statement of her own doubly thwarted desire, a desire that she routes interestingly enough through Virginia Woolf, whom she quotes at length on the significance of Knole. Woolf located the meaning of Knole in the people who had built it and lived in it, the 'Richards, Johns, Annes, Elizabeths, not one of whom has left a token of himself behind him, yet all, working together with their spades and their needles, their love-making and their child-bearing, have left this' (qtd in V. Sackville West, p. 215). For Woolf, the people holding the spades and needles are as significant to the house's history as those who produced heirs to the estate, and for Vita they figure even more vividly:

> Great state was observed here once, when well over a hundred servants sat down daily to eat at long tables in the Great Hall; the very list of their employments suggests the sound and activity which stirred within the walls of this self-contained encampment, this private burg: the armourer, the falconer, the slaughterman, the brewer, the baker, the barber, the huntsman, the yeoman of the granary, the farrier, the grooms of the great horse, and the stranger's horse, the men to carry wood, Solomon the bird-catcher, and many others besides, all coming in from their both-ies and outhouses to share in the communal meal with their master, his lady, their children, their guests, and the mob of indoor servants whose avocations ranged from His Lordship's Favourite through innumerable pages, attendants, grooms and yeomen of various chambers, scriveners, pantry-men, maids, clerks of the kitchen and the buttery, down to the humble Grace Robinson and John Morockoe, both blackamoors. (V. Sackville-West, p. 217)

Vita's Knole, then, was embodied not just in the ancient plants and ancestral stones, not just in the memories of the statesmen, soldiers and beauties who had stayed there, but in a centuries-old conglomeration of the collective lives constituting a 'private burg', a community on a scale no twentieth-century patron could afford to maintain. As part of the National Trust, Knole now belongs, theo-retically, to the British people, among them the descendants of all those workers who kept it going for all those years, though parts of the house are still inhabited privately by the bearer of the title, Lord Sackville, and his family.

In which we (maybe) uncover a dark-hearted villain

Mortimer, Lord Sackville, a younger brother – for that matter, a *fourth* brother – who, through a series of accidents including an aunt's capricious will and an older brother's suicide, inherited Knole in 1873, was one of Scharf's grand connections.[4] Or at least, so we assumed when we came upon those enchanting Knole menus in Scharf's collection. The better acquainted we became with George

Scharf's Lord Sackville and the more closely we inspected the circumstances surrounding his tenure at Knole, the less overawed we were by Scharf's association with him. For one thing, as Robert Sackville-West notes, Knole, despite or in part because of its enormousness, was not now what it once had been. The treasures of the art collection and the grandeur of the house notwithstanding, the Knole of the 1870s and 1880s was a diminished place. The division of the family property had resulted in two separate titles (Baron Buckhurst, which went to the elder son, and Lord Sackville, which went to the younger), neither of which was sufficiently endowed. Knole in particular suffered by virtue of its size and the fact that the income from the property was only half that of Buckhurst: at the time by far the bigger and more glamorous property, Knole was also much more expensive to run. The agricultural depression of the 1870s and 1880s that wiped out the livelihood of so many country estates also affected Mortimer's finances, as did the lawsuits among the Sackville brothers over the rightful disposition of their inheritance (R. Sackville-West, p. 164). All of this legal wrangling could not have added to the dignity of Knole and to Mortimer's stature nationally or in the local community.

And certainly, the newly minted Lord Sackville was not the stuff of heroic narratives, national or otherwise. Robert Sackville-West describes Mortimer as a 'courtier' holding 'a series of arcane court appointments [such as Gentleman Usher and Groom in Waiting]', whose career was marked by 'desperately trying to wangle his next appointment' (p. 156). He notes that Mortimer's career, like that of his younger brother, Lionel (an assistant précis writer for the Secretary of State for Foreign Affairs),

> remained bastions of the aristocratic closed shop, with recruitment by connection rather than by competition. It was no coincidence that two future Lord Sackvilles, Mortimer and Lionel, neither of whom, dare I say it, was that able or dynamic himself, had chosen to make their way in two of the least demanding of the careers available. (R. Sackville-West, p. 156)

When we first met Mortimer in the pages of Scharf's diaries, he seemed to us a somewhat harmless and perhaps ineffectual figure. Perhaps this was because he did not appear in the year-end summaries alongside other landmark connections. Although the diaries characteristically do not report a word that Mortimer said to Scharf, we did read many entries in which they spent hours walking alone and conversing together around the estate, especially – for some reason – in the now-no-longer-extant hops garden. The small but persistent mystery of what these two men, born in the same year, might have had to say to each other dissolved into a general sense of their fitness for each other.

That sense of Lord Sackville and George Scharf's essential similarity became more disturbing as we reread what little information is available about the former, who enters the public record, the history of Knole and the history of the English country house (see Mandler, p. 210) for his infamous decisions in 1874 to close Knole House to the public and, later, in 1883, to close Knole Park. Peter Mandler sees Mortimer's decision to deny the house to visitors as in some ways part of a more general reaction on the part of the aristocracy to an increasing influx of tourists of almost all classes eager to tour great houses. Mortimer, like many of his fellow aristocrats, framed his decision as 'a defence of private property' and as a way of protecting Knole from damage (p. 201). Mandler notes the possible link between Mortimer's decision and his 'struggle[s]' to inherit Knole:

> It may have been out of a desire to enjoy fully the fruits for which he had struggled; it may have been resentment at the lordly way in which Buckhurst had pretended to carry on the Knole tradition; or it may have been (as many contemporaries claimed) that Mortimer was just a particularly sour and stuck-up old Tory who hated the dirty and ungrateful *canaille*. (pp. 200–1)

Finally, Mandler seems to side with those 'contemporaries'; Mortimer's last appearance in Mandler's text comes with the epithet 'unpleasant' (p. 210).

Robert Sackville-West's description of his ancestor's closing of Knole Park to the public suggests that this first Lord Sackville was not only a bully but something of a coward. In 1883, after Mortimer added a series of wooden posts around the locked gates at Knole – 'prevent[ing] horses and even prams from entering' – the villagers of Sevenoaks, who had been accustomed to strolling, riding and wheeling babies through the Park, rose in protest. On Bonfire Night they carried a 'giant sketch' through the town, 'showing a bridleway through the park, and a pig – Mortimer – perched on top of Knole House' (R. Sackville West, p. 166). The following year Mortimer was subject to even more carnivalesque protests, including men dressed as women wheeling prams and forcing themselves into the Park. About one thousand inhabitants of Sevenoaks stormed the Park on two consecutive days, damaging some windows and other property and terrifying the inhabitants of Knole. Mortimer called in the police on more than one occasion, becoming the subject of public demonstrations in Sevenoaks on Guy Fawkes Day in 1883 and again in 1884, as villagers carried a coffin through the streets (R. Sackville-West, pp. 166–7). Eventually a compromise was reached allowing pedestrian access to the footpaths in Knole Park, but not before a traumatised Mortimer had temporarily vacated the premises to hide out for a while with Lady Sackville in the Grand Hotel at Scarborough (R. Sackville-West, p. 167). It is sometimes hard to see Mortimer in a 'direct line' of battle-tested Sackvilles.

Mortimer also figures unheroically in the inheritance plot, not so much because he (like his brothers and sisters) scrabbled for decades over possession of Knole, but because of his not leaving in his will any money to his nephews and nieces, whom he refused to speak to when he was alive.[5] To be sure, his descendants do not remember him with much affection. Robert Sackville-West says that '[a] pair of gloomy portraits of Mortimer and his wife were consigned to a dilapidated passage in the house, where his whiskery, dark-hearted presence still casts a pall' (p. 168). It is hard not to see Mortimer as a petty old man and to wonder what Scharf might have seen in him.

Another way of posing this question is to ask what it was that Scharf was doing at Knole besides eating dinners followed by walks with his host in the hops garden. We know that he speaks of 'arranging', or 'altering' the hanging of, paintings (D 2 August 1877), and his sketchbooks are full of portrait sketches from Knole from this period as well as earlier. Most of his work with the portraits seems to have been done with the supervision – or at least in the company – of Lady Sackville; perhaps Mortimer, like Vita's grandfather, knew 'nothing whatever about the works of art in the house'; perhaps he saw them only in terms of their monetary value and in the context of family legal battles.

As one might expect, Scharf does not comment directly on the family lawsuits in which his host is involved. On several occasions, while Scharf was visiting, Lord Sackville went to London; just once, on 2 August 1877, Scharf connects his host's journey to 'an appeal in the House of Lords', noting that Lord Sackville returned with 'good news'. There must have been many visits to London, much scheming and planning that, for whatever reason, do not make it into the diary, although, as we shall see later, the legal and the domestic do come together briefly, registering in Scharf's bodily experiences in Knole House.

Scharf's cheerful invocation of 'good news' shows him to be at least somewhat in the know about Mortimer's legal proceedings; it is also, of course, clear that Scharf takes Mortimer's side. It is easy to see Scharf's careful work with the family portraits as aligned with Mortimer's interests, either in a general way as producing for Mortimer a sense of lineage and possession or, more specifically, as clarifying the provenance and value of individual paintings. Scharf's talents – his love of detail, his penchant for hard work and his professional interest in family portraits, as well as his predilections – his snobbery, his love of good food, his sense (which we will discuss below) that portraits are about the sitter – fit almost too neatly with Mortimer's agenda for Knole.

Days and nights at Knole

In asking what it was, exactly, that Scharf was doing at Knole, we came up against a new challenge to our disciplinary assumptions and to our long relationship with the idea of George Scharf. While, as we discuss below, many of Scharf's activities fell outside narrow definitions of 'work', we had, at some point, to contend with the nature of the work he did: with its central protocols, knowledges and practices. We had, in other words, to take on Scharf's place in the history of portraiture. Because we had turned early on – and predictably – to his obituary, we knew the best that could be said about him; because we had read for mentions of Scharf in the London *Times* after his death, we had some idea of his influence at the turn of the twentieth century as an authenticator and historian of portraits. We imagined that a small but satisfying part of our own work would be to showcase him: to put him back, as it were, into his proper place in museum studies and in the history of portraiture – two fields about which we knew very little. Part of this endeavour involved, finally, looking at his published works – the articles for the *Journal of the Antiquarian Society*, the *Athenaeum* and *The Times*, for example. What we found was, in a word, disappointing. We found someone who could be called (again there is no word for this identity) a Great Describer. Like his sketches, but with less verve and energy, his written texts stick close to the surface of his objects of study, describing rather than analysing them.

It was, in part, this descriptive modality that made Scharf's work

Fig. 4.2 Aphra Behn: typical sketch of a portrait
from GS's sketchbooks, May 1873.
©National Portrait Gallery, London.

on portraits so problematic for us. We had already flipped through
hundreds of pages of his sketches of portraits and noted their
repeated characteristics: the quick outline of the sitter's body, geo-
metric and undetailed, surrounded by careful notes about clothing
and colour (Fig. 4.2). There was, to our eyes, something compelling in the authority and – in our ignorance we fumbled for words
– *sketchiness* of the figural outlines: the listing of eye and hair colour,

the shades and details of fabric. There was, however, something almost ungainly, perhaps even flat-footed, about the translation of the colours of the original portrait into the colour-words of the black-and-white sketches. And, yet, especially *en masse*, we were able to see, even in these flattened representations, Scharf's visual energy and imagination at work.

We found a similar flatness in Scharf's writing about portraits, especially in what were probably his most influential pieces on portrait authentication. In a book by his successor at the NPG, dedicated to Scharf and based on Scharf's research on portraits of Mary, Queen of Scots, Lionel Cust presents Scharf as the 'first person [. . .] to approach the subject by a really scientific method' (Cust, *Notes*, p. 3). Intrigued by this promise of innovation and, indeed, by the appearance of 'science', we imagined early versions of current protocols for dating paint and canvas or for the identification of characteristic lines. Instead, we were repeatedly sent back to Scharf's elaborate and painstaking lexicon of colour – in this case eye colour, the crucial element in authentication. In 1888, Scharf wrote four letters to *The Times* about genuine and spurious portraits of Mary Stuart. He argues in them that most purported portraits of her were not 'reliable':

> The reliable portraits are few in number, and they are easily distinguished by peculiarities which they all possess in common. Among these the most remarkable is the colour of the eyes. They are decidedly brown, sometimes of a yellowish hue (hazel), but more frequently of an absolute reddish colour like chestnut and the paint known to artists as 'burnt sienna'. (Scharf, 'Portraits of Mary, Queen of Scots')

The eye-colour test is crucial to Scharf's work on a portrait that he reidentifies as being of Mary's mother and not of Mary herself, because the woman pictured has blue eyes (Scharf, 'Portraits of Mary, Queen of Scots'). Years after Scharf's death, in 1928, Cust wrote a letter to *The Times* about Scharf's method: 'Scharf used to say that the only item of herself which a woman could not alter or disguise was the colour of her eyes' (Cust, 'Mary, Queen of Scots'). Agency (and duplicity) in representation here is completely given over to the (woman) sitter; there is no sense that the painter could have purposely or otherwise 'altered' the sitter's eye colour, no indication that a portrait's colours could have faded or changed with age or that eye colour itself could have varied with light or mood.

Of course, eye colour is not the whole story; Scharf also paid quite a bit of attention to costume, to provenance and to a portrait's role in family history. But all of these elements focus on the sitter and, indeed, on the sitter-as-person. This emphasis should not have come as a surprise to us; after all, the NPG collection is arranged by sitter, as Scharf's correspondence about portrait acquisition throughout his time as secretary makes clear. Still, it was difficult for us not to see Scharf's person-centred work as in some ways co-extensive with his snobbery.

Our uneasiness was not entirely about Scharf's snobbery, however, nor even about how it might play into a not-too-dignified quarrel over possession. We were less than impressed by the principles Scharf applied in rehanging the collection at Knole. As we have suggested, when we first realised that Scharf spent a great deal of time arranging the collection, we originally imagined his work proceeding from some principle of painting or history or portraiture of which we were ignorant (and about which we would be obliged to learn). What we saw in the daily entries, however, was somewhat anti-climactic: for example, Scharf's diary entry for 20 August 1877 has him '[w]ith Lady Sackville shifting some of the pictures, especially horse subjects'. We admit we do not know all that goes into the hanging of paintings, but our first thought was to wonder whether Lady Sackville truly needed a professional to sort out the horses from, say, the sheep or the goats.

It was only much later, after the publication of Pergam's book on Scharf's early work with the Manchester Art Treasures Exhibition, that we began to understand Scharf as an innovator in the history of display. As we note in our introduction, Scharf's 'chronological hangs' at public exhibitions allowed for a 'comparative methodology' between national traditions (Pergam, p. 65). Although the comparative scheme would not have been part of his work in private collections, he might have had equally interesting ideas about the arrangement of family portraits. In the absence of scholarship on the private catalogues, we simply do not know. We do know, however – and again we discuss this briefly in the introduction – that Scharf was critical of the arrangements of family portraits in situ, especially for their 'poor lighting' and 'awkward' placement (Pergam, p. 59). Perhaps, then, we had underestimated what Scharf was accomplishing at Knole.

Back to the table

If during the day Scharf was often the portrait rearranger, family historian and unofficial docent of the collection, in the evenings – when he sat down to the dinners immortalised in those folding menu boxes – he would share a table with the likes of a 'Sir Howard Elphinstone' (D 16 July 1877); a 'Lady Janet Taylor' (sister of Marquess of Tweeddale) (D 8 November 1877) and a 'Prince Solms & Lord Dunchaux' (D 2 August 1877). After dinner Scharf participated in card games ('fortunetelling and fishponds'; D 27 August 1877), played piano duets (D 29 August 1877); listened to fellow guests' singing of French and Italian songs (D 7 July 1877); and sometimes sat up past midnight in the smoking room with other gentlemen (D 8 November 1877). Some evenings the guests would assemble in the music-room to listen to the orchestrion, a device resembling an oversized music box that could play various cartridges to imitate the sound of a symphony orchestra. In all these interactions, the scholar whose presence hinged on work he was doing for the proprietor seems to have taken on the same status as the invited guests with whom he passed the time.

As far as we are concerned, the chief attraction of staying with the Sackvilles in those days had to be the dinners. Ah, those dinners! The Knole menus are, after all, the thing that enticed us into this project with their over-the-top presentation of pure gustatory luxury. At their most expansive, dinners at Knole could be inconceivably elaborate, like this one from 16 July 1877 (we have translated some of the less familiar culinary terms):

Diner du 16 Juillet
Potage Gaufret [soup garnished with miniature waffles]
Potage Crécy au Riz [soup of carrots and rice]
Filets de Sole Cardinale [sole in a reddish sauce, probably garnished with lobster]
Filets de Laperaux Chasseur [2–4–month-old hare, prepared with mushrooms and shallots]
Ballottines de Volaille au Jardinière [poultry boned, stuffed, rolled, poached, coated in aspic and sliced, with mixed vegetables]
Tête de Veau Financière [calf's head with rich garnish of truffled chicken quenelles, cockscombs and kidneys, olives, mushroom caps and demi-glace sauce flavoured with Madeira and truffle essence]
Quartier d'Agneau rôti S[au]ce. Absinthe
Pigeons rôti [roasted pigeons]

Pois à l'Anglaise [peas with butter, sugar and herbs]
Aspics de Foie Gras
Croûte à l'Espagnole [crusts of fried bread, filled with anchovy butter
and chopped boiled eggs, bound with tartare sauce,
garnished with olives]
Puddings glacé au Thé [an iced dessert flavoured with tea]
Pains à la Duchesse [choux pastry with sweet filling or,
possibly, macaroons]

The next day's dinner was a little less fancy but, nonetheless, pro-
digious. To stay at Knole was, for Scharf, to eat this way night after
night after night.

Until the night, that is, when Scharf reports that he arrived at
Knole to find 'Lord and Lady Sackville alone & most of the servants gone'. In his entry for 14 October 1878, Scharf reports that
the butler, the housekeeper, both footmen and the lady's maid had
'all been dismissed', leaving only two servants and the underbutler
to run the enormous household (D 14 October 1878). Scharf was
there alone with the Sackvilles, in keeping with his quasi-familial
position in the house. Three days after his arrival Scharf notes,
'A small question of servants' wages settled in the County Court
against Lord Sackville' (D 17 October 1878). Like so many details
of Victorian diaries, this, of course, raises more (small) questions
than it answers: did Lord Sackville refuse to pay the servants their
back wages? Tradition has it that at some point Mortimer dismissed
servants he thought had been poisoning him. Was this an early
instantiation of that fantasy? On Thursday, 24 October, Scharf
reports having 'advised Thomas the underbutler [he of the uncon-
summated romance plot of Chapter 2] to remain a few days longer'
(D 24 October 1878). 'Advised' implies that Thomas asked Scharf
what he should do. Why would the underbutler turn to the houseguest for help? Why did Scharf think Thomas ought to stay? Why
did Thomas – or the others – want to go? The diary does not tell
us more, though the menus in Scharf's album show the meals were
comparatively plain and the French menus very inexpertly written during this period. From this we have concluded that, as with
financial accounts, much can be learned through the close reading
of menus.

And also through the close reading of architecture. When he
stayed at Knole, Scharf apparently was assigned to a particular
bedroom that he came to call 'my room, next to the chapel with
the Benedictus fireplace' (D 18 August 1877, D 1 February 1879).

During his visit in October of 1878, Scharf spent the better part of a week 'sketching in Lady Sackville's room' (D 24–5, 28 October 1878). On our first pass through the diaries, we wondered about the propriety of a single gentleman's spending so much time in a lady's boudoir, though the more specific notation of 28 October, 'Sketching picture in Lady Sackville's room', was reassuring (D 28 October 1878). We did not dream of any connection between the little room with the Benedictus fireplace and the bedroom of the lady of the house until we went ourselves to explore the private quarters of the great house where Scharf had come to feel so much at home.

In which we become guests of the Sackvilles (sort of)

In the summer of 2012, having contacted the present Lord Sackville about our book project, we were delighted to receive an invitation to come to Knole to locate the settings of Scharf's experiences there. Lord Sackville was to be away from home during the weekend we proposed for our visit, but he told us his mother would be glad to show us the house. We were greeted at the visitors' gate by Mrs Bridget West, whose late husband was the previous Lord Sackville, and who has lived at Knole for some forty years. The house is so large and so rambling in its interior architecture, even Mrs West is capable of being surprised by what lies behind some of its doors.

With good humour and great spirit, Mrs West took us into the private spaces we knew from Scharf's diaries: the music-room, now a sitting-room; the Poets' Parlour, now a formal dining-room still decorated with the old portraits of the English literary greats; and the Retainers' Gallery, a ruined barracks at the top of the house. We saw family portraits that had not made it into the public rooms, including, in a narrow passageway, the matched pair of Mortimer and Elizabeth Sackville. It is this portrait of Mortimer that led Robert Sackville to describe its subject as 'gloomy [. . .] whiskery [and] dark hearted'. Mortimer stands stiffly in front of what at first appeared to us to be Knole itself. Elizabeth, her face turned to the left, is royally dressed in red velvet and ermine. The building in the background of her portrait, probably the same as the one in Mortimer's, has a slightly more European air; her small white hand emerges from her sleeve to rest on a tomb or a ruin. With their massive gilt frames, the Mortimer and Elizabeth portraits seemed to us too big for the human scale of the run-down hallway carved out of the enormity of Knole. Everything about the portraits – from the frames to the costumes and the poses of their central figures, to their geographical conceits – suggested that these were meant to be publicly displayed, to present a public face in a home whose negotiation of the public and the private had been an issue for so long.[6] Averse as he was to letting the public inside the house, Mortimer now moulders in a space where no one but the family can see him, and where no one pays him much attention at all.

Like the visit to the paper archive, the archival home visit unfolds within an idiom of discovery and, thus, of privacy and secrecy. When we set out on the journey to and through Knole, we tried to quash any expectation that we would unearth something new that would be relevant to our project. After all, we had only a few hours in a house that had been continuously inhabited since Scharf's visits to the Sackvilles. Our archival self-disciplining worked well for the first hour or so; we were there to see and inhabit the space where Scharf had spent so much time; this was a re-enactment project and not a truly archival one. We confess, however, that what Jane Eyre might call a less 'tempered' narrative broke down (as did Jane's) when we found ourselves in the capacious attics above the private rooms at Knole. The attic is, after all, where secrets, archival and otherwise, are to be found: who has not dreamed of finding the missing manuscript in the attic? The letter in the trunk?

At first these rooms were a disappointment. There were so many of them, and they were all empty and quite clean. We identified the 'barracks room' to which Scharf had led a tour; there was no trace of his presence on the floors or in the air of the room. One upstairs room, however, looked like the attic of our archival fantasy. It was full of discarded objects: lamps, mysterious glass cases, broken furniture, trunks and pictures stacked on the floor. As we walked between the uneven rows of things, we felt both the excitement of the archival journey and a more quotidian (and to Helena, personally familiar) despair in the face of household junk. We were not, of course, responsible for tidying the attic or for cleaning it, but we were there to bring a different kind of order that depended on a mental if not a physical sorting: we had to separate what was important to our project from what was not. While the paper archive produces some of the same urgencies, this was different: we had only a few minutes, we did not want to waste our hostess' time and these were objects – many of them heavy or awkward – that had to be lifted, turned, got at.

Our first 'find' – we think this was the word we must unconsciously have borrowed from the idiom of our shared antique shopping – was, perhaps, appropriately, not related to Scharf, but to Vita. It was a large mounted photograph of the twenty-one-year-old Vita's wedding to Nigel Nicholson in 1913 that served as a reminder of how we, psychologically speaking, got to Knole in the first place. Picking our way to the middle of the room, we made another discovery, a trace of another marriage more immediately relevant to our story: two matching red velvet cases, which, when opened, proved to be what Mrs West recognised as 'travelling' portraits of Mortimer and Elizabeth. Although not miniatures by any means, these middle-sized encased portraits would have accompanied their owners and subjects on journeys – perhaps in this case even on the Sackvilles' trip to the Continent to avoid the repercussions of the footpath scandal. Despite the jewel-box sumptuousness of their velvet cases, these travelling portraits seemed homier, more intimate, than the ones on the downstairs wall. Their subjects were older, less formally dressed, far less grandly posed. Outfitted for a rather chilly outdoors against an indeterminate background, they could have been a country squire and his wife. This was the quotidian Mortimer, the slightly second-rate one; we both liked this Mortimer better.

Of course, our fondness for the portraits derived in part from how we found them; face down, and abandoned to the attic, they spoke not only of the marginality of these particular Sackvilles to the history of the house but to the romance of the archive. It was as if the portraits of these marginal figures had been placed there (left there?) by an archival divinity for us to find, rescue and reintroduce into the story of Knole, most immediately by photographing them. Robyn's iPhone camera, which had already produced unexpectedly lucid pictures of Scharf's sketches and diary pages, as well as pictures of other rooms at Knole, allowed us to do Scharf's work of replicating portraits in more portable genres. We had our own travelling versions of these not-so-travelling portraits, to be transferred from phone to computer desktop.

Our most exciting discovery, though, came when Mrs West welcomed us into her own spacious apartment in what used to be the guest wing of the great house. Leading us down the corridor adjacent to her apartment, she remarked that the subject of our study must have stayed in one of these bedrooms, far from the part of the house where Lord Sackville's young family lives. We told her about Scharf's references to 'the Benedictus fireplace' (having no clue what that meant) in the 'little room by the chapel'. Seeming puzzled, she took us across the vast courtyard to the centre of the house, where we entered a chapel the size of a small parish church, with its vaulted ceiling, wooden pews, ancient organ and stained-glass windows. We climbed a back staircase from the chapel to a hallway leading us into a small room where we found a fireplace with 'Benedictus' carved into the mantelpiece. This had to be Scharf's 'own little room'. Mrs West was visibly surprised, and even more so when we stepped out of that room to find ourselves in the hallway where Lady Sackville's room used to be. 'Well!' she said, 'That *is* strange.'

Knowing George Scharf the way we flatter ourselves we do, we are certain that the proximity of his room to Lady Sackville's reflected no impropriety. What it suggests to us is intimacy of a different kind. Lord and Lady Sackville placed Scharf in a room where a close relative might stay. If he began his sojourns at Knole as a quasi-employee and continued there in the guise of a guest, by the time the 'Benedictus fireplace' room had become his own, he was something like family. We looked out of the windows onto the lovely views from Lady Sackville's room, remembering that Scharf had spent many days there helping his hostess arrange the portraits on her walls.

Buzzing with the thrill of having followed Scharf into Knole's most intimate spaces, we drove away towards the village of Sevenoaks and towards Chevening. Still in thrall to the primacy of Knole, our decision to 'stop by' Chevening was an afterthought. Our English friend, who had kindly driven us down to Kent from London, gently informed us of something we should have known: Chevening is now an official government residence. It is no surprise that Chevening is a high-security site; as we drove its perimeter it was impossible to see anything but the top of its roof. While, as its recent website notes, Chevening is open to the public only a few times a year, it functions very much as a sort of anti-Knole, free of tourists, tea-rooms, and – by and large – researchers and scholars. 'Occupied' but not 'owned' by government officials nominated under the 1987 amended Chevening Estate Act, it, too, negotiates public and private functions, but it does so in a seclusion that Mortimer Sackville might well have envied.

We had not prepared for this second visit. Like the villagers of Sevenoaks under Mortimer's reign at Knole, we were destined to remain on the outside, looking at a national treasure from a distance. Even as we circled Chevening, unable to penetrate its perimeter, much less its mysteries, we knew we would have to come to terms with the power it had over George Scharf's story. We would have to confront what may have been the central – and in all senses most powerful – relationship of Scharf's life: with the 6th Earl Stanhope, intellectual, patron of the arts, Tory member of Parliament and chairman of the Board of Trustees of the NPG. The way in – at least for now – was not through the home but through the paper archive, official and ephemeral.

Friends at Chevening

One of us – Helena – now owns two pieces of Scharf ephemera of her own. Sometimes buried on her desk among student papers, fragments of the manuscript of this book and medical bills (Helena is the messy one), one piece occasionally resurfaces to produce a shock of (mis)recognition; the well-known handwriting that signals to her the heft and distance of London is oddly at home on her desk. Although she cannot always lay her hand on this piece of paper, she has never searched for it in vain or for very long. The handwriting, more familiar than her own since she has stopped writing in longhand, calls to her from beneath other things. If this call seems too mystical, there is another explanation that perhaps is more mystical still. It is the only piece of paper on her desk with a black border; it is a fragment of mourning, a *memento mori* (Fig. 4.3). Like Jack's confessional letter to George, it produces a little shock every time she sees it.

We call this object a piece of paper rather than a letter or a note because there is no context for this single sheet on which are written two sentences very similar to ones from Scharf's diary. The paper says:

> The last time I saw Lord Stanhope was at Chevening 20th November 1875. I had almost up to the last moment been reading to him 'Advice to Julia' by Henry Lutterell [sic] illegitimate son of Lord Carhampton, published by Murray 1820. Lord Stanhope enjoyed it very much. (underlining in the original)

In the bottom right-hand corner of the page are the initials 'GS'; across the bottom of the paper is written in small letters and in a different hand, 'Sir G. Scharf director N.P.G'. The label vaguely implies the paper belongs to some archive, but it provides no origin or context for the isolated existence of these two sentences.

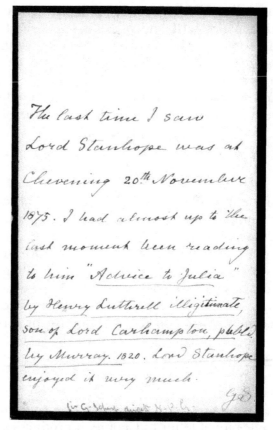

Fig. 4.3 Scharfiana: fragment of GS's handwriting referring to
Lord Stanhope's death. From Private Collection of Helena Michie.

Scharf's writing, in his customary black ink, begins one quarter
of the way down the page. Without salutation or title, the writing seems unanchored – or rather anchored only to the bottom
of the page by the painterly initials and to the sides by the black
frame. Although its content is precise about dates, the page itself is
undated. It is a small surviving miracle of specificity, but it gives no
specifics about itself.

The content of the two sentences echoes but does not precisely
replicate Scharf's much more elaborate diary entry of 20 November
1875:

At 4 o'clock read more of Lutterell's [sic] Advice to Julia to LS which he
enjoyed very much. When near 5 he dismissed me to take some tea with

Lady Mahon [Stanhope's daughter-in-law] in the drawing room before
starting. I kissed his hand, and alas never saw him again. I feel most grateful to have been allowed latterly to be so intimate with him, & rejoice
that I gave up all other engagements & invitations to be with him at
Chevening. I never had a truer friend. [In his artist's hand at the bottom
of the page:] He died 24th December 1875. R. I. P.

Both of these accounts attempt to record a fragment of time; the
diurnal rhythms of the diary add to the year, the month and the
day a time of day: 4 o'clock, teatime. The diary entry records, as do
other entries about Chevening, a domestic context. Both accounts
give the name of the book Scharf read to his friend;[7] both register
Lord Stanhope's enjoyment of it. Oddly, the shorter piece offers
an extended genealogy of the writer, Henry Luttrell; this seems
to take the place of the more intimate genealogy of the diary in
which Scharf moves from deathbed to tea table, from father- to
daughter-in-law.

It is hard to know whether the piece of ephemera is a fragment of something else – a letter, perhaps, or an enclosure in a
letter – or whether it is something (but what?) in its entirety. On
Helena's desk and on her VISA bill, which records her payment to
the Internet rare-book site Abebooks, it is an object unto itself. Like
many objects, however, it requires context – if not page numbers,
if not a provenance, at least some account of what work it might
have done in the world. Like many objects, it points outward away
from itself along a metonymic chain. Does this item somehow stand
for Scharf's relationship with his truest friend? In the absence of
other pages, this scrap of writing reads like a declaration. The two
sentences are self-authorising, establishing their own importance.
More than the diary entries about Stanhope, the simple announcement without context declares the end of Stanhope's life – and
Scharf's participation in it – to be important.

We have once again begun a story of a key relationship tha-
nocentrically, as we implicitly compare Stanhope's death as it is
represented in the diaries to accounts of the deaths of Scharf's
father and mother. What follows is an attempt to break with the
finality of Stanhope's death and to read the relationship of these
two men from something like a beginning. This involves turning to another archive, supplementing the diary, the fragment
and Scharf's general correspondence with a collection of letters
from Stanhope to Scharf from the time that Scharf was appointed

secretary of the NPG in 1857 to 1875, the year Lord Stanhope died and Scharf recorded his death in his diary. Part of the NPG collection, these letters chronicle the setting up of the Gallery; the acquisition, authentication and hanging of portraits; the evolution of the Gallery catalogue; and, implicitly, the changing role of the secretary who was to become director. This particular archive ends, of course, with Lord Stanhope's death, but the energy of this collection rests with the earlier letters between two men in mid-life, making and remaking a relationship at once personal and professional.

The archivist of this particular collection of letters is Scharf himself, the collection an act of self-archiving. Scharf does include a file of letters written by Stanhope to William Hookham Carpenter, acting secretary of the Gallery before Scharf was able to take over in October of 1857. The very first letter from Stanhope to Carpenter makes it clear that Carpenter has asked that his own son be considered for the job. Stanhope responds, in effect, that the naming of the new secretary is a *fait accompli*:

> My Dear Sir, I thank you for your communication of this morning. Will you allow me to assure you that although I am not personally acquainted with your son, I should have felt pleasure from the respect I entertain for you, if the choice of the Treasury had devolved on him. Mr Scharf is however I believe highly qualified to fill the post. (SC 5 March 1857)

The tone of Stanhope's letter is respectful enough, but somewhat dismissive of Carpenter; it also does not spend time dwelling on Scharf's qualifications. It is hard to tell whether the brevity of the comment about Scharf derives from Stanhope's reluctance to engage in detail with Carpenter's request or from unfamiliarity with Scharf's actual training and experience.

A later Stanhope letter, presumably to a Treasury official, suggests more intimate knowledge of Scharf's *vita*. In it, Stanhope asks that the secretary be paid a 'liberal salary' and that the position include 'apartments in the house or gallery allotted to our Board'. The general principle Stanhope articulates here is, by the end of the letter, framed in terms of the new secretary's particular 'merit': 'I must also add that I think the merit & reputation of Mr Scharf add another strong reason against assigning him any low & depreciated stipend for his services. I had much rather that we had less money to spend for pictures than that our Secretary be underpaid' (SC 14 March 1857).

We cannot say for certain how well Stanhope knew Scharf at this point. The two men might have met as early as the 1840s; Stanhope – or Lord Mahon as he was then – signed Scharf's certificate of election as a fellow of the Society of Antiquaries in 1852.[8] Indeed, the first year's worth of correspondence suggests that the two men are hardly acquainted outside the Gallery. The letters from Stanhope mirror the form of his address to Carpenter, beginning with the formal 'My dear Sir' and ending 'very sincerely yours, Stanhope'. On 9 October 1857, Stanhope makes a point of informing Scharf of his out-of-town address, 'Chevening, Sevenoaks', although the name and location of Stanhope's ancestral estate would have been public knowledge – and, we might add, knowledge of a kind Scharf was especially inclined to possess. Similarly, Stanhope gave Scharf his London address in Grosvenor Square in a letter dated 16 October, despite having previously written to Scharf on the letterhead of his town house (SC 1857). It is hard to read Stanhope's motive in informing Scharf of what he probably already knew: he could be making a small personal opening in the relationship through the mention of his homes or, on the contrary, he could be signalling, consciously or not, that Scharf was not personally part of the world to which he was requested to send professional letters and parcels; or he could be enacting a form of courtesy (or feigned modesty) by pretending to assume that he was not a famous earl whose residence was well known.

In the winter of 1857 we perceive a slight warming in the tone and content of Stanhope's letters to Scharf. In November he signs for the first time 'I am Sir your very faithful servant' (SC 18 November). A few weeks later he delivers his first written praise of Scharf's work, noting that 'the device for numbering [portraits] pleases me very much' and (about the catalogue Scharf was constructing) 'the goodness of your handwriting is a very real advantage to us in this as in other respects' (SC 8 December 1857). One might at this point be tempted to call Stanhope's comments faint praise, or at least praise for accomplishments of a relatively banal kind. Certainly the emphasis on numbering and handwriting suggests that at this time, despite his respect for Scharf's 'reputation', Stanhope saw the secretary's job in very narrow terms.

Around Christmas of the same year a serious conflict arose between the two men over issues of authority. Scharf had asked for permission to take a 'week's holiday at Christmas', but the letter granting the request goes on to criticise Scharf quite sharply for arrogating to himself too much authority in other areas:

[W]hile you have consulted me upon this point [the Christmas break] you have omitted to consult me upon another much more material – namely your communications with the public press. Of these you only inform me after they have taken place. Now I must take the liberty of frankly telling you that as I conceive you as Secretary of the National Portrait Commission are not entitled to send for publication any matter relative to the business of that commission without the authority and permission of the Board.

You say that you would have written to consult me 'but time was too pressing'. I have yet to learn however why assuming that any publication at all was to take place in the Atheneum or Notes & Queries it was of such pressing importance that the publication should take place in this week rather than next.

I decline to give you any opinion as to the propriety or impropriety of any such publication, or of the articles you have prepared, but I protest against the course you have taken without the smallest sanction from the Board or from myself as present Chairman. (SC 18 December 1857)

Clearly the two men were operating with different visions of what constituted a secretaryship – and perhaps of the relation between themselves. A man who has been praised for the clarity of his handwriting is perhaps unlikely to be thought of primarily in terms of his potential for contributing to the leading journals of the day. A heavily edited draft of Scharf's response, included in the file of Stanhope's letters, offers both an apology and a defence. Scharf notes that he 'receive[d] your note with great pain because it reminds me that I have overstepped the limits that I ought to have observed', but he maintains that the editors of the journals contacted him (SC 19 December 1857). Stanhope's rebuke and Scharf's apology constituted a crucial early moment in a professional relationship, when Scharf consented to defer to his boss and social superior.

We do not have any evidentiary trace of what must have been a reconciliation between the two men, but the collection begins to include items that cross what was to become – for Scharf if not also for Stanhope – the porous line between the professional and the social. On 30 January 1858 came the first invitation to Grosvenor Place to 'join two or three persons'. Soon, some letters begin to reveal in Stanhope an increasing sense of a shared project; in February Stanhope writes that he is 'excitedly pleased' with a portrait of Marvell from the Bishop of Ely (SC 5 February 1858). This missive is signed only with Stanhope's initial, although he goes back to his full name in other letters.

Throughout that spring, however, most of Stanhope's letters

retain their tone of command. On 15 February, for example, Stanhope wrote on House of Lords letterhead to register another complaint:

> Just now – here in the House of Lords – I have been very greatly vexed to hear from Lord Ellenborough to whom I had given an Order of Admission [to the Gallery] & who yesterday availed himself of it, that the Catalogue which was handed him by the servant attending was quite at fault [sic] the numbers in the Catalogue not agreeing with those affixed to the pictures. This defect cannot fail to give any visitor [. . .] a very unfavourable idea of our proceedings.

Demanding that Scharf correct the problem 'with the least possible delay', Stanhope underscores, with his resort to the imperative, the difference in their professional positions (SC 5 February 1858). Perhaps more important here are the way the signs of rank convey the sense that Stanhope is talking to a *social* inferior. The House of Lords letterhead, followed on the page by the strangely insistent phrase 'Just now, here in the House of Lords', invokes a physical and social place to which Scharf could never have access. The 'here' emphasises the distance between the place of writing and the place of receiving the letter; the 'now' suggests an aristocratic urgency that collapses the temporal distance between the chastiser and the chastised, the mistake and the necessity of fixing it without 'delay'.

Stanhope invokes what we take to be an aristocratic temporality in another chastising letter expressing his incredulity at Scharf's having scheduled a meeting of the NPG trustees at ten o'clock in the morning. Scharf had obviously misinterpreted a directive from Stanhope, who tells him:

> I never dreamt of any Meeting at ten o'clock, which [. . .] would have been a most extraordinary time to name, but intended to name to you the hour of Four [. . .] You must therefore at once issue a Circular stating that the Meeting which in the former Circular was from a misapprehension fixed at Ten O'clock will in reality take place the same day at Four. Lose no time if you please in doing this. (SC 15 June 1858)

This letter is reminiscent of an earlier missive Stanhope sent to Carpenter about scheduling a trustee meeting. Carpenter, according to Stanhope, sent the announcement out too soon: by the time of the meeting, the trustees would 'have forgotten all about it' (SC 27 February 1857). In both letters Stanhope is obviously pointing to the difference between the attitude towards time of the Board, a group composed largely of aristocrats,[9] and that of civil servants like the secretary of the NPG. Scharf, Stanhope seems to say, might be ready to work at ten in the morning, but the Board members would not; ten in the morning belongs to civil-service time and not to the temporalities that define the days of men like Lord Stanhope.

And it is here that we come to an unpredictable turning point in the story of Scharf and Stanhope. For the first time in the written history of his relationship with Scharf, Lord Stanhope tells a joke. Readers who remember our account of our very first archival error – positing that Scharf's dream of being beheaded immediately preceded the hosting of his very first dinner party – might rightly be a little suspicious here. To say that something happens for the first time is to assume a certain completeness in the archive; in a collection like the Stanhope letters there are long and uneven gaps between items. There may well have been other – and funnier – jokes in letters between Scharf's appointment in 1857 and August of 1858 that, for whatever reason, escaped Scharf's self- and institutional-archiving project. For that matter, Stanhope may have told Scharf hundreds of jokes in the Gallery, on the street or at the meetings of the Antiquarian Society; these jokes, if they were spoken, have not left a trace. But there is a joke, a small one, in a letter of 4 August: 'I thought our day at Canterbury was very pleasant & I hope that you may have found it so. But there was certainly a drawback in our bad & scanty dinner' (SC 4 August 1858). Perhaps, on second thought, 'joke' is the wrong word. It is an in-joke without being a joke, a shared allusion to a 'bad' experience despite which, or perhaps partly because of which, the two men had a 'pleasant' day. Funny or not, the not-quite joke (dare we say it) marks for us, at least, a new phase in the relationship as represented in these letters. Stanhope changed his salutation and started writing 'My dear Mr Scharf' (SC 11 August 1858). Together, the two men entered somewhat awkwardly the Scharfean gift economy: Stanhope sent Scharf one of his own books, *The History of the War of the Succession in Spain* (1832), but Scharf already had bought a copy, so Stanhope substituted his *Life of Belisarius* (1829). Scharf then sent a book to Stanhope's town house, and Stanhope wrote to thank him and to say he had not received it because he was still at Chevening. Stanhope acknowledged the gift in anticipation: 'meanwhile [. . .] accept my cordial thanks for it, with the assurance that I shall value it highly both for the giver's sake & its own' (SC 15 August 1858). Although this gift exchange was delayed, they can be seen as cementing a relationship of near-equals – at least professionally speaking. After 4 August, Lord Stanhope always says please when he asks Scharf to do something by letter, and Scharf visited Chevening with increasing regularity.

What happened at Canterbury besides the bad and scanty dinner? (How) did whatever happened change the relationship between the two men? Although there is no invitation in the folder of letters, and we found no mention there of a visit to Chevening around those dates, we know from Scharf's sketchbooks and diaries that he spent time at Knole and Chevening in late July and early August. It seems that Scharf must have used Chevening as a home base for local visits because on 27 July Scharf records a tip to a servant at Chevening on 30 July 1858 when he also writes 'to Canterbury' (D 30 July 1858). There is no indication of what the two men were doing during their time in that cathedral city.

We do not intend to suggest, readers might be relieved to know, that the night(s) in Canterbury included sex, romance or even a wish for these on the part of either man. Although we are naturally tempted to overread Scharf's silence and Stanhope's joke in the most classical Freudian ways, it does not feel quite right to do so as we did with silences and dinners involving Jack. We are willing to say that Canterbury changed everything, but we do not know why. Stanhope does not joke about the meals they most likely shared at Chevening, even though the only other connection we have traced between Stanhope, eating and joking happened at Chevening when Lady Stanhope, the funny person in the family, served Stanhope a meal deliberately made up of his least favourite foods (Newman, p. 313). There is something about travelling to Canterbury, that shared and isolated moment, which might have served as a metonymy for the whole visit or might have seemed quite distinct from it. The exchange of gifts that followed put the relationship, as it were, into conversation with Scharf's other male friendships, making them legible in a new way. For the first time, we see a mention of the Stanhopes efficiently incorporated into the summary for 1858; Chevening appears alongside Dutch lessons, breakfasts with London friends and the health of Scharf's mother and aunt.

The next year – 1859 – is perhaps the most crucial one for the relationship and the first one in which Scharf speaks of a 'friend-ship' between himself and Stanhope. As we have noted in Chapter 2, Scharf uses the word 'friend' in a variety of ways – to designate the professional men with whom he associates in London and also the titled connections whom we might understand as 'friends' in an older sense, more closely approximating 'patron' or 'advisor'. Stanhope is, of course, not literally a patron in that he does not directly support Scharf financially; as we shall see over the next few years, however, Stanhope was to take a variety of steps to promote Scharf's career, offering professional advice, introducing him to other titled 'friends' (and portrait owners) and even presenting him at court. But the older meaning of 'friend' is insufficient to describe the relationship from 1859 onward; in that year, Scharf emerges as what we would now call a 'family friend', a frequent visitor to Lord Stanhope's country home. As with Knole, it is dif-ficult to say what exactly Scharf was doing at Chevening (we take this issue up in its place), but at Chevening there is a bigger issue, which has to do with the meaning of the word 'friend' and the dif-ficulty of describing a relationship that borrows from the ancient discourse of patronage, the emerging modern discourse of emo-tional closeness and a Victorian discourse of professionalism and collegiality.[10]

The year 1859 opens with a New Year's letter from Stanhope (SC 1 January 1859) and, three days later, a second, better or at least more extended joke that underscores the Earl's growing profes-sional identification with Scharf:

> I thank you for the list you have sent me of the rejected pictures. Our choice last year has been so good that I do not think the disappointed picture dealers will be able to console themselves like the young lady's suitors in a contemporary poem:
> 'It soothes the awkward squad of the rejected
> To see how very badly she selected!' (SC 4 January 1859)

In quoting Byron's *Don Juan* (canto XII, stanza 36), Stanhope playfully compares picture-buying to marriage. Perhaps more tell-ing, however, is Stanhope's use of 'Our choice' to signify not only a single act of rejection and selection but a whole year of such actions, which have remade the two men into a first-person plural. Stanhope's note is a form of Scharf-like annualising, prompted no doubt by Scharf's careful list of the year in pictures; it is significant both that Stanhope shares the credit and that they come together over a list, a history of a year spent in each other's professional company.

In this crucial year we also begin to see Scharf emerging in a new light as a bona fide family friend. Two days after the last letter, Stanhope mentions Lady Stanhope for the first time in the correspondence: 'Lady Stanhope desires to join with me in returning to you our cordial thanks for the two copies of your interesting tract. How very excellent though slight are the engraved illustrations with which you have adorned it!' (SC 6 January 1859). In naming and representing Lady Stanhope, Lord Stanhope presents himself, interpolates himself, as a married man, opening a link to his private life that is arguably in some ways more powerful than an invitation to Chevening. Later in the year Stanhope will represent his daughter, too, in an expanded gift economy: 'My daughter desires me to return to you her cordial thanks for your kind remembrance & large accession to her cypher-book' (SC 14 December 1859). While it is possible that Scharf has contributed a 'cypher' to the book, it is more likely that he was contributing some of the sketches that would become an important currency of his visits to great houses. If he was included – although in a mediated way – in an exchange network with the women of the Stanhope family, he was also included in more formal and public family events, including a coming-of-age party for Stanhope's son, Lord Mahon, at which George danced all night before returning home to London (D 1 January 1860).

February 1859 marked a real moment of public triumph for Scharf, in large part due to the interventions of Lord Stanhope, who presented his protégé to the queen at a levee on the 23rd of the month. While we do not know who suggested the presentation, Stanhope seems quite enthusiastic about it, reminding Scharf, who has been invited to the Duke of Marlborough's at Blenheim, to be sure to be back in London for the presentation. 'Only remember that if there be a Levee on the 23rd (as is now reported) that is the one which I shall attend, & at which my name will be gladly at your service for your presentation. I have this day sent in your name in due form to the Lord Chamberlain's office for Presentation at the next Levee' (SC 15 February 1859). Scharf's diary duly records on the 23rd, 'Queen's Levee. To be presented by Earl Stanhope' (D 23 February 1859), and includes the event in the year-end summary.

The 1859 letters also indicate that Scharf is making connections with other owners of great houses. In August Scharf has to refuse an invitation to Chevening because of a prior invitation to Blenheim. This is clearly work-related, as he is cataloguing the portraits in the Blenheim connection, but Stanhope's gracious letter about the conflict de-emphasises Scharf's professional role:

> We were very sorry not to see you here on Saturday but should have regretted still much more your putting off your other engagements on our account. You will have fine weather I trust for your week at so beautiful a place as Blenheim. Pray ask the Duke of Marlborough to be so kind as to let us know if he hears (as he is likely to do at some time or other) of any good portraits for sale of the first Duke or of the Duchess. (D 16 August 1859)

The mention of the portraits is framed as an afterthought; Stanhope's remarks about the beauties of Blenheim discreetly imply that Scharf will simply be there to enjoy them.

It is from Blenheim and on Blenheim letter-paper that Scharf writes the year-end summary for 1859 on 1 January 1860, quoted at greater length in Chapter 2:

> To Woodstock Church with the Duke and Duchess of Marlborough & family [. . .] The occupation & locality which ring the new year upon me were perhaps to indicate a pleasing event both in the past year & my future life. My position in the Portrait Gallery is excellent & the confidence of the Trustees unreserved. Lord & Lady Stanhope several times invited me to Chevening & especially on the occasion of Ld. Mahon's coming of age. Their friendship was strikingly shewn [. . .] My presentation at Court was also an Event.

Although Scharf has used the word 'friends' many times in the diary to mean everything from 'pals' to people who lend him money, this is the first time he has used the term for Lord Stanhope. Perhaps he is emphasising the personal nature of the relationship when he includes Lady Stanhope – who is not, after all, involved in the business affairs of the NPG – in the pluralised, abstracted form of the words: 'Their friendship'.

What the year-end summary does not include, of course, is the dailiness of the working relationship between Scharf and Stanhope, an element that is also not strongly present in the diary. We do get a taste of the changes in that relationship from Stanhope's letters to Scharf, which, as we have seen, grow more intimate in tone as they begin to rely on the idiom of shared vision and labour. Nowhere is this clearer than in the relatively rare instances where Stanhope feels he must correct Scharf's work. If we contrast the early, abrupt letters of correction with one written in June of 1860, we will see a substantial change in tone and address:

> In all these it is very important that we should have our dates scrupulously accurate. Now you have given the 17th of April as the day on which Hastings' trial concluded; I believe that you will find it to have been the 23rd. (SC 27 June 1859)

More remarkable than the politeness of the 'I believe' is the 'we' of the first sentence. A celebrated historian in his own right, Stanhope is identifying with Scharf and taking shared responsibility, not for this mistake, but for the accuracy of their joint representations to the public. It is during this year that Stanhope also refers to 'our' letter to *The Times* – surely a sign of having worked through the issues having to do with Scharf's relations to the 'public press' (SC 17 March 1859).

'Friend', of course, can also extend to family connections. It might have been around this time that Lady Stanhope wrote to Scharf a quite intimate note asking him to ask the gallery assistant, Mr Lee, to help transport her younger son, Philip, from London to Chevening. The tone of the letter is playful, even intimate:

> Dear Mr Scharf –
>
> My young scamp Philip goes thro' London on <u>Friday</u> next – do you think it would be very wrong if I were so far to divert Lee from the public service as to ask him to see Philip safe from our Grosvenor Place house [. . .] in a cab & lodge him in the Sevenoaks Omnibus which you know leaves Charing Cross at 3 o'ck.
>
> Philip is to arrive early at the Victoria Station from Brighton.
>
> If you can arrange this for me, I know you will – and it would be very kind, for Philip is terribly independent & keeps me in a constant motherly fidget till I see him safe! I have not of course written to Lee but leave it in your kind hands. (SC undated; underlining in original)

In asking Scharf to contact Lee, Lady Stanhope is also 'diverting' Scharf himself from 'public service'. Despite her apologies and her jokes, Lady Stanhope is, of course, indirectly issuing a demand, if not a command, on the authority of that other more exalted public servant, her husband, Scharf's boss. By pointing out that she has not written to Lee directly, she indicates her grasp of the proper chain of command. In more ways than the exchange of books and sketches might suggest, Lady Stanhope is part of an extended network of connection along which those gifts (and tellingly children) travel from London to Chevening and back.

Throughout the 1860s Scharf continues his formal acknowledgement of the Stanhopes in his year-end summaries, but the mentions
of his time with the family at Chevening grow more specific, more
intimate and more detailed. While the year-end summary for 1862,
from which we have quoted before, takes on the contours of a professional narrative that comes to include other titled friends ('all
my views well understood & my pursuits so thoroughly supported
by Ld. Stanhope, the Duke of Marlborough and Lord Derby'),
his diary emphasises domestic connections. One such anniversary
entry comes on Scharf's birthday in 1864:

> My 44th Birthday finds me very honourably and pleasantly located in the
> house of my *patron and friend* Earl Stanhope where I have been residing
> on a visit since Wednesday the 7th instant. The friendly terms on which I
> am received by the family is exceedingly agreeable. Soon after breakfast
> I went into the Library where Lord Stanhope was altering some of the
> book presses and where he had introduced a very pleasant open fire for
> sitting by [. . .] Charles Lewes wrote to offer to come see me on my birth-
> day, but my engagement to remain at Chevening till Monday prevent[ed]
> me from accepting it [. . .] I enjoyed a good deal of music in the course
> of the day with Lady Mary and Lord Mahon. Henry Stanhope came &
> chatted in my room [. . .] The chief part of the afternoon was devoted
> to a general sketch of the events of 1864 for Lady Stanhope's album
> [. . .] Lady Mary gave me a piece of India rubber and drank my health at
> dinner. We had various games in the evening whilst others played at whist
> [. . .] Lady Mary gave me a pair of slippers she had been working for me,
> & on Sunday showed me in her room all her evening dresses, tiaras and
> ball dresses. Spent a large portion of Saturday in the Tapestry room with
> Lady Stanhope & Lady Mary in painting fans & copying various pictures
> from Knole. (D 16 December 1864; italics added)

This is the only instance we have found in which Scharf refers to
Stanhope as a 'patron'; rhetorically, the pairing of 'patron and
friend' allows him to empty the term 'friend' of the connotations of
patronage and to emphasise its private nature.[11] The unidiomatic
locution of 'residing on a visit' suggests how much he feels at home
at Chevening, where he presents himself as having access not only
to Lord Stanhope's inner sanctum – to his cosy library – but to the
domain of the women of the family. Resisting invitations from his
London friends like Charles Lewes, Scharf remains ensconced at
Chevening on his birthday in what appears to be a quasi-familial
role. Lady Mary, the daughter of the house, opens her closets for
his inspection, works slippers for him and gives him the small but
significant birthday gift of an India rubber, suggesting an allusion

to and appreciation of his role as a producer of sketches. While Scharf does not appear in this entry as a professional draughtsman, he does note participating in the more communal and familial pursuit of painting fans. While Mary's handmade slippers are perhaps the most obvious sign of intimacy, the detail Scharf offers about contributing a 'general sketch of the events of 1864 for Lady Stanhope's album' seems in some ways even more telling. Whether 'sketch' means drawing or timeline here, we must imagine Scharf not only absorbing the Stanhope family into his own chronologies within the diary but also producing chronologies for them. These are temporal as well as spatial intimacies.

In 1865, Scharf apparently took another important professional step for which he sought advice from his 'patron and friend'. On Christmas Day of 1864, Scharf notes in his diary that he has 'put by a letter which I had received three days before from Lord Derby requesting me to make him a Catalogue Raisonné of his pictures at Knowlsey, together with a kind letter of advice which Lord Stanhope had sent me respecting it'. The letter from Lord Derby asked Scharf to name an 'honorarium' for the work (DC 23 December 1864). Although we do not have Scharf's letter, he apparently wrote to Stanhope asking if, given his position at the NPG, he could accept money for making the catalogue. Stanhope wrote back immediately, assuring Scharf that he felt his confidence in Scharf to be justified. He notes that, 'apart from our official ties' he feels an 'interest' in Scharf's 'welfare and prosperity' (DC 23 December 1864). Stanhope is very positive about Lord Derby's offer, telling Scharf he would be 'doing an injustice to yourself & your family were you to hesitate as to accepting the commission which Lord Derby offers & receiving an Honorarium'. In this same letter Stanhope tells Scharf that the NPG 'trustees [. . .] have the first claim on [his] time' and, then, continues: '[B]ut when your duty to them is fully discharged – as you have always fully and amply discharged it, the remainder of your time is your own'. Scharf apparently wrote to Derby soon afterwards; an undated draft shows him fumbling to phrase his requirements, but finally requesting 'one Hundred guineas' (DC 25 December 1864).

We cannot be sure if this was the first time Scharf received an honorarium for his work at a country house, but we cannot find any trace of income for his work at Blenheim two years previously. The correspondence with Stanhope suggests that this is a major professional step and shows us that Stanhope was completely supportive of what must have been a unique professional career that grew up around connections, developing expertise and happenstance.

Reading for death

It is hard to characterise Lord Stanhope's letters from the late 1860s and early 1870s except to say that they indicate a stable relationship between him and Scharf. The letters become more businesslike; although Scharf is no longer the target of a renewed aristocratic abruptness, one gets the impression of a man more opinionated or more hurried. Partly, this is because Lord Stanhope now talks more directly about rejecting portraits. Some sample comments from 1864 capture the mood of many of his letters:

> My own opinion is that a bust of Francis Duke of Bedford ought not to find a place in the Gallery. He had given signs of considerable promise in the House of Lords; but of promise only; he died when little more than thirty years of age. (SC 30 May 1864)

> We ought to be much obliged to Mr Millais for his kind intentions though I must own myself quite astonished how he could think Mr Leech entitled to representation in our Gallery. For a different reason – that is as not being British – I must own that I would greatly demur [?] to Philip the second. (SC 29 November 1864)

There is something almost necessarily *ad hominem* about these decisions, since portraits were never explicitly rejected for aesthetic reasons. The focus on the sitter assumed from the beginning the Gallery's mission to serve as a national, that is to say British, representational project. Stanhope is also quite grumpy (on Scharf's behalf) about the 'cheeseparing' Treasury (SC 23 July 1870). He tends to interpret national events in terms of their cost to the Portrait Gallery. His only recorded reaction to the death of Dickens in 1870 is to say that the novelist's portrait 'will go up to a very high sum' (SC 25 June 1870).

Though it surprised us a little, we think we might have detected a return of the snobbery manifested in Stanhope's communications from the earlier period. In 1873 Stanhope writes to Scharf to question his identification of a portrait. He asks, '[A]re you sure you are right as to the portrait being of the Earl of Ossory? I doubt it very much since you mention him as bearing the Garter which it is most unusual for an eldest son to obtain in his father's life-time.' At the bottom of the letter, in Scharf's handwriting, is the typically precise notation, 'Sir Thos Butler earl of Ossory was no 478 on the list of Knights of the Garter, Elected Sept & installed 25th October 1672' (SC 7 June 1873). Reading this silent debate, and this apparently groundless objection on Stanhope's part, we could not help thinking that Stanhope was once again asserting his experiential knowledge of the aristocracy to keep Scharf in his proper place.

Of course, we could have been dead wrong. And we would not have leapt to the conclusion that Stanhope was undergoing some kind of personality change if not for two archival signs. The first was that Stanhope's handwriting deteriorated markedly from about 1862 on. Since handwriting is so crucial to the archival experience, and since for the reader in the archive it comes before, and can serve as a barrier to, content it can colour the reading it enables or makes difficult. A change in handwriting is a change in the archival experience; it is the lens through which all readings – and all interpretations – take place. For Helena, in particular, who had taken on the task of reading through the Stanhope letters sequentially, it was difficult not to thematise the difficulty of the handwriting – to see Stanhope as himself deteriorating morally or physically.

The other sign was that the folder of letters was nearing its end. Decline is part of the archival experience in different ways. What qualifies most documents in the archive to be archived at all is that they are written by people who are no longer alive. In many cases – and certainly in this one – archival readers know the date of the writer's death. To move chronologically through the archive is to approach, knowingly, the death of the archival subject; it is hard not to look for signs of that death. Robyn, who was the one to read sequentially George Scharf's later diaries, noted with a pang that the pages he had filled daily for five decades with beautiful penmanship began in his last year to be marred by ink-blots when they were not left altogether empty. By the final month's record, she remarked with sorrow that the narrative of Scharf's life had devolved into brief lists of disgusting physical symptoms, discouraging doctor's visits and, yes, rich foods consumed. It was all body and all decay. The last entries became too painful for Robyn to transcribe verbatim, given the palpable fact of running out of pages and years, and the immutable, historical event of Scharf's death in 1895. Although Stanhope's letters did not similarly record symptoms of his own, to us those symptoms are legible on the page. Helena knew as she read that Lord Stanhope would be dead by 1875 and that Lady Stanhope's death would come first, at the end of 1873. She wondered if Stanhope would allude to the loss of his wife, Scharf's friend, in this professional correspondence or whether perhaps the letters would break off for a while or altogether. As it happened, the content of the letters did not change, but their appearance did. Starting in 1874, Lord Stanhope's letters have black borders, thick at first and then progressively narrower as mourning protocol required. Many of the letters have obviously been dictated to someone who took the words down with perfect, youthful handwriting. They are materially different, different materially. The letters written within the sombre borders suggest a man slightly out of touch, his mind perhaps elsewhere, with his dead wife, with his own impending death.

In Helena's case the move from the end of the folder of Stanhope's letters to the next archival source was a moving back to the different exigencies and temporalities of Scharf's diaries. She began again, wondering where to start waiting for Lord Stanhope's death in the diary. Her instinctive solution was to begin with Lady Stanhope's death and with a post- (post)marital plot; reading this way, between the deaths of husband and wife, was to imagine that one death could have led to, or at least paved the way for, the other. As she read through Scharf's mentions of Stanhope, she could hear the murmur of conventional thanatic conjugal metonymies: 'He had nothing left to live for', 'without her he lost his will to live', 'she was everything to him'. In fact, Stanhope's few biographers say very little about the closeness of the marriage – and even less, as is biographers' wont – about the meaning of that marriage in late life. There is no support for any narrative, medical or psychological, that would link the deaths. But in waiting for death one must start somewhere.

Nevertheless, the central figure for us in this story of double mourning has to be George Scharf, a figure who, depending on how you read the archives, could have been near the centre of that marriage or those deaths or of no relevance at all. The diary and also the black-bordered fragment now belonging to Helena make George central, of course. Whatever its initial purpose, this is the archival work accomplished by that fragment of we-know-not-what: the announcement that George Scharf figured in the story of the Earl of Stanhope's death.

As has so often been the case, reading the diary became for us an act of diagnosis at a distance; in archival retrospect the moment of diagnosis arrives on 18 November 1875. Scharf's diary tells us that in September he was at a house party at Madresfield with 'the Stanhopes', presumably Lord Stanhope and some other family members, since Lady Stanhope is no more (D no day, September 1875). There is no mention that anything is wrong. By November Scharf is at Chevening and Stanhope is ill with bronchitis; Scharf reads to him from *The Times*; a portrait of Stanhope by Walter William Ouless (later to become the painter of Scharf's own official portrait) arrives at Chevening. Lord Stanhope feels a little better and comes downstairs. On 18 November there is an accident. Scharf writes, and then crosses out, an account of Stanhope falling in the drawing-room and pulling a glass fireplace screen down on himself. We do not know why or when Scharf crossed out this part of the entry. It is unlikely that he had made a mistake and that Stanhope did not fall; the crossing-out seems to signify denial, at the time or in retrospect. Perhaps it is an attempt to save Stanhope's dignity, although we assume that Scharf did not imagine an archival reader of his diaries. Whatever the reason for his running the pen through the sentence, the crossing-out only emphasises the moment for Helena as archival rereader and for Robyn, who first transcribed this particular entry. Robyn solemnly noted the crossing-out; Helena made much of it. This was the beginning of the end – and George was unable to face the truth.

As we know from the fragment and the diary entry so similar to it with which we began this section, Scharf was not present at Stanhope's death. He was not destined to play a part in this death-bed scene, missing the actual moment as he missed the moment of his father's passing. One possible reason is that Scharf was experiencing his own serious illness that December. Later, he would blame a cab ride to his friend Beauford's for his contracting scarlet fever, the symptoms of which began to show themselves on 18 December (D 1 January 1876). Reading his entry for that day, one can actually trace the arrival of the symptoms through the deterioration of Scharf's handwriting. After a relatively neat list of expenses, presumably written early in the evening on that day, Scharf describes the onset of his symptoms in a most uncharacteristically illegible scrawl:

> Came in through a damp foggy Atmosphere. Pleasant evening reading Macready's memoirs. Putting away papers and writing letters. At 1/2 past 1 whilst taking some seltzer water I suddenly perceived an obstruction in the throat. It continued all night through & in the morning sent for Charlie Sangster [Scharf's doctor]. Miss Jolliffe [a visiting nurse] went

off in a cab. Lunch at Gallery [. . .] I was very ill all night vomiting bile & worn by diarrhoea. Intensely miserable and quite alone till Mrs Lee came.

The end of this entry was presumably written the next morning or later; his drive to record through the pain of his illness is moving, as is the transparency of the connection between body and (hand) writing. Although the question of when he wrote is confusing, the archive is finally, unequivocally registering bodily distress. If the entry is a moment of archival triumph for the archivists, a fleeting image of body and text in alignment, it is also, as we shall see, probably the lowest point in Scharf's long mid-life.

Scharf's own illness mutes the impact – at least orthographically speaking – of Lord Stanhope's death on Christmas Eve. Scharf hears of his friend's death through a mutual friend and records it in pencil, rather than his usual black ink: 'Mr William Smith called bringing the news of Lord Stanhope's death at Bournemouth [in Dorset] at 9:30 a.m. that same morning' (D 24 December 1875). Scharf was not to comment on what must have been terrible news for several weeks, as he continued to focus on his own body. He could not attend Stanhope's funeral on 30 December and depended once again on William Smith for information. His handwriting was still terrible when he wrote, on 31 December:

> Mr Smith called & gave me an account of the funeral of Lord Stanhope. Sangster found I was going on favourably. All the skin peels off from my left hand. It comes off freely & in large pieces like orange peel.

Caught up in the horror of his own symptoms as they unfold, Scharf thus marks the last day of 1875 with an entry in the present tense. He does not write a year-end summary. His entries for the next few days, however, initiate a temporality that looks simultaneously forward and back as he brings together his own illness and deaths past and present. On the interstitial space of the diary's fly-leaf, a place outside of time, he writes:

> A sad year this opens for me, having lost my best friend Lord Stanhope (who died on the 24th), and being myself prostrate with a severe attack of Scarlet Fever, which first showed itself on the 18th. I have been fortunate in the medical aid of Charlie Sangster & Collambull. I also have a very good nurse from the Nursing Institute, Mrs Roberts. (D 1 January 1876)

This entry struggles to negotiate two different kinds of pain and two temporalities. The mention of Stanhope's death, cordoned off by parentheses, evokes the idiom of finality, while the date that marks the day of his own presumed infection betrays a desire for origin, which was to persist in the reappearance of the story of the disastrous cab ride as an anniversary entry for years to come. It is as if Scharf is puzzling out the meaning of his illness and, perhaps, of his continued life in juxtaposition to the other, grimmer, if in some ways less horrific, story of his friend's death from pleurisy. It is important also to see Scharf at the beginning of two other temporal processes: recovery from illness and mourning. It might be, of course, that these are linked. Scharf's entry for New Year's Day characteristically has him looking forward as the 'sad year [. . .] opens'.

Fast on the heels of this entry comes the anniversary of his mother's death, always noted on 6 January, and the anniversary three days after that of his mother's funeral and the arrival many years earlier of his father in London; this is a connection, as we mention in Chapter 3, that he has noted before, although not every year. One death recalls another, not least because of a coincidence of the calendar. During his long recovery in Brighton, which must have reminded him of Stanhope's attempts to regain his health in that other seaside resort town, Bournemouth, Scharf turns to reading *Middlemarch* and to what are probably his most literary entries. On 23 January 1876 he 'entered with interest into the characters after the Casaubon engagement'; he tried to keep reading in the coffee-room at the place where he was staying, but was interrupted by 'a strange rednosed inquisitive man rather like an American in manner' who 'pestered me with questions' (D 24 January 1876). As long as he stayed in his bedroom, though, Scharf could read unmolested. On 1 February he 'finished Middlemarch & was disappointed with the conclusion'. As we have said in our preface, we would certainly have loved to know why he was disappointed, but the diary does not venture into literary criticism. For the first but not the last time in the diaries, George is at rest, his time punctuated, not by visits, but by the rhythms of George Eliot's prose.

So far we have spoken as if the reason that George Scharf was not at his 'best friend's' bedside was that he was too sick to attend. Of course, this is only half – perhaps less than half – of the story. Scharf might well have been absent even if he had been in perfect health. It is possible, even likely, that in this moment of dying, Lord Stanhope had no thought of Scharf, that from the Earl's perspective Scharf was not his best and truest friend, that the relationship was as asymmetrical as their class positions. Stanhope's letters to

213

other correspondents and the biographies of him we have found are silent on the subject of George Scharf. Without a doubt, if Lord Stanhope on his deathbed at Bournemouth did not feel the absence of his professional subordinate, this self-made and self-educated immigrant's son, that fact would meet the expectations of the British historians and literary scholars with whom we have discussed Scharf's career. The question of what Stanhope thought of Scharf is linked but not identical to the question that structures our third and fourth chapters: what class was George Scharf, anyway? We can restate the problem here like this: in what ways was Scharf visible to Lord Stanhope and to the Stanhope family? When they invited him to Chevening were they inviting a family friend, an avuncular figure, a professional cataloguer, an appendage to the Chevening portrait collection, a colleague of Lord Stanhope, his employee, his true friend? Did the Stanhopes prepare a special room for him, look forward to his visits, consult his tastes? What did they get from his visits and what did they give? If Scharf had not been ill, would he have been invited to give a eulogy, to sit in a special place at the service?

We have, as usual, no definitive answer. For a long time both of us remained sceptical that Scharf was in any way thought of as an equal or even an intimate at Chevening, just as we were hesitant to see him as a quasi-family member at Knole. It was easy to see Scharf's insistence on the vocabulary of friendship, at least in more modern terms, as a projection of his own feelings. Scharf himself might have understood the relationship as essentially and necessarily one-sided; his professions of friendship might have taken for granted that for all the visits to Chevening, all Scharf's 'residences' there, someone of his social origins could never be part of the Stanhopes' emotional world. This would certainly be aligned with the perspective of many British scholars of the nineteenth century who have spoken to us about our project. One of those conversations stands out for us most vividly, the one in which a British history professor informed us that the story we were telling was 'impossible': it was simply inconceivable that a son of an immigrant debtor without formal education could have been an actual friend and houseguest to the titled. His certainty wavered, though, when we pulled out our secret weapon: those slippers, the ones Lady Mary Stanhope made for Scharf and presented to him on his birthday. It is hard to imagine a young girl, the daughter of an aristocratic household, making something so intimate for a middle-aged professional subordinate of her father's. For an uncle, maybe, an older brother – or a long-time family friend.

For Helena, who did not have much difficulty persuading Robyn, there came a moment when she began to believe in the possibility of a real intimacy – whatever that might have meant – between Scharf and the Stanhopes. It had nothing to do with Scharf's year-end diary summaries or even with the deathbed scenes. It came to her when she turned from the textual archive, with which she felt a certain comfort, to the visual archive in which she continued to feel out of her depth. It was not the sketches made by Scharf of the portrait collections at Chevening (of which there are many) nor of the interior of the house (there is a stunning sketch of the main staircase more experimental in style than many of Scharf's drawings) that got to her. It was those other sketches of the family at leisure: intimate moments of card playing, a lady with a frog in her hair and – long after Lord Stanhope's death – a sketch of his grandson curled up, fast asleep. The very first moment when Helena began doubting the class asymmetry narrative and started to believe was when she saw in the sketchbooks a drawing of Lady Mary, the youthful worker of slippers, in a boat with two young women friends, whom Scharf identifies as Miss Henniker and Miss Alice Henniker (Fig. 4.4). In the sketch dated 14 July 1865, a fore-shortened rowboat cradles the three women. One is resting with her back to the viewer, one is sitting up reading or sketching to the viewer's left and, in what is probably the bow, a third young woman is sprawled on her back asleep, her pretty cheek turned towards the sky. The boat is visually supported by what the sketcher has helpfully pointed out is a 'reflection of the boat on the Water'. Together, the boards that make up the gunnels of the boat and its shadow form concentric circles around the young women, who fill the interior with their bodies and dresses. The boat looks crowded, but not dangerously so; its angle and roundness suggest not so much a craft as a walnut shell: there is something miniature and magical about the way the young women are floating. The sleeping woman is the one who arrests attention; she takes up a good half of the boat's interior space. She sleeps voluptuously, visually interrupting the reading of her companions. It was, finally, the sketches and, perhaps especially, this sketch of Lady Mary that convinced us that Scharf and the Stanhopes were friends in all of the rich and evocative meanings of the word. It was Scharf's own visual idiom that opened up for us an unfamiliar story of Victorian class ascendance

Fig. 4.4 GS sketch of Lady Mary Stanhope and friends in a boat, July 1865.
©National Portrait Gallery, London.

at odds with our previous assumptions – and of those with whom we had so far shared the stories of George Scharf's life.

We could, of course, be overreading. This possibility came abruptly home to us when we presented part of this chapter at the 2013 annual North American Victorian Studies Association meeting. At the end of the talk, we projected Scharf's sketch of Lady Mary as part of a PowerPoint presentation, noting not only the general intimacy of the picture but the fact that there was something written in the folds of Lady Mary's skirt. Hours before, in our hotel room, we had both peered closely at that writing, although we had not (yet) seen the picture enlarged as it would be when projected. We had – excitedly, and with much pulling on and taking off of our glasses – discovered that the letters in Lady Mary's skirt spelled out 'with love, GS'. This was a find that took us back to other climactic visual moments, including the discovery of Jack's name on the back of the portrait of his friends. Imagine our feelings when our friend and fellow Victorianist, Rebecca Stern, asked from the back of the room whether the words on Lady Mary's skirt might be, in fact, 'black lace'. Rebecca could not have known how quickly her question put an end to all doubt. She was unaware, after all, of Scharf's habit of writing notations of colour and fabric into his portrait sketches. As we turned to look at the projected version of the picture, we realised that we had read those initials, that expression of love, into and onto the dress. Scharf was in some ways treating the portrait of his own making like the historical portraits at Knole, Chevening and other private and public collections. The personal – and we still believed in it – was inseparable for George, for Scharf, from the professional.

We would like to end this chapter, this book and this partial Life with another of George Scharf's manuscript pieces that came into Helena's possession several months after her first foray into the Scharfian consumer archive. This full letter signed by Scharf was a birthday gift from Helena's husband, Scott. Unlike the memorial fragment, this piece of the archive and of the gift economy contains the generic features of the letter. Although addressed only to 'dear Squire', it does at least have a salutation. Scharf has signed his full name. It is dated (10 October 1887), and it is written on station-ery with the embossed heading 'Chevening, Sevenoaks'. The letter concerns an attempt on Scharf's part to trace a story 'of Dryden acting as umpire for the Duke of Dorset at Knole'. Although he reports that he has looked at a number of print sources but not yet at the 'gossipy' Bridgeman's guidebook to Knole, he is 'sure that he did not <u>invent</u> it [emphasis his]'. At this relatively late moment in Scharf's relationship to Knole and Chevening, he is still doing research, still moving at least mentally between houses. We see Scharf at work, although we do not know much of the context for his enquiries. More crucial for our purposes, however, is the second paragraph, where he describes his relation to Chevening. At this date, of course, Scharf's patron, the 5th Earl Stanhope, would have been long dead, and he would have been visiting the family of the 6th Earl. Scharf's position at Chevening seems in his own somewhat wry telling to be stronger than ever:

> I am enjoying myself here very much; being promoted to the state Bedroom known as the Chatham room with a large canopied four post bed & a flight of steps at the side to help me up. A lovely portrait of Lady Chatham William Pitt's Mother by Hudson, and a splendid portrait of John second earl Chatham by Romney. I gaze upon them from the depths of my bed. (Punctuation sic)

In a reflexive act of scholarship, and with much sorting through images of the Chatham family, Helena finally traced the portrait at which Scharf had been gazing by writing to the archivist at

Chevening. Perhaps the exact identity of the portrait matters, but again, perhaps it does not. We love to think of the aging, brittle and corpulent George 'promoted' to the Chatham room, ensconced in a four-poster bed and surrounded by Stanhope family portraits.[12] We love the detail of the flight of steps, put there perhaps as a literal and figurative accommodation of this family friend. Our introduction begins with the painful details of Scharf's final illness, but we do not want to end our book with his death. Instead we leave him here, enjoying himself in the state bedroom of the house that meant so much to him. We love that he is still using stationery from great houses, and that he seems able, late in life, to stop working if only for a moment, to gaze at the portraits that represent his social and professional success.

Coda:
our archivist, ourselves

B UT PERHAPS GEORGE SCHARF would not have wanted us to end
with him at rest. He was, after all – and this is a modern term
for an old-fashioned value – a hard worker. This was, for both of
us, another point of identification with Scharf, although we sus-
pect he would be as puzzled by the kind of work we do as we sometimes were by his professional activities. By the end of our work
on and with him, however, we realised that our jobs – Scharf's
job and our own – had something in common and that this com-
monality might produce a final attempt at an identity term to add
to bachelor, diner, sketcher, fat man, extra man and the other
categories we tried out for Scharf. It took us arguably too long
to realise that Scharf, too, was an archival researcher subject to
the exigencies and fantasies of the archive. That realisation came
to us after Helena's trip to the Laing archive at the University of
Edinburgh, whose holdings include letters from Scharf to David
Laing, librarian of the Signet Library in Edinburgh and member
of the Society of Antiquaries of Scotland. Scharf used Laing as a
resource for the NPG portrait collection, although his letters also
deal in gossip and speculation about open positions in the world
of libraries and curatorships. An unmistakably Scharfian question at the end of a letter asks for 'the exact colour of the eyes of
Mary, Queen of Scots in the Morton portrait' (DL 23 November
1869). Further reading of the letters shows Scharf to have been
particularly interested in obtaining a portrait of Walter Scott.
As he puts it in a letter from Chevening on 2 September 1863,
'Had Mr Raeburn the son of the great painter, any portraits of

eminent persons? We want a good Sir Walter Scott terribly' (DL 2 September 1863).

Later letters show, however, that Scharf is not simply interested in the acquisition or authentication of portraits; he is eager to find out as much about them as possible. An 1871 letter to Laing asks for further information about a portrait already in his hands:

> You are doubtless aware that we were so fortunate as to secure for this Gallery the portrait of Sir Walter Scott seated in his study at Abbotsford painted by Sir William Allan. He is represented reading the Proclamation of Mary Queen of Scots previous to her marriage to Darnley. It would be interesting to know where that proclamation now is, and I feel that I cannot do better than appeal to your honoured self for the information. I should very much indeed like to see it. Has it been facsimilied? The writing in the picture appears readable, but on applying a glass, only a very few words reveal themselves. I hope that you will excuse my troubling you with this question, but I consider it a matter of public interest. (DL 24 May 1871)

Like many an archival researcher, Scharf identifies a document that piques his curiosity and that he sees through the lens of his larger research project. Never did we feel closer to Scharf as archivist than when we read his brief reference to using a literal lens, 'applying a glass', to the tiny (and reversed) writing of the proclamation. While it would be too much to say we saw through Scharf's (prosthetic) eyes at this moment, it felt that way as we remembered all the moments in our research when visual technologies from eyeglasses to contact lenses to iPhone cameras to PowerPoint projections to magnification buttons on computer screens revealed – or failed to reveal – new information.

While we do not have Laing's response to Scharf's query, Scharf's next letter to Laing suggests a familiar mix of archival deflation and a determination to persevere.

> I am greatly obliged by your kind and interesting letter. The circumstance of Sir Wm [sic] Allan having paraded this large proclamation made me suppose that it was some special document, perhaps the original for approval by the Council or for Scribes to copy from, which might have come into Sir Walter's own possession. I do not know the treasures of Abbotsford having only been there for one single morning. Has any list or catalogue of his books and literary treasures been published? The Proclamation has the following appearance in the picture. Sir Walter holds it exactly like a newspaper. [Scharf includes a sketch of the proclamation held between two hands.]

The main body of the writing is seen reversed through the transparent
paper on parchment, & only the indorsement [sic] reads the right way
[. . .] (DL 3 June 1871)

Laing has obviously suggested that the proclamation was an
invention of the painter rather than a copy of a 'special document'.
We empathised with Scharf's disappointment, and perhaps even
more with the brevity of his time at Abbotsford: we, too, had felt the
inadequacy of 'one single morning' in the archive. We are also, of
course, familiar with Scharf's reaction to an apparent archival dead-
end: the explosion of further questions and the continual return
to the document. We only wish that, in our letters to archivists, we,
too, could produce a sketch of what we wanted; Scharf has access
here to an archival tool not in our arsenal.

Scharf, then, was also, or perhaps predominantly, an archivist in
two senses: a preserver of records and documents and a researcher
in the archives. Perhaps his own, somewhat clumsy locution works
even better as an ultimate identity for him – and for us. In a letter
to Laing he praised the recently deceased Royal Librarian, Bernard
Bolingbroke Woodward, for transforming his own position and
thus making it hard to replace him: 'There seems to be a good deal
of difficulty about the duties of the post. Woodward has by his intel-
ligence & zeal raised it from a mere Conservator to an Elucidator
– both of books & of drawings and paintings' (DL 23 November
1869). After trying on various identities for the professional Scharf,
we can think of nothing better than 'Elucidator'; indeed, as writers
of Scharf's lives, we aspire to no better identity for ourselves.

Notes

Chapter 1

1. The album is listed in the British Library Catalogue as 'A Collection of Invitation Cards, Menus, etc. from 1869 to 1876 formed by Sir George Scharf'. See Works Cited (under Other unpublished archival sources) for details.
2. Slatter, p. 13. See also O'Donoghue and Jackson, *DNB*.
3. We are indebted to a conversation with Lara Kriegel, early on in our research, for helping us to think about how this project might have been shaped differently by scholars in different disciplines.
4. Scharf entered paintings in the Art Union of London's annual contests in 1845 and 1846. His paintings – a series of illustrations of the Ten Commandments and a 'Non Angli sed Angeli' – earned him honourable mentions. Additionally, he displayed two paintings of Xanthus at the Royal Academy in 1845 and four more the following year, plus a large painting at the British Institution.
5. According to the *New York Times* (23 October 1981), 'The Extra Man at Dinner Parties May Be a Thing of the Past'. That article states that an 'uneven table' was by then acceptable.
6. For a discussion of fatness as a (queer) identity, see Moon and Sedgwick, Whitesel and Lebesco. For a social science perspective on coming out as fat see Saguy, especially Chaps 2 and 4; fatness as an identity category is further explored in Rothblum and Solovay, Kirkland and Farrell.
7. The meals at Knole would have been served à la russe; servants would pass around plates of food to the guests who could decline a particular dish. See Colquhoun, *Taste*, pp. 251–6.
8. Many of the menus we found ended with a savoury pastry served

222

either alongside or after the sweets, and often the savoury dessert featured either parmesan cheese or anchovies.

9. Most historians of the English middle class point to the problem of definition of social class more generally, and of the middle class specifically. Early twentieth-century historian R. H. Gretton, looking back on the recent past, notes the 'inherent vagueness' of the term, and argues that it is 'essentially a negative one' whose 'inclusions can be nothing but the exclusions of two other terms' (pp. 1–2). He also sees the 'distinctions' between classes - and perhaps between the middle and other classes - as 'of all distinctions the least permanent' (p. 1). Other historians, like Lawrence and Jeanne Stone, agree that the middle class was actually made up of many smaller class identities. It 'was sliced and sliced again to extremely slim status layers subtly separated from each other by the delicate but infinitely resistant lines of snobbery' (Stone and Stone, p. 423). Hobsbawm catalogues the different ways the middle class has been defined: from income, to profession, to the employment of servants, concluding only that whatever the definition, the 'genuine middle class was not large' (p. 134). The relation between the middle class and Marxist notions of the bourgeoisie is no more definitive, especially if we begin to see 'bourgeois' as naming a series of attitudes that were typical of all English classes as well as a particular relation to production (Langland, p. 25). For an argument about the political use of the term 'middle-class' in the early years of the nineteenth century see Wahrman, Chap. 11.

10. His, for example, is the very last name on a five-column list of attendees at a levee in honour of Victoria's birthday on 27 May 1867. (See 'Her Majesty's Birthday'.) On 18 June 1866, *The Times* again puts him last, where his name is actually followed by an '&c'. (See 'Lady Derby's Assembly'.)

11. The obituary also notes, remarkably, that Scharf had a 'curiously unwieldy figure that was a perpetual difficulty to him', a phrase more than any other that brings his body, as it were, to life for us.

12. The painting can be viewed at the NPG website: <http://www.npg.org. uk/collections/search/portraitExtended/mw00049/Private-View-of-the-Old-Masters-Exhibition-Royal-Academy-1888?> (last accessed 16 December 2014).

13. See Geddes Poole, Chaps 1 and 4, especially p. 96.

14. We do not know when the two men met, although Lord Stanhope (at the time Viscount Mahon) signed Scharf's certificate of election on 12 February 1852. Thanks to Adrian James of the Society of Antiquarians for this information.

15. Katherine V. Snyder has written about bourgeois domesticity among bachelors in the English novel of Scharf's period, offering historical background on the 'trouble with bachelors'.

16. The literature of 'the archive' seems still to be dominated by two figures, Derrida and Foucault. In treating the archive as an origin, Derrida, in *Archive Fever*, necessarily stresses its singular (if collective) nature. Derrida's book has itself become a point of origin for writers on the archive: Steedman, Velody, Joyce and Lynch all begin by addressing *Archive Fever* and by riffing on its central term.

17. Mary Addyman links feelings for certain kinds of objects to James George Frazer's idea of 'sympathetic magic'. The most useful of her terms for our purposes is the profoundly metonymic 'association objects', or 'items that have become hallowed in some way by coming into contact with a celebrated person, gaining significance through their physical association with that person' (p. 2).

18. One way of becoming a Victorianist in this triumphal sense is (also and almost) to become a historian. The spectre of historical truth for literary critics is often mediated by the figure of the historian who might have done/be doing something different with the archive. That 'something different' will crop up as a possibility, a fantasy, an obligation and a limitation at various points in this story.

19. Lewis and Barlow's transnational 'Ephemera Project' defines the term more vividly and with a sense of the collective: 'Ephemera are detritus or garbage that people produce without intending it to survive the moment' (last accessed 26 June 2014).

20. Our self-archiving, alas, did not extend to writing down the day we first accessed the online catalogue. We made up the month and day, in homage to Virginia Woolf.

21. The recent consensus on Victorian diaries is that they should be read as reflections of cultural forms and expectations rather than unmediated expressions of individual feeling. (See Steinitz, for example, pp. 6–7; Bellanca, Chap. 1; and Millim pp. 22–5.)

22. For our Victorian diarist, the inherent interest of the weather was, we think, its impact on light and, hence, on the way things looked, including the portraits he catalogued.

23. Bellanca observes that 'weather is omnipresent in British diaries because the constant meteorological shifts' in the climate simply commanded people's attention. We agree, but we part ways with Bellanca when she looks to diarists' weather reports as 'an emotional barometer linking the writer's inner and outer worlds' (p. 31).

24. For a complete description of the banquet and our comments on it, see Rice University's Victorian Studies Seminar's George Scharf Banquet page at <http://www.ruf.rice.edu/~nineteen/scharf.html> (last accessed 28 January 2014).

25. For a scathing account of re-enactment, see Agnew (p. 301). Alexander Cook offers something of a defence of the practice (p. 488) and para-

phrases Collingwood's claim that all history is a form of re-enactment (p. 491).

26. We would like to thank Victoria Ford Smith for her help in editing and regularising this document. Although even she could not make it more exciting, she did – literally – make it more colourful and easier to manipulate.

27. See Brownley, p. xvii. We are thinking particularly of the contribution of feminist autobiography theorists like Smith and Watson.

28. See Warhol's categories of unnarratability in 'Neonarrative, or, How to Render the Unnarratable in Fiction and Film'.

29. Pergam also notes Scharf's understanding of how best to light individual paintings for exhibition (p. 58).

Chapter 2

1. Until 1857, George used the single-volume 'Letts Diary'. In January of 1857, doubtless in connection with his new responsibilities at the NPG, Scharf upgraded to a larger format, called – appropriately enough – 'Letts Professional or Monthly Diary'. John Letts, the publisher and printer of the Letts line, has his place in the diary craze of the early-to-mid-nineteenth century, urging potential customers to 'conceal nothing from its pages nor suffer any eye but your own to scan them' (Martin Hewitt, qtd in Amigoni, p. 27).

2. For a discussion of the ubiquity of the marriage plot and its imbrication in the history of the novel, see Boone (p. 65). The marriage plot is a literary device, a dominant genre and a cultural imperative.

3. For the anti-narrative imperative of queerness, see D. A. Miller (pp. 45–6), Morrison, pp. 61–3 and Edelman.

4. Of course, this is a method with a history – and a history of critique – even in purely literary contexts, as the rise of the New Formalism suggests. The poststructuralist dismissal of formalism is summed up in DeMan. For the New Historicist repudiation of formalism, see Liu. For more recent defences of close reading in the service of a contextualised criticism, see Strier, Levinson and Levine.

5. For Elizabeth Barrett Browning's remarks about the Kenyon–Bayley relationship, see, for example, her letter to Mary Russell Mitford (28 December 1842) in Raymond and Sullivan. For Kenyon's will, see *The Times*, 27 January 1857, p. 9, column E.

6. Our own form of name-dropping compels us to note that Lewes was George Eliot's stepson. Eliot knew Scharf through her friend Barbara Bodichon and mentions him once (in passing) in her correspondence (George Eliot to Mme Eugene Bodichon, 15 Februrary 1862, in Haight, 4:13).

7. See the Peerage website, compiled by Darryl Lundy, available at <http:

//thepeerage.com/p42630.htm#i426297> (last accessed 19 August 2013).

8. This is, of course, the effect of Scharf's being the narratee of his own diary; clearly he was not writing for posterity.

9. As we shall see in Chapter 3, Elizabeth Scharf's diaries are full of references to gifts of food and drink from her son. Of course, the menus George transcribes and collects are souvenirs not only of meals but of networks of high-status relationships.

10. During George's final illness, female friends, including the younger Lady Mahon (Lord Stanhope's daughter-in-law) and Winnie Pattisson (Jack's daughter), did visit him at Ashley Place.

11. Sometimes Scharf wrote year-end reflections on his birthday as well as on New Year's Eve. Since his birthday was in mid-December, this sometimes led to summaries of the same year occurring within just two weeks of each other.

12. And an 'Event' worth a footnote. Scharf was presented at the queen's levee by Lord Stanhope on 23 Februrary 1859. See Chap. 4 (Necrological Notice in Announcements and Occasional Papers, 1864).

13. James Morant Lockyer, architect, Egyptologist and specialist in the history of ancient medals died, perhaps of suicide, in 1864 at the age of forty-one. A 'Necrological Notice' in the *Sessional Papers of the Royal Institute of British Architecture* notes that 'the loss of the wife he loved was a stroke under which his gentle spirit succumbed' (pp. 2–3).

14. Scharf does not often record waning friendships – or engage with any form of dysphoric narrative – so the mention of Charles Cordell is unusual. Although Scharf is in the diaries very loyal to his friends, marriage is acknowledged to make a change in his relationships. See the year-end summary for 1864; he writes: 'Marriage has separated me from several former friends, namely Howard & Percy Carpenter, the latter through having formed a most imprudent match. Charles Lewes also is on the point of being married & not likely to continue a frequent visitor' (D 31 December 1864). Carpenter – but not his wife – is welcomed back into the Scharf's circle three years later: 'Percy Carpenter has regained his intimacy with us. His wife is not likely ever to obtain a footing in my mother's house' (D 31 December 1867).

15. We are indebted to Marlene Tromp for the knowledge of the significance of 'Woodstocks'.

16. According to Peter King Smith, on a web page called 'Secretary to Lord of the Admiralty', Pattisson was a co-investor (along with two of his brothers and an uncle) in a mortgage taken out on the building, then called the Tregullow Offices, in 1891. None of the principal was paid back, but when the property was sold in 1902, Jacob Pattisson collected all the interest due.

17. See Peter King Smith, 'The Zimapanners'. This constantly evolving site contains genealogical histories of families associated with Zimapanner House in Cornwall, including the Pattissons.

18. Details about Jacob Howell Pattisson's career, disappearance, bankruptcy, disgrace and re-establishment in polite society available at Peter King Smith, 'Jacob H. Pattisson's Children'.

19. Details from Peter King Smith, 'Secretary to Lord of the Admiralty'.

20. The list of Pattisson's professional positions in *Who's Who* does not include his affiliation with the National Portrait Gallery, evidence that his work there was voluntary. See Addison et al., *Who's Who: An Annual Biographical Dictionary*.

21. The *Wikipedia* article states that Felsted School, founded in 1564, developed rapidly into a model English boarding school in the mid-nineteenth century due to the discovery of an infusion of income. See 'Felsted School', <http://en.wikipedia.org/wiki/Felsted_School> (last accessed 24 August 2013).

22. Country home of the Earl Cowper in Hertfordshire. Earl Cowper had lent paintings to the Manchester Art Treasures Exhibition. See National Gallery of Art website, available at <http://www.nga.gov/content/ngaweb/research/library/imagecollections/research-in-the-collection.html> (last accessed 13 August 2013).

23. According to Bryony Millan, the Acting Archivist at the Heinz Library, the items from the correspondence with Jack were probably selected 'because they reveal a more private, affectionate side to Scharf than is generally seen in his other correspondence and papers. These items are indicative of a strong friendship and very touching' (private email to Helena 28 September 2011).

24. This was not strictly true. George's 'Jackiana' apparently included all correspondence with and about Jack from 1872 on. The NPG divided this file into two – one from 1872, the year of Jack's marriage, and one for the later correspondence.

25. It was only after a few passes through the file that we began to wonder who had put the calendar page and the letter in the same clear folder and to think about an earlier archival reader, this one with more authority to construct the archive. We do not know whether the placement of the calendar page was purely a matter of chronology or whether the anonymous archivist was reading with the romance plot.

26. The reference to Dick Worsley's birthday suggests another set of competing temporalities: the annual (anniversary) event of the birthday, noted and probably celebrated each year, and the exceptional event of Jack's departure from this group and what we might call a bachelor temporality through marriage.

27. We have written elsewhere about the second-marriage-plot's prevalence in *People* magazine. See Warhol and Michie.

28. O'Donoghue died in 1929 just before his eighty-first birthday; he would have been about thirty-eight years old when the photograph for the cabinet card was taken.

29. *Dictionary of National Biography*, 1st edn, *s.v.* 'Scharf, George'.

30. Responses to Terry Castle's review of Deirdre LeFaye's edition of Austen's letters show that many readers of the *London Review of Books* (*LRB*) in 1995 mistakenly thought that Castle was calling Austen 'lesbian' and were accordingly outraged. See Castle.

31. See, for example, Wilson's review of *The Devonshires: The Story of a Family and a Nation*, by Roy Hattersley, in which Wilson confidently asserts, 'William Cavendish, the sixth, "Bachelor Duke", wasn't gay.' Pope praises Kate Colquhoun for not 'making any simplistic interpretation of the Duke [of Devonshire]'s motives, but the fact that he wrote in his diary "[Paxton] is everything for me", conveys the poignancy of unrequited love'. For a nuanced speculation about the relationship between the two men, see Clayton, pp. 33–4.

32. For the most detailed account of male homosexual culture at this period (beginning the year of Scharf's death), see Matt Cook. One site that he includes as 'important [. . .] for many men' is the British Museum, particularly the Hellenic galleries (p. 33). For information about patterns of arrest and prosecution, see Cocks.

33. C. R. Ashbee's biographer, Alan Crawford, says it was 'a normal part of Victorian respectability for [an upper-middle- and upper-class man to] have had rooms and habits of life that were separate from, and not to be questioned by, his household and family' (Crawford, p. 4, qtd in Cook, p. 31).

Chapter 3

1. The launch plot and marriage plot are closely connected. Social historians have noted a longstanding, uniquely Anglo-American expectation that married children should form their own households. See Stone, *Family*, p. 408 and Macfarlane, pp. 92–7.

2. See Kerr for an outline of the family-systems approach.

3. We use 'disnarration' in the sense elaborated by Warhol ('Neonarrative'). The disnarrated is similar but not identical to the way Andrew Miller uses Stuart Hampshire's 'optative mode' to talk about counterfactual storytelling (Miller, p. 77).

4. Jackson describes a similar dynamic relating to British politics. He argues that GSS had no interest in the outcome of elections but saw the political process as an opportunity to draw people and street life (*George Scharf's London*, p. 4).

5. GSS uses pages after his December entries to calculate his total earn-

ings for a given year. Unlike his later attempts at accounting, these calculations do, in fact, come out right.

6. For examples of how inventive couples could be in shaping their marriages (and separations) in an earlier period, see Stone's case studies in *Uncertain Unions*. See also his *Road to Divorce*.

7. As Stewart puts it, 'Some characters must die in any period of novel writing. As everyone allows, characters die more often, more slowly, and more vocally, in the Victorian age than ever before or since' (Stewart, p. 8).

8. At no point in George Jr's descriptions of his mother's (or his aunt's) health is there the sense that we get from parallel entries about his father, that the invalid is partly to blame for being sick.

9. Mrs Scharf's observation depends on some eccentricities of handwriting, and what she probably said to George was that 'chump' reads the same backwards *and* upside-down. Mrs. Scharf must have written the word in cursive script, making the tops of the 'm' angular rather than rounded, and not closing the final 'p' too tightly. Experiments with writing 'chump' this way indicate that upside down it does look very much like the same word.

10. We distinguish anxiety from actual financial conditions, here, in part, because, as we shall see later, the steps the family took to document and to resolve their difficulties do not always seem rational and, in part, because our own (limited) accounting abilities were severely challenged by what was available and unavailable in the archives.

11. This is still an important issue for feminist economists who point out the limits, for women and children, of economic statistics based, for example, on ideas of a unified household and the idea of 'household income'. See Agarwal, p. 2.

12. A proper family-systems analysis would examine birth order and triangles within and across three generations, but we have no information about George Jr's grandparents or his own parents' families of origin. See Jenny Brown, and for literary family-systems analysis, see Cohen and Schiff.

13. <http://digital.lib.lehigh.edu/remain/120/> The note in which Dickens refers to the letter is not included in the complete edition of Dickens's letters but has been transcribed by Margaret Brown and Angus Easson, editors of *The Letters of Charles Dickens*, and reproduced on this website along with a description of the handbill's contents.

14. Mrs Scharf kept up a correspondence with 'my dear Henry' in America (ESD 1 January 1859), and George Sr was in the habit of marking his diary pages with a large 'H' on the days a letter from Henry arrived from the United States.

15. If this fact invokes the image of a Henry Scharf who was refined, prosperous and comfortably set up in a respectable position to rival the one

his brother was to achieve back in London, then we must recall that the University of Virginia – growing fast in the 1840s and 1850s – was not the genteel establishment it later became. Indeed, it was a chaotic and violent place. In 1840 a professor was fatally shot trying to intervene in a fight between two students. The year 1843 'was principally character-ized by the remarkable frequency with which pistols were drawn in affrays amongst the students' (Barringer and Garnett, p. 150).

16. Henry does not actually seem to have been a faculty member at the University of Virginia, but to have been doing what we would call adjunct work there. Apparently his pay for teaching would have come not from the university but from individual students.

Chapter 4

1. For a new reading of sensation fiction and the immunitary paradigm that talks about the genre in precisely terms of belonging, see Hsu.

2. As with many great country houses, there are still private quarters housing family members as well as parts of the house that are open to the public through the National Trust, which owns and maintains the building.

3. The younger sons of Elizabeth – Reginald, Mortimer, Lionel – each inherited Knole in succession; it is important that both Charles, the eldest son, and Reginald, the second, fought with their respective next brothers to retain Knole and its associated titles as well as Buckhurst, whose baronetcy they held by right of primogeniture.

4. Mortimer's inheritance was the end of a series of legal struggles among male heirs for family titles and for possession of the house, all deriv-ing from Mary's will and a problematic codicil. The mind-bogglingly complex terms of that will and codicil are spelled out in *Inheritance* (R. Sackville-West, p. 162).

5. Much of his personal estate was left to Queen Victoria's four maids of honour. The will was (of course) contested by Lionel (R. Sackville-West, p. 168).

6. In 1890 the guidebook to Knole stated that 'the Park is always open to the public' (R. Sackville-West, p. 168).

7. *Advice,* by Henry Luttrell, is a book-length society satire in rhyming couplets.

8. Thanks to Adrian James, the assistant librarian of the Society of Antiquaries in London, for access to this certificate. According to the *Dictionary of National Biography,* Stanhope was elected vice president of the Society in 1841 and president in 1846 (see Pollard).

9. For a more detailed discussion of the balance of aristocrats and civil servants on the boards of museums and galleries in the period, see Geddes-Poole, Chap. 1.

10. Stanhope himself, of course, marks a transition in the idea of patronage. He is not a patron of a single artist but in a broader sense, through his chairmanship of the NPG and other organisations, a 'patron of the arts'. This is a relatively new form of what we might call institutional patronage that survives today on the walls and letterheads of museums and arts foundations in the donor categories of 'patron' and the usually less exalted 'friend'.

11. The link between 'patron' and 'friend' reminds us once again of Joseph Paxton's cross-class relationship with the Duke of Devonshire. Whatever term we might use for the relationship, it is clear that Lord Stanhope became increasingly invested in Scharf's social and professional success.

12. The 3rd Earl Stanhope married Lady Hester Pitt, daughter of the Countess Chatham and William Pitt the Elder and sister of William Pitt the Younger (1720–1803).

Works cited

Ackroyd, Peter. *London: The Biography.* New York: Nan A. Talese, 2001.

Addison, Henry Robert et al. *Who's Who: An Annual Biographical Dictionary.* London: Adam and Charles Black, 1907.

Addyman, Mary. *Association Objects and Contagion.* <curiousworldofvictori ancollecting.blogspot.com> (last accessed 10 July 2014).

Agarwal, Bina. 'Bargaining and Gender Relations: Within and Beyond the Household'. *Feminist Economics* 3.1 (1997): 1–51.

Agnew, Vanessa. 'History's Affective Turn: Historical Reenactment and Its Work in the Present'. *Rethinking History: The Journal of Theory and Practice* 11.3 (2007): 299–312.

Alighieri, Dante. *The Divine Comedy, with Fifty Illustrations [. . .] by George Scharf.* Trans. Frederick Pollack. London: Chapman and Hall, 1854.

Alsop, Susan Mary. *Lady Sackville: A Biography.* Garden City, NY: Doubleday, 1978.

Amigoni, David J. *Life Writing and Victorian Culture.* Burlington: Ashgate, 2006.

Arendt, Hannah. *The Human Condition.* 1958. Second Edition. Chicago: University of Chicago Press, 1998.

Barker, Juliet. *The Brontës.* New York: St Martin's Press, 1995.

Barringer, Paul B. and James Mercer Garnett. *University of Virginia: Its History, Influence, Equipment, and Characteristics.* New York: Lewis, 1904.

Bartlett, Neil. *Who Was That Man?: A Present for Mr Oscar Wilde.* London: Serpent's Tail, 1988.

Bellanca, Mary Ellen. *Daybooks of Discovery: Nature Diaries in Britain, 1770–1870.* Charlottesville: University of Virginia Press, 2007.

Boone, Joseph. *Tradition Counter Tradition: Love and the Form of Fiction.* Chicago: University of Chicago Press, 1987.

Works cited

Bridgman, John. *An Historical and Topographical Sketch of Knole, in Kent; with a Brief Genealogy of the Sackville Family*. London: W. Lindsell, 1817.

Brontë, Charlotte. *Jane Eyre*. London: Smith, Elder, 1847.

—. *Villette*. London: Smith, Elder, 1853.

Brooks, Peter. *Reading for the Plot: Design and Intention in Narrative*. New York: Knopf, 1984.

Brown, Jenny. 'Bowen Family Systems Theory and Practice: Illustration and Critique'. *Australian and New Zealand Journal of Family Therapy* 20 (1999): 94–103.

Brown, T. Allston. *A History of the New York Stage from the First Performance in 1732 to 1901*. New York: Dodd, Mead, 1903.

Brownley, Martine Watson. *Reconsidering Biography: Contexts, Controversies, and Sir John Hawkin's 'Life of Johnson'*. Lewisburg, PA: Bucknell University Press, 2011.

Byatt, A. S. *Possession: A Romance*. London: Chatto and Windus, 1990.

Castle, Terry. 'Sister-Sister'. *London Review of Books*, 3 August 1995, pp. 3–6.

Clayton, Jay. *Charles Dickens in Cyberspace: The Afterlife of the Nineteenth Century in Postmodern Culture*. New York: Oxford, 2003.

Cocks, H. G. *Nameless Offences: Homosexual Desire in Nineteenth-Century London*. London: I. B. Tauris, 2009.

Cohen, Paula Marantz. *The Daughter's Dilemma: Family Process and the Nineteenth-Century Domestic Novel*. Ann Arbor: University of Michigan Press, 1991.

Collingwood, R. G. *The Idea of History*. Oxford: Clarendon Press, 1946.

Collins, Wilkie. *The Woman in White*. 1859. Harmondsworth: Penguin, 2003.

Colquhoun, Kate. *A Thing in Disguise: The Visionary Life of Joseph Paxton*. London: Harper Collins, 2003.

—. *Taste: The Story of Britain through Its Cooking*. New York: Bloomsbury, 2007.

Cook, Alexander. 'The Use and Abuse of Historical Reenactment: Thoughts on Recent Trends in Public History'. *Criticism* 46.3 (2004): 487–96.

Cook, Matt. *London and the Culture of Homosexuality, 1885–1914*. Cambridge: Cambridge University Press, 2003.

Crawford, Alan. *C. R. Ashbee: Architect, Designer, and Romantic Socialist*. New Haven, CT: Yale University Press, 1985.

Cust, Lionel. *Notes on the Authentic Portraits of Mary, Queen of Scots Based on the Researches of the Late Sir George Scharf, K.C.B., Rewritten in the Light of New Information*. London: John Murray, 1903.

—. 'Mary Queen of Scots'. *London Times*, 3 November 1928.

Davis, Natalie Zemon. *The Return of Martin Guerre*. Cambridge, MA: Harvard University Press, 1983.

—. *Women on the Margins: Three Seventeenth-Century Lives.* Cambridge, MA: Harvard University Press, 1995.

de Certeau, Michel. *The Practice of Everyday Life.* Trans. Steven Rendall. Berkeley: University of California Press, 1984.

DeMan, Paul. 'The Dead-End of Formalist Criticism'. In *Blindness and Insight: Essays in the Rhetoric of Contemporary Criticism.* New York: Routledge, 1983. 233–7.

Derrida, Jacques. *Archive Fever.* Trans. Eric Prenowitz. Chicago: University of Chicago Press, 1998.

Dickens, Charles. *Bleak House: An Authoritative and Annotated Text.* George Ford and Sylvère Monod (eds). 1853. New York: Norton Critical Editions, 1977.

—. *Our Mutual Friend.* 1865. Oxford: Oxford University Press, 1989.

—. *Great Expectations.* 1860. New York: Oxford University Press, 1993.

—. *The Pilgrim Edition of the Letters of Charles Dickens.* Ed. Kathleen Tillotson, Graham Storey et al. Vol. 10, *1862–1864*, ed. Graham Storey. Oxford: Oxford University Press, 1998.

—. *Sketches by Boz.* 1836. Harmondsworth: Penguin, 1995.

Dictionary of National Biography. 'George Scharf'. London, n.d.

Edelman, Lee. *No Future: Queer Theory and the Death Drive.* Durham, NC: Duke University Press, 2004.

Eliot, George. *Middlemarch.* 1874. Harmondsworth: Penguin, 2003.

Farrell, Amy Erdman. *Fat Shame: Stigma and the Fat Body in America.* New York: New York University Press, 2011.

Farwell, Marilyn. *Heterosexual Plots and Lesbian Narratives.* New York: New York University Press, 1996.

Fellows, Sir Charles. *An Account of Discoveries in Lycia, being a Journal Kept during a Second Excursion in Asia Minor.* London: John Murray, 1841.

—. *Introductory Remarks to Lycia, Caria, Lydia, illustrated by Mr. G. Scharf.* London: J. Murray, 1847.

Frazer, James G. *The Golden Bough: A Study in Magic and Religion.* 2nd edn. Vol I. New York: Macmillan, 1900.

Freedgood, Elaine. *The Ideas in Things: Fugitive Meaning in the Victorian Novel.* Chicago: University of Chicago Press, 2006.

Geddes Poole, Andrea. *Stewards of the Nation's Art: Contested Cultural Authority, 1890–1939.* Toronto: University of Toronto Press, 2010.

Gretton, R. H. *The English Middle Class.* London: G. Bell and Sons, 1917.

Guizot, François Pierre Guillaume. *The Fine Arts: Their Nature and Relations* [. . .] *with illustrations* [. . .] *by G. Scharf, Junior.* Trans. G. Grove. London, 1853.

Haight, Gordon (ed.). *The George Eliot Letters.* 7 vols. New Haven, CT: Yale University Press, 1954–78.

Hobsbawm, Eric. *Industry and Empire.* Harmondsworth: Penguin, 1968.

Horace. *The Works of Q. Horatius Flaccus Illustrated, chiefly from the remains of ancient art* [. . .] *by George Scharf.* London: John Murray, 1849.

Hsu, Sophia. 'Domestic Governmentality: Family, Italy, and the Liberal State in *The Woman in White*'. Unpublished article, 2014.

Hughes-Hallett, Penelope. *The Immortal Dinner: A Famous Evening of Genius and Laughter in Literary London, 1817.* Chicago: New Amsterdam Books, 2002.

Hulme, Graham, Brian Buchanan and Kenneth Powell. *The National Portrait Gallery: An Architectural History.* London: National Portrait Gallery, 2000.

Ishiguru, Kazuo. *The Remains of the Day.* New York: Vintage, 1989.

Jackson, Peter. *George Scharf's London: Sketches and Watercolours of a Changing City, 1820–50.* London: John Murray, 1987.

—. *Drawings of Westminster by Sir George Scharf.* London: London Topographical Society, 1994.

Jalland, Patricia. *Death in the Victorian Family.* Oxford: Oxford University Press, 1996.

Joyce, Patrick. 'The Politics of the Liberal Archive'. *History of the Human Sciences* 12.2 (1999): 35–49.

Karusseit, Catherine. *Victorian Respectability and Gendered Domestic Space.* <http://repository.up.ac.za/bitstream/handle/2263/5523/Karusseit_ Victorian (2007).pdf?sequence=7l> (last accessed 23 August 2013).

Keats, John. *The Poetical Works of John Keats, Illustrated* [. . .] *by George Scharf, Junior.* London: Edward Moxon, 1854.

Keen, Suzanne. *Romances of the Archive in Contemporary British Fiction.* Toronto: University of Toronto Press, 2001.

Kerr, Michael and Murray Bowen. *Family Evaluation: An Approach Based on Bowen Theory.* New York: W. W. Norton, 1988.

King, Katie. *Networked Reenactments: Stories Transdisciplinary Knowledges Tell.* Durham, NC: Duke University Press, 2012.

Kirkland, Anna. *Fat History.* New York: New York University Press, 2008.

Koven, Seth. 'The Whitechapel Picture Exhibitions and the Politics of Seeing'. In Daniel J. Sherman and Irit Rogoff (eds), *Museum Culture: Histories, Discourses, Spectacles.* Minneapolis: University of Minnesota Press, 1994. 22–48.

—. *Slumming: Sexual and Social Politics in Victorian London.* Princeton: Princeton University Press, 2004.

Krafft-Ebing, Richard. *Psychopathia Sexualis.* 1886. Trans. Franklin S. Klaf. New York: Arcade, 2011.

Kriegel, Lara. *Grand Designs: Labor, Empire, and the Museum in Victorian Culture.* Durham, NC: Duke University Press, 2008.

Langland, Elizabeth. *Nobody's Angels: Middle-Class Women and Domestic Ideology in Victorian Culture.* Ithaca, NY: Cornell University Press, 1995.

Lebesco, Kathleen. *Revolting Bodies: The Struggle to Redefine Fat Identities.* Boston: University of Massachusetts Press, 2004.

Lebrecht, Norman. 'A Romantic Spirit'. *Wall Street Journal* online. New York, 12 December 2012. <http://online.wsj.com/article/SB1000142 412788732402400457817154080835899­4.html> (last accessed 17 May 2013).

Levine, Caroline. 'Strategic Formalism: Toward a New Method in Cultural Studies'. *Victorian Studies* 48.4 (2006): 625–57.

Levinson, Marjorie. 'What Is New Formalism?'. *PMLA* 122.2 (2007): 558–69.

Lewis, Stephen and Tani Barlow (eds). *The Ephemera Project.* <chaocenter. rice.edu/ephemera/about.aspx> (last accessed 1 April 2014).

Liu, Alan. 'The Power of Formalism in the New Historicism'. *ELH* (1989): 721–71.

London *Times.* 'Figure Drawing for Ladies – Mr. George Scharf, Junior'. 25 September 1854.

—. 'Art Treasures Exhibition'. 24 October 1856.

—. 'Mr. Kenyon's Will'. 27 January 1857.

—. 'Deaths'. 14 November 1860.

—. 'Lady Darby's Assembly'. 18 June 1866.

—. 'Her Majesty's Birthday'. 27 May 1867.

—. 'Knole'. 14 November 1877.

—. 'Lord de la Warr', 14 November 1877.

Luttrell, Henry. *Advice to Julia: A Letter in Rhyme.* London: Murray, 1820.

Lynch, Michael. 'Archives in Formation: Privileged Spaces, Popular Archives and Paper Trails'. *History of the Human Sciences* 12.2 (1999): 65–87.

Macaulay, Thomas. *Lays of Ancient Rome, with Illustrations [. . .] by George Scharf, Junior.* London: Longman, 1860.

Macfarlane, Alan. *Marriage and Love in England, 1300–1840.* Oxford: Blackwell, 1986.

Mandler, Peter. *The Fall and Rise of the Stately Home.* New Haven, CT: Yale University Press, 1999.

Marsh, Jan. *Pre-Raphaelite Sisterhood.* London: Quartet, 1985.

Mayhew, Henry. *London Labour and the London Poor.* Ed. Robert Douglas-Fairhurst. Oxford: Oxford University Press, 2010.

Michie, Helena. *Victorian Honeymoons: Journeys to the Conjugal.* Cambridge: Cambridge University Press, 2006.

—. 'Victorian(ist) "Whiles" and the Tenses of Historicism'. *Narrative* 17.3 (2009): 274–90.

Miller, Andrew. *The Burdens of Perfection: On Ethics and Reading in Nineteenth-Century British Literature.* Ithaca, NY: Cornell University Press, 2008.

Miller, D. A. *Narrative and Its Discontents: Problems of Closure in the Novel.* Princeton: Princeton University Press, 1989.

Works cited

Millim, Anne Marie. *The Victorian Diary: Authorship and Emotional Labour.* Burlington: Ashgate, 2013.

Milton, John. *L'Allegro and Il Penseroso, with* [. . .] *illustrations* [. . .] *by George Scharf.* London: Art-Union of London, 1848.

Moffat, Wendy. *A Great Unrecorded History: A New Life of E. M. Forster.* New York: Farrar, Straus and Giroux, 2010.

Moon, Michael and Eve Kosofsky Sedgwick. 'Divinity: A Dossier, a Performance Piece, a Little-Understood Emotion'. In J. E. Braziel and K. LeBesco (eds), *Bodies Out of Bounds: Fatness and Transgression.* Berkeley and Los Angeles: University of California Press, 2001. 292–328.

Morrison, Paul. 'End Pleasure'. In Paul Morrison, *The Explanation for Everything: Essays on Sexual Subjectivity.* New York: New York Unversity Press, 2001. 54–72.

Munden, Thomas Shepherd. *Memoirs of Joseph Shepherd Munden, Comedian.* London: R. Bentley, 1844.

Munich, Adrienne. 'Good and Plenty: Queen Victoria Figures the Imperial Body'. In Tamar Heller and Patricia Moran (eds), *Scenes of the Apple: Food and the Female Body in Nineteenth- and Twentieth-Century Women's Writing.* Albany: SUNY Press, 2003. 45–64.

National Gallery of Art. <http://www.nga.gov/content/ngaweb/research/library/imagecollections/research-in-te-collection.html> (last accessed 23 August 2013).

National Portrait Gallery London. <npg.org.uk> (last accessed 10 July 2014).

'Necrological Notice in Announcements and Occasional Papers'. *Sessional Papers of the Royal Institute of British Architecture* (1864): 2–3.

New York Times. 'The Extra Man at Dinner Parties May Be a Thing of the Past'. 23 October 1981.

—. 'An Old Actor Disappears'. 8 July 1887.

Newman, Aubrey. *The Stanhopes of Chevening: A Family Biography.* London: Macmillan, 1969.

O'Gorman, Marcel. *E-Crit: Digital Media, Critical Theory, and the Humanities.* Toronto: University of Toronto Press, 2002.

Panofka, Theodor. *Manners and Customs of the Greeks.* Ed. Sir C. T. Newton. London: T. C. Newby, 1849.

Pergam, Elizabeth A. *The Manchester Art Treasures Exhibition of 1857: Entrepreneurs, Connoisseurs and the Public.* Burlington: Ashgate, 2011.

Pollard, Albert Frederick. 'Stanhope, Philip Henry'. *Dictionary of National Biography, 1885–1900,* vol. 54. <http://en.wikisource.org/wiki/Stanhope,_Philip_Henry_(DNB00)> (last accessed June 2012).

Pope, Catherine. Review of *A Thing in Disguise: The Visionary Life of Joseph Paxton,* by Kate Colquhoun. 23 July 2012. <blog.catherinepope.co.uk> (last accessed 6 June 2014).

Porter, Roy and G. S. Rousseau. *Gout: The Patrician Malady.* New Haven, CT: Yale University Press, 1998.

Raymond, Meredith B. and Mary Rose Sullivan. *The Letters of Elizabeth Barrett Browning to Mary Russell Mitford, 1836–1854.* Winfield: Armstrong Browning Library of Baylor University, Browning Institute, Wedgestone Press and Wellesley College, 1983.

Rothblum, Esther and Sondra Solovay. *The Fat Studies Reader.* New York: New York University Press, 2009.

Royal Institute of British Architects. '*Necrological Notice*'. London: J. H. and James Parker, 1864.

Sackville-West, Robert. *Inheritance: The Story of Knole and the Sackvilles.* London: Bloomsbury, 2010.

Sackville-West, Vita. *Knole and the Sackvilles.* London: Trafalgar Square, 1992.

Saguy, Abigail. 'Coming Out as Fat'. *Social Psychology Quarterly* 20.10 (2011): 1–23.

Scharf, Sir George. *Recollections of the Scenic Effects of Covent Garden Theatre, 1838–39.* London: J. Pattie, 1839.

—. *Letters and Testimonials in Favour of G Scharf, Jun.* London: Privately printed, 1854.

—. 'Portraits of Mary Queen of Scots'. *London Times*, 7 May 1888.

Schiff, Sarah Eden. 'Family Systems Theory as Literary Analysis: The Case of Philip Roth'. *Philip Roth Studies* 2 (2006): 25–46.

Segal, Erich. *Love Story.* New York: Harper and Row, 1970.

Shattuck, Charles H. *The Shakespeare Promptbooks: A Descriptive Catalogue.* London and Urbana: University of Illinois Press, 1965.

Sherman, Stuart. *Telling Time: Clocks, Diaries, and English Diurnal Form, 1600–1785.* Chicago: University of Chicago Press, 1996.

Slatter, Enid. *Xanthus: Travels of Discoveries in Turkey.* London: Rubicon Press, 1990.

Smith, Peter King. 'Secretary to Lord of the Admiralty: Jacob Luard Pattisson'. The Zimapanners: The Complete History. <www.zimapan ners.com/pattisson,-jacob-luard.html> (last accessed 11 February 2014).

Smith, Sidonie. *Performativity, Autobiographical Practice, Resistance.* Madison: University of Wisconsin Press, 1998.

—. *Resisting the Gaze of Embodiment: Women's Autobiography in the Nineteenth Century.* Madison: University of Wisconsin Press, 1992.

—. Smith, Sidonie and Julia Watson. *Reading Autobiography: A Guide for Interpreting Life Narratives.* Minneapolis: University of Minnesota Press, 2010.

Snyder, Katherine V. *Bachelors, Manhood, and the Novel, 1850–1925.* Cambridge: Cambridge University Press, 1999.

Solomon, Maynard. 'Franz Schubert and the Peacocks of Benvenuto Cellini'. *Nineteenth-Century Music* 12 (1989): 193–206.

Soyer, Alexis. *The Gastronomic Regenerator*. London: Simpkin, Marshall, 1861.

Stanhope, Philip Henry. *The Life of Belisarius*. London, 1829.

—. *The History of the War of the Succession in Spain*. London, 1832.

Steblin, Rita. 'The Peacock's Tale: Schubert's Sexuality Reconsidered'. *Nineteenth-Century Music* 17 (1993): 5–13.

Steedman, Carolyn. *Dust: The Archive and Cultural History*. New Brunswick, NJ: Rutgers University Press, 2002.

Steinitz, Rebecca. *Time, Space, and Gender in the Nineteenth-Century British Diary*. New York: Palgrave Macmillan, 2011.

Stewart, Garrett. *Death Sentences: Styles of Dying in British Fiction*. Cambridge, MA: Harvard University Press, 1984.

Stone, Lawrence. *The Family, Sex, and Marriage in England, 1500–1800*. Abridged. New York: Harper and Row, 1979.

—. *Road to Divorce: A History of the Making and Breaking of Marriage in England*. Oxford and New York: Oxford University Press, 1990.

—. *Uncertain Unions & Broken Lives*. Oxford and New York: Oxford University Press, 1992.

Stone, Lawrence and Jeanne C. Fawtier Stone. Oxford: Clarendon Press, 1984.

Strier, Richard. 'How Formalism Became a Dirty Word and Why We Can't Do Without It'. In Mark Rasmussen (ed.), *Renaissance Literature and Its Formal Engagements*. New York: Palgrave, 2002. 207–15.

Suleiman, Susan Rubin. 'Writing and Motherhood'. In Shirley Nelson Garner, Claire Kahane and Madelon Sprengnether (eds), *The Mother Tongue: Essays in Feminist Psychoanalytic Interpretation*. Ithaca, NY: Cornell University Press, 1985. 352–77.

Tosh, John. *A Man's Place: Masculinity and the Middle-Class Home in Victorian England*. New Haven, CT: Yale University Press, 1999.

Velody, Irving. 'The Archive and the Human Sciences: Notes towards a Theory of the Archive'. *History of the Human Sciences* 11.4 (1998): 1–16.

Victorian Studies Seminar at Rice University. *VSS George Scharf Banquet*. 3 May 2009. www.ruf.rice.edu/nineteen/scharf.html (last accessed 1 April 2014).

Wahrman, Dror. *Imagining the Middle Class: The Political Representation of Class in Britain, c.1780–1840*. Cambridge: Cambridge University Press, 1995.

Warhol, Robyn. 'Neonarrative, or, How to Render the Unnarratable in Fiction and Film'. In James Phelan and Peter Rabinowitz (eds), *Blackwell Companion to Narrative Theory*. Oxford: Blackwell, 2005. 220–31.

Warhol, Robyn R. and Helena Michie. 'Twelve-Step Teleology: Narratives of Recovery/Recovery as Narrative'. In Sidonie Smith and Julia Watson (eds), *Getting a Life: Everyday Uses of Autobiography in Postmodern America*. Minneapolis: University of Minnesota Press, 1996. 327–50.

Whitesel, Jason. *Fat Gay Men: Girth, Mirth, and the Politics of Stigma.* New York: New York University Press, 2014.

Wilson, A. N. 'Unfinished History: An Aristocratic Family Chronicle – As Far as It Goes'. *Financial Times*, 24 May 2013.

Woolf, Virginia. *Orlando.* London: Hogarth Press, 1928.

Unpublished and archival sources

Heinz Archive and Library, National Portrait Gallery, London

AB 59 Scharf, Sir George. Appointment Book 'To call and see' [1859–80] NPG7/1/2/1/1/1.

AB 80 Appointment Book 'To call and see' [1880–95] NPG7/1/2/1/1/2.

D [Sir George Scharf's] Diaries NPG7/3/1. Diaries for each year are individually numbered from 1845 (NPG7/3/1/1) to 1895 (NPG7/3/1/52).

ESC Letters from George Scharf [to Elizabeth Scharf] NPG7/3/7/3/3/1.

ESD Diaries [of Elizabeth Scharf] NPG7/3/7/3/1.

GSS Scharf, George Johann. Journals NPG7/3/7/2/1. (Individual journals are numbered sequentially from 1833 to 1860. The journal for 1840–5 is NPG7/3/7/2/1/3; the journal for 1845 is NPG7/3/7/2/1/4 and the journal from 1852 to 1859 is NPG7/3/7/2/1/14.)

JP 72 [Sir George Scharf's] Correspondence with Jacob ('Jack') Luard Pattisson, 1872 NPG7/3/5/1/1.

JP 73 Correspondence with Jacob ('Jack') Luard Pattisson, 1873–4 NPG7/3/5/1/2.

LES Letters from various senders [to Elizabeth Scharf] NPG7/3/7/3/3/2.

MH Diaries [of Mary Hicks] NPG7/3/7/4/1. Diaries are individually numbered from 1856 (NPG7/3/7/4/1/1) to 1864 (NPG7/3/7/4/1/13).

SB [Sir George] Scharf sketchbooks NPG7/3/4/2.

SC Letters from the chairmen of the Board of Trustees to the secretary NPG7/1/1/4/1.

Other unpublished archival sources

A Scharf, Sir George. *A Collection of Invitation Cards, Menus, etc. from 1869 to 1876 formed by Sir George Scharf.* Unpublished manuscript in the British Library, London, 1887.

DL Sir George Scharf correspondence with David Laing. The Papers of David Laing, Edinburgh University Special Collections Centre for Research. La. IV. 17. Folders 8265–8281.

Index

241

temporality (*cont.*)
  and letters, 93, 96, 101, 210
  of lifewriting, 54
  and history, 175, 177, 178
  and the marriage plot, 89–90, 93–4,
    107
  and recursion, 63, 73, 119, 141,
    168
  and simultaneity, 57–8, 153–4
Tosh, John, 84
triangles *see* family systems
Trollope, Anthony, 70, 94

vita(e), 6, 49–50, 53, 168

Weeks, Sophie, 45
Wilde, Oscar, 51–2, 116
Womack, Elizabeth, 47
Worsley, Richard, 73, 74, 78, 102, 108,
  115, 148

Xanthian Marbles, 5, 7, 42–4
Xanthus, 41–4, 48, 77, 222

Zimapan House, 83, 85, 226n, 227n